AMERICAN POWER AFTER THE FINANCIAL CRISIS

A volume in the series

<small>CORNELL STUDIES IN MONEY</small>

edited by Eric Helleiner and Jonathan Kirshner

A list of titles in this series is available at www.cornellpress.cornell.edu.

AMERICAN POWER AFTER THE FINANCIAL CRISIS

JONATHAN KIRSHNER

CORNELL UNIVERSITY PRESS

ITHACA AND LONDON

First published 2014 by Cornell University Press
Printed in the United States of America

Library of Congress Cataloging-in-Publication Data

Kirshner, Jonathan, author.
  American power after the financial crisis / Jonathan Kirshner.
    pages cm
  Includes bibliographical references and index.
  ISBN 978-0-8014-5099-0 (cloth : alk. paper)
  1. Global Financial Crisis, 2008–2009—Political aspects. 2. United
States—Foreign economic relations—21st century. 3. United States—
Foreign economic relations—20th century. 4. National security—
Economic aspects—United States. I. Title.
  HF1455.K56   2014
  337.73—dc23   2014008088

Cornell University Press strives to use environmentally responsible suppliers and materials to the fullest extent possible in the publishing of its books. Such materials include vegetable-based, low-VOC inks and acid-free papers that are recycled, totally chlorine-free, or partly composed of nonwood fibers. For further information, visit our website at www.cornellpress.cornell.edu.

Cloth printing   10   9   8   7   6   5   4   3   2   1

To ABS, EJL, DKS, TJC, and REA

CONTENTS

Preface

This book, like all books, reflects the intellectual trajectory of its author, and it is especially worthwhile in this instance—or at least, I think, clarifying—to call attention to aspects of my own analytical orientation that provide context for its main arguments. Three elements in particular, all notably unfashionable, have shaped my perspective: my specialization in the economics of national security, an emphasis on the weight of history, and the influence of some elements of the writings of Keynes.

Trained initially as an economist, I switched to political science in graduate school. As a specialist in international relations, I retained an active interest in macroeconomics, and, more specifically, I was not surprisingly drawn toward questions that considered the role of economic factors in questions of war and peace. At that time, scholarship in international relations was strictly divided between "security studies" and "international political economy," an academic vestige of the Cold War, which I erroneously predicted would be unsustainable in the post–Cold War environment.[1] Nevertheless, when the financial crisis developed, I was irresistibly drawn to the question of its effects on national security questions.

I also retained, as a student of both economics and international politics, a perspective that valued the role of history. In practice, to hold the view that "history matters" means two things: (1) that the events of history, judiciously placed in context, offer analytical lessons for the present; and (2) the choices made by actors are influenced by their own historical experiences and by their interpretations of the "lessons of the past." To many, if not most, nonacademic readers of this book, these may seem like obvious banalities. But among academic specialists such views are increasingly anachronistic. Economists have almost completely shed their historians; it is a rare PhD student from a top program who has taken a single course in economic history. Political science, in the envious thrall of its more prestigious cousin, is moving in that direction as well, running both from its own past and from the idea that knowing about the past is of any disciplinary value. (The editor of a top journal once told me that his aspiration was for "a political science that did not have to resort to formal names.")

My own commitment to the value of the past has meant that economic historians—Charles Kindleberger is the most obvious but by no means only example of this—have had a great influence on my own thinking and analytical orientation.[2] These same instincts, especially once stimulated by debates with colleagues about macroeconomics, led me to a great curiosity about Keynes—and to the vast trove of Keynes's original writings—at a time when Keynes was in considerable disfavor (to say nothing of his original, largely unread work). The influence of Keynes on this book, in today's political context, necessitates some clarification or at least inoculation. Because, in contrast to Kindleberger, about whom I have never heard anyone utter an unkind word, there is something about Keynes that makes many people's blood boil.

Keynes is a lightning-rod, most likely, not because of his own writings, but because of the political choices suggested by the practice of contemporary Keynesianism (quite a different animal from the original work of Keynes) and the association of his ideas in the United States with the New Deal and the Great Society, and programs such as Social Security and Medicare, which were bitterly opposed by some at the moment of their creation as socialistic interference in the free market. But Keynes is a greatly misunderstood figure.[3] Untangling this history is beside the point here: for virulent anti-Keynesians, I would simply note that the arguments in this book draw heavily on only two or three insights from Keynes's writings—on uncertainty, capital controls, and, to some extent, economism. None of them are special to Keynes; none of them are elements of the postwar practice of "Keynesianism."[4] Nevertheless, I should be very clear that thinkers like Keynes and Kindleberger did imprint in me a great wariness about the dangers inherent to an unregulated financial sector; in the 1990s these informed my reactions to financial deregulations such as the repeal of the Glass Steagall Act and how I interpreted the Asian financial crisis. And this in turn has shaped my interpretation of the global financial crisis. As I emphasize throughout this book, however, one need not share my interpretation of the crisis to agree with my arguments about its effects on American power and world politics.

Finally, a word about evaluating those arguments: this book offers an interpretation of the past that informs expectations about likely political developments in the future. However, as I emphasize most explicitly in chapter 8, the trajectory of history is uncertain, contingent, and ultimately unknowable. For students of international politics, proffering forecasts of the future is a card trick of dubious virtue. And the game is not even worth the candle: explanation, elucidation, and anticipation are where the real value is added. This book, then, will stand or fall not on the accuracy of its "predictions" but on the cogency of its analysis and the logic of its argumentation, which lead us to anticipate certain pathways along which history might unfold.

Most of this book was written when I was the World Politics visiting fellow at the Princeton Institute for International and Regional Studies, and I am very appreciative of the support of the World Politics editorial committee and the generous hospitality of Mark Beissinger, Susan Bindig, and the PIIRS staff. I have also benefitted from comments and suggestions offered by participants at seminars and workshops where I presented various portions of this project-in-progress, at Cornell, Princeton, Rutgers, Johns Hopkins University's School of Advanced International Studies, the University of Texas at Austin, Texas A&M, the Nobel Institute, and two events hosted by the Tobin Project on Sustainable National Security Strategy. I also thank Maria Sperandei and Wendy Leutert for valuable research assistance (and Wendy again for all of the translations). I am most especially appreciative of the close readings, critical eyes, and essential support of Rawi Abdelal, Benjamin Cohen, Burt Diamond, Ilene Grabel, Roger Haydon, Eric Helleiner, and Peter Katzenstein; several anonymous readers also provided a number of very helpful suggestions. My greatest debts are to Esty, Elie, and Ari, who did some heavy lifting to make this book possible, and with such apparent ease that it might have gone unnoticed. It did not.

AMERICAN POWER AFTER THE FINANCIAL CRISIS

1

The Global Financial Crisis as World Politics

The 2007–8 global financial crisis was a watershed event. With the flicker of screens—overlooking Times Square, on desktop computers, on hand-held devices—trillions of dollars of wealth simply drained away, as if pouring uncontrollably down city streets and vanishing into the sewer. The US financial economy threatened to implode and, with it, the entire global economy. The world was on the brink of another Great Depression. Luckily, the real economic wreckage wrought by the 2007-8 crisis, the worst economic downturn since the Great Depression, wasn't quite as bad as that earlier catastrophe. Nevertheless, after the initial dust settled, people found themselves, if not in a different country, surely in a different economy, which was dispiritingly different from the one that came before. And recovery from the crisis, within societies and from country to country, was wildly uneven: relatively swift for some, virtually nonexistent for others.

Not surprisingly, such a seismic event has attracted considerable attention. Many books have been written about the crisis, the overwhelming majority of which have focused on (very important) issues such as its economic causes, prospects for reforms designed to prevent its recurrence, and political factors attendant on each of those questions. Less attention has been paid to issues of international relations, although there has been a renewed interest in global economic governance. But with regard to how the crisis might have altered the international balance of power or affected the patterns and rhythms of world politics into the future, there are still more questions than answers—in fact, many such questions have yet to be asked. This book is about the international political meaning and implications of the global financial crisis of 2007–8, with an emphasis on its consequences for American power and influence in world politics.

The global financial crisis was an important inflection point in the trajectory of international relations, and it will be increasingly recognized as such as the events themselves recede into history. This proposition is built on three principal, interrelated contentions, each of which is contestable— indeed, much of the stuffing of this book is designed to establish, provide context for, and support these core claims. First, the crisis brought about an end to what I call the "second US postwar order" (which I define as the period of US hegemony *after* the Cold War and associated with its project of domestic and international financial deregulation), due to a collapse of its international legitimacy. Second, for both material and ideational reasons (tangible economic factors and changing ideas about economic choices, policies, and orientations), the crisis has accelerated two pre-existing underlying international political trends. One is the relative erosion of the power, and political influence, of the United States in general, and the other is the increased political influence of other states, including China. Third, the crisis has brought about what I term "a new heterogeneity of thinking" with regard to ideas about how to best manage domestic and international money and finance. These divergences are largely the result of new thinking outside of the United States, which will increasingly contrast with the essentially unchanged attitudes suggested by American policy preferences in these areas. This "new heterogeneity" will matter greatly because it will contribute to increased discord between countries with regard to efforts designed to manage and supervise the international economy. This will, in turn, inhibit the prospects for solutions to problems that will inevitably arise, and for consequential reform of existing international institutions.

This book is concerned with international politics, and that is where its novel contributions will be found. But to understand the material and ideational factors that will contribute to the consequences for international relations that I anticipate, it is necessary to work through a good bit of history and political economy. Nothing comes from nowhere, and revisiting the Great Depression, the evolution of post–World War II US hegemony, and the Asian financial crisis of 1997–98 are crucial for my argument and for the implications of the current crisis. Similarly, reviewing how the US economy came to be dominated by its financial sector, competing narratives about the causes of the global financial crisis, and the role of the dollar as an international currency are essential parts of the story. This chapter offers a general overview of the book and previews how these elements link together.

Learning and Unlearning the Lessons of the Past

Although this is a book concerned with the present, informed by the recent past and with an eye on the future, I begin with a discussion of the Great Depression, which is an indispensable excursion for understanding and contextualizing contemporary events. The interwar catastrophe mattered for the reasons that history typically matters—it is rich with lessons for the present, and it was a formative experience that shaped public policy for generations. Although history does not repeat itself, the course of the Great Depression, the general contours of its origins and initial eruption of its crises, offers a hauntingly similar echo of the panic of 2007–8 and its causes. This time around, the result was "the great recession," which, as the most debilitating economic distress since World War II, is not to be underestimated. But the more recent distress nevertheless pales in comparison with the economic ruin of the Depression, which in turn contributed importantly to the bloodbath of World War II.

The more recent crisis did not spiral out of control, partly because the lessons of the Depression had been learned. It is easy to criticize the policy choices made by various governments; especially after economies pulled back from the brink of the chasm and politicians, no longer desperately scrambling to jointly put out the fire, resumed their normal business of fighting over who should pay for the repairs. But, crucially, those initial choices, to increase spending and assure adequate liquidity, did put the fire out. In the interwar years, by well-remembered contrast, austerity measures (cutting government spending), monetary orthodoxy (especially adherence to the gold standard), and collectively disastrous protectionism shoved the teetering world economy into the abyss.[1]

Learning—that is, avoiding the blunders of the past—was only part of the story. Luck also played a role, then and now. In the interwar years, economic squabbles were quick to escalate, leaving everyone worse off, partly because security dilemmas between states were especially intense. World War I had traumatized Europe; it shattered the political equilibrium on the Continent and generated more international problems than it resolved. Suspicious and insecure, countries were wary of cooperating with potentially dangerous rivals. In contrast, despite the fact that rivalry is a perennial attribute of international politics, the recent crisis took place in a great power security environment that was markedly benign. None of the major participants hesitated to reach for a policy lever out of fear of an imminent military threat.

But lessons can be unlearned—in fact, unlearning the lessons of the Depression contributed mightily to the global financial crisis—and there are no guarantees that the international security environment will remain benign indefinitely. All the more reason to touch base with the interwar years, which also serve as a useful proving ground to illustrate general attributes about the politics of international money and finance that remain acutely relevant for contemporary politics. One lesson is that because of the unique nature of money—it has value solely because people think it has value—ideas about money, good or bad, right or wrong, have a powerful, formative effect on the choices made by states, and for whether a given macroeconomic policy will succeed or fail.[2] Not far behind ideas, it should be added, is power. As Robert Gilpin observed, "every international monetary regime rests on a particular political order."[3] Yet another issue is that international monetary relations have a tendency to be acrimonious because the policy choices of one country tend to put pressure on the politically sensitive interest and exchange rate policies of other countries, often unintentionally. Finally, the interwar years also offer yet another warning with contemporary relevance: international macroeconomic disarray can affect politics within states, helping to empower, as it did in Germany and Japan in the 1930s, political factions that reject cooperative foreign and economic policies.

The lessons of the Great Depression provided the essential building blocks of the financial order constructed after World War II. Although the period from that time to the global financial crisis is commonly described as a period of continuous American hegemony, in fact the United States orchestrated two distinct international orders, each based on a distinct economic ideology and geopolitical vision. The first order, associated with the remarkable quarter-century of economic growth that took place from 1948 to 1973, bore the stamp of John Maynard Keynes's intellectual influence and was shaped by the Cold War confrontation between the United States and the Soviet Union. (The United States was eager to help its military allies recover from the war, and, in the context of an ideological struggle with the USSR, was tolerant of experimentation with varieties of capitalism.) But these lessons were unlearned in the 1980s and 1990s, setting the stage for the more recent crisis. The "second US postwar order," which I date from 1994 (as the foreign policy agenda of the Clinton administration took shape) through 2007, was based on an anti-Keynesian economic philosophy, "market fundamentalism," and coincided with the emergence of unrivaled US unipolarity. Market fundamentalism holds that unfettered markets—even financial markets—left to govern themselves always know best and that there is one singularly correct cocktail of economic policies that applies to all countries in all circumstances.

This was, of course, the antithesis of the first US postwar order. The architects of that earlier system built institutions such as the International Monetary Fund (IMF) and the General Agreement on Tariffs and Trade (GATT), which were designed to respond to the lessons of the Depression and the war.[4] They wished to encourage countries to cooperate, to embrace the international economy, and to respond to the incentives presented by market forces. But, at the same time, they understood that unmediated market forces would generate considerable economic distress and create pressures for unwelcome and inappropriate uniformity across countries' economic policies. The system was thus designed for international institutions and domestic policies to insulate economies from the bitter winds inherent in unbridled capitalism. John Ruggie dubbed this "the compromise of embedded liberalism," an understanding that market forces would be embraced, but mediated, so that individual states could pursue domestic political and social agendas as each saw fit.[5]

Keynes was the key intellectual influence on the embedded liberal order, and he understood that it was macroeconomic pressures, and especially short-term capital flows, that presented the gravest danger to these arrangements. Envisioning the postwar monetary order, he emphasized repeatedly that various forms of capital controls, especially those designed to inhibit destabilizing short-run speculation, were essential.[6] Given the balance of power between the United States and Britain at the time, it is not surprising that the IMF, as established, was closer to the American vision. But capital controls were a basic part of its charter.[7]

Keynes's ideas and the practice of postwar economic policy known as Keynesianism were two different things. The latter, enormously influential in the 1950s and 1960s, got fairly well beaten up first by academic critiques and then by the stagflation of the 1970s. In the 1980s, Keynesianism was declared dead, and a new approach, new classical macroeconomics, was on the rise. Central to this approach was rational expectations theory and its fellow traveler, the efficient markets hypothesis. Rational expectations holds that all actors in the economy share an understanding of the same singularly correct model of how the economy works, and make choices in the context of known risk.[8] The efficient markets hypothesis, which holds that current market prices accurately express the intrinsic underlying value of an asset, flows naturally from this position, as those prices reflect the sum of the collective wisdom of savvy market actors.

By the 1990s, what was rebranded as a "new Keynesianism" heralded the convergence of mainstream macroeconomic theory, as both new classicals and new Keynesians embraced rational expectations. But despite the labels, this was even further removed from Keynes, who did not hold "rational expectations." Rather, Keynes held that investors more often grope in the dark than calculate risk: they can't assign precise probabilities to all potential eventualities because too many factors are unknowable. In a world of uncertainty, financial markets are susceptible to—even driven by—what he called "animal spirits," unpredictable shifts in the attitudes and emotions of investors. It should be noted that one need not be a Keynesian to reject rational expectations theory. Both his most famous intellectual opponent, Friedrich von Hayek, and one of the most prominent and passionate anti-Keynesians of his day, Frank Knight, offered analyses that were fundamentally at odds with rational expectations. (Knight saw uncertainty, which he distinguished from risk, as the very engine of capitalism.)[9] But the modern mainstream academic convergence around rational expectations—a theory that, it turned out, did not perform well when subjected to empirical tests—provided an important intellectual foundation of the second US postwar order. If financial markets always know best, they need not be regulated. They can, as Federal Reserve chairman Alan Greenspan insisted, supervise themselves. This idea meshed well with political developments—the increasing influence of the growing financial sector and rise of the "New Democrats," who, in the 1990s, cultivated Wall Street as a source of support—that provided the impetus behind the second US order.

Joining forces with the Republican Party, the Clinton White House orchestrated the deregulation of the US financial sector. The repeal of the Glass-Steagall Act (the Depression-era law designed to create protective firewalls within the financial sector) and the passage of the Commodity Futures Modernization Act (which prevented the regulation of derivatives, including the credit-default swaps that would play a central role in the 2007–8 financial crisis) completed the transition of the US economy from one in which the financial sector was regulated and supervised and whose role in the economy was subordinate (that is, it allocated capital in the service of real economic activity) to an economy dominated by its financial sector. Finance became the largest, the fastest growing, and the most profitable sector in the American economy. And it wielded enormous political influence.

The Second US Postwar Order and the Origins of the Global Financial Crisis

The American financial liberalization project had an international component. In partnership with its new benefactors on Wall Street, officials of the Clinton administration fanned the globe encouraging states to liberalize and to open their domestic markets to US banks, insurance companies, and brokerage houses. From the US perspective all good things went together: financial deregulation was assumed to be good public policy; it was clearly good for US firms, and financial globalization suggested an international environment in which US political power and influence would be relatively enhanced.

Not coincidentally, in the mid-1990s the IMF was reaching similar conclusions about the appeal of unfettered capital. In a radical and bold power play, the Fund moved to abandon its original charter with a planned revision of its articles of agreement. Instead of accommodating capital controls, the IMF would now force its members to renounce their use as a condition of membership in the Fund. But this was not simply a question of the Fund falling into step with American commands: ideas mattered. The US government, the financial sector, economists at the IMF, and the professors who trained them shared the same views on the benefits of uninhibited finance.[10]

In explaining the move toward capital liberalization in the 1990s, as is true of most questions regarding the politics of money, it is hard to disentangle the roles of power, ideas, and interests.[11] It is notable, however, that in this particular case, the ideas were castles made of sand. Economic theory strongly *tends* to see the free play of market forces as efficient and optimal from an economic perspective. But there are exceptions, including "market failures," where the free market goes wrong. And although there are good reasons to believe that capital mobility is a good thing, there are also good reasons to believe that completely unregulated capital flows are too much of a good thing.[12] As a matter of fact, studies have repeatedly failed to show a positive relationship between capital liberalization and economic growth, or a host of other desirable economic outcomes.[13]

At the same time, it is well established that countries that dismantle their capital controls *are* more vulnerable to very costly and disruptive financial crises, even when they are following what orthodox observers and advisers would deem "appropriate" economic policies. More generally, throughout history, periods of high international capital mobility are associated with an increase in the number of financial crises. Nor should this really be all that startling. Charles Kindleberger showed decades ago (and recent studies only confirm) that financial crises are common occurrences throughout economic history and the factors that contribute to them are well understood. More puzzling is why the ideology of completely uninhibited capital endures.[14]

Not surprisingly, then, the momentum to liberalize capital flows coincided with an increase in international financial instability, most notably seen in the Asian financial crisis of 1997–98. That devastating crisis came as a surprise, however, to the IMF, which not only failed to see it coming but had been touting the sound macroeconomic policies of the countries that bore the brunt of its destructive force. Even as the storm was surging the Fund failed to recognize its implications. A team of its specialists visited Korea in October 1997 and confidently, and erroneously, predicted that the unfolding crisis would not reach its shores.

The Asian financial crisis and its immediate aftermath planted the seeds of doubt that would eventually delegitimize the second US order by exposing an ideological fissure with regard to its interpretation. The US government and the IMF saw the crisis as the result of policy failures *within* the affected countries and as evidence of the superiority of the US economic model. In Japan and China, and throughout Asia more generally, it was seen as a classic international financial crisis, and one that illustrated the dangers of too much capital mobility. This divergence was exacerbated by dissatisfaction with the austerity measures imposed by the IMF and resentment about the opportunistic way the United States took advantage of the political leverage the crisis afforded it in negotiations with its Asian partners.

The IMF also won few friends by forging ahead with its plans to revise its charter. With the plan now facing growing opposition, the Clinton administration dropped its posture of arm's-length indifference to the Fund's capital liberalization drive and rallied to support it.[15] But the continuing eruption of financial crises, now in Russia and Latin America, stalled the initiative. New amendment or not, however, the ideology of free capital remained in place at the IMF and in the United States. In fact, the United States entered the twenty-first century even more powerful, and ever more confident, than before. But that confidence—hubris, really—encouraged the nation to overlook warning signs of dangers lurking in its finance-driven, deregulated economy. The US financial model might have been the only one left standing, but the fortunes being accumulated masked a metastasizing systemic risk. In addition, the United States underestimated how the crisis of the 1990s atrophied the enthusiasm of others for the American way, though such doubts and disenchantments mattered little as long as things were going well.

Things stopped going well in 2007, when the financial system imploded in the worst crisis since the Great Depression.[16] That disaster was rooted in the financialization of the US economy and the flawed foundations of the second US order. (One need not share my interpretation of the crisis to agree with my assessment of its consequences for world politics. But attention to competing interpretations is a crucial element of my argument.) The US financial sector grew so fast, and generated so much wealth for its participants, that it skewed the balance of the economy. Top students from the best universities were irresistibly drawn by the prospect of fantastic wealth. And not just business majors—physicists and engineers wanted a piece of the action, too. In 2006, almost half of Princeton's graduating class took jobs in finance. Financial firms were also becoming much larger, and a small number of gigantic, intricately enmeshed firms dominated the industry. Was this a good thing? Could the financial sector become "too large"? At what point did it become "too concentrated"? Were the major firms "too interdependent"? These are questions that cannot even be asked (and therefore were not asked) if a bedrock assumption of analysis is that market outcomes must inherently be good or, at the very least, are optimally efficient.

Finance was not simply growing; its business model was changing—in ways that made a crisis more likely. In the old days, banking was boring: borrow money at 3 percent, lend it at 6, and be on the golf course at three; at least so went the joke. Back then, banks followed an "originate and hold" model, which meant they would retain the mortgages they issued until maturity. But the innovation of securitization—the slicing up, repackaging, and selling of mortgages and other instruments—changed the nature of banking. The model shifted to one of "originate and distribute," that is, sell the mortgage, which was usually broken up into a myriad of tiny components. In such a model, of course, there is less incentive to subject borrowers to intense scrutiny. In contrast, given the money to be made, there are tremendous incentives to create product (issue loans) and move them along (sell securitized assets to other investors). Also enormously profitable was the alchemy of creating new and fantastically complex financial products that blended together fragments of all kinds of instruments. Trends in the industry, such as the increasing ratio of bonuses to base pay, further encouraged star performers to value the present over the future and to make gambles that promised immediate rewards with risks shoved just over the horizon.

Two types of risks were building, massively and unchecked, in this new financial world. *Individual risk*—risk associated with particular instruments and specific players—might have been mitigated by credit rating agencies (CRAs). It was simply impossible, even for savvy, sophisticated, experienced investors to assess the underlying value and safety of the tens of thousands of exotic financial instruments floating around. A triple-A rating from a CRA offered a Good Housekeeping seal of approval for investors in no position to inspect the kitchen themselves. But the new US financial order was riddled with fundamental conflicts of interest, and one of them was that CRAs were paid by, and beholden to, the issuers of securities, not the investors who bought them. Triple-A ratings were handed out all too easily.

Systemic risk was also growing. Because of the unique nature of finance, even sensible levels of risk taken by individual firms can produce an unhealthy level of risk for the financial system as a whole. With increasing leverage—less money commanding more assets (and, necessarily, more liabilities and obligations)—and an environment that encouraged greater risk taking, the fact that financial firms were routinely counterparties for each other meant that one unlucky (not to mention reckless) bank could easily imperil another, which would threaten another, and so on. That's what a financial crisis looks like.

But the very idea of systemic risk was anathema to the ideology of what I refer to as the "new American model." A harbinger of this shift was the transition at the Federal Reserve from the leadership of the conservative cop-on-the-beat Paul Volcker to the libertarian financial market cheerleader Alan Greenspan. And the Bush administration outdid even the Clinton administration in financial permissiveness, disdaining not only regulation but (like Greenspan), government oversight and supervision as well. Conflicts of interest continued to proliferate, not simply within the industry, but between government and finance as well. Bankers, politicians, and regulators became so enmeshed that the metaphor of the revolving door between public- and private-sector employment—which was spinning dizzily at every level of government—is inadequate. The intertwined connections looked more like a double helix, imprinting the shared DNA of efficient financial markets.

Concerns for systemic risk were not just vanishing from government, they were vanishing from economics textbooks as well. The widespread embrace of rational expectations theory led to a convergence in the discipline around macroeconomic models that not only failed to see the financial crisis coming but were designed in such a way that they could not account for even the possibility of such a crisis. A similar type of problem plagued the risk-management models in vogue on Wall Street. Deploying science-fiction levels of mathematical prowess, these models fed the impression that today's geniuses knew better than yesterday's fools and had, for all practical purposes, solved the perennial problem of unanticipated and dangerous risk.

There were some voices of dissent. All models, no matter how sophisticated, are utterly dependent on their assumptions, and critics warned that the new financial models built their expectations based on the experiences of the recent string of good years and the assumption that those good times would continue to roll.[17] But such critics, along with Cassandras like Paul Volcker and the rare mainstream, finance-friendly economists who expressed cautious, qualified concerns about systemic risk, were ignored.[18]

Concern for systemic risk, assumed away in the new American model, was nevertheless a central component of an older approach that held that unregulated finance was naturally prone to crisis.[19] Paradoxically, periods of stability encourage greater risk taking and financial innovation, which draws in crowds following in the footsteps of successful pioneers. This leads to a classic form of market failure: the behavior of each individual is rational, but their actions collectively create a risk that is not taken into account by any individual.

There are, then, two distinct interpretations of the causes of the financial crisis of 2007–8. From the new American perspective, it was a terrible, unfortunate, exceptionally unlucky strike of lightning, a freak event that was extremely unlikely and essentially unpredictable. But for the older school of thought, some sort of crisis was virtually inevitable; it was a question not of if but of when. Deregulation encouraged the financial sector to become dangerously large and interconnected; an efficient markets culture encouraged those who might guard against the buildup of systemic risk to abandon their posts.

Which of these perspectives is right obviously matters for the future of the US economy. I am a member of the old school; but this book is not about settling that debate. It is about the implications of the financial crisis for the future of American power and the nature of international relations. For these questions, the "correct" interpretation of the crisis is beside the point. Crucial for my argument are four much less controversial claims: (1) for much of the world, the global financial crisis was the second major financial crisis within ten years; (2) the United States was at the epicenter of the crisis; (3) for many, the crisis raised new doubts about the wisdom of the new American model; (4) the US financial system following the crisis is characterized by greater continuity than change.

Power, Ideas, and International Political Consequences

It is these new developments that will have consequences for international relations. The delegitimization of the second US postwar order will encourage a new heterogeneity of thinking about how best to govern money and finance. As a result, policy choices by states will reflect an increased desire for greater autonomy and some insulation from the US economy. These changes will complicate the prospects for international cooperation.

A variety of macroeconomic policy innovations (most obviously the increased deployment of various forms of capital controls) are already being introduced in a wide variety of countries throughout the world, reflecting the new heterogeneity.[20] But new thinking and its consequences can be seen most plainly in China. Before the crisis, even though Beijing was always very cautious about capital deregulation, especially as its controls had protected it from the Asian financial crisis, its policies were nevertheless tacking slowly and cautiously toward the American model. This was heartily encouraged by US officials, who, in the years leading up to the 2007–8 crisis, had but three words of advice for developing countries in general and China in particular: liberalize, liberalize, liberalize. American elites pressed vigorously for dismantling controls and eliminating all barriers to the free flow of capital.

For years, such advice, and a tacit acknowledgement that the US financial model represented what all states should aspire to, was the moral equivalent of being told to eat more vegetables—in theory it was the right thing to do, but in practice the effort was uneven and halfhearted. This all changed as a result of the global financial crisis, which exposed basic flaws in the American way. The crisis, and assessments of its causes, ended the belief that the American model was singularly correct, or even a good idea. In China, it provided yet another lesson about the perils of finance unbound and also elicited what I call "buyer's remorse," remorse about a development model that left it with massive, historically unprecedented holdings of US dollars and that had bound it so tightly to the US economy.

Loss of faith in the American model and, close on the heels of that change of heart, disenchantment with the way the United States was managing its economy and its currency, as well as its general stewardship of the global economy, has altered China's economic strategy. Searching for space from the dollar, and eager to entertain new ideas of how to best organize the world's money and finance, Beijing has now moved to promote the international role of its own currency, the renminbi (RMB), also known as the yuan.

There are barriers to RMB internationalization, especially fragilities within China's own domestic financial sector.[21] And any disruption in China's remarkable record of high annual economic growth—a scenario not to be underestimated—would further complicate such ambitions. But Beijing is on track to increase the international use of the yuan and, as a long-run project, aspires to see it as the international money of East Asia. The emergence of the RMB as an important international currency, in addition to reducing China's dependence on the dollar and pushing back against the second US order, will enhance its economic autonomy and its political influence, objectives accelerated by the financial crisis. Moreover, in the wake of the crisis, it is not simply that China is more willing to see its currency play a larger role in global economic affairs, but other countries, reaching similar conclusions about the second US order, are more receptive to such advances and newly eager to embrace opportunities for diversification. The new heterogeneity of thinking—and its consequences—is a widespread phenomenon.

These developments also suggest that the postcrisis environment will be characterized by increased macroeconomic conflicts between countries. International monetary relations are commonly tempestuous and cooperation elusive, the result of inherent difficulties that can be mitigated by a concentration of monetary power, ideological homogeneity, and shared, salient security concerns. But all of these variables are now moving in the "wrong" direction. Political power (and monetary power) is becoming somewhat more dispersed in the international system. Ideas about money and finance are much less homogeneous than they once were. And the security interests of key players at the monetary table are more varied than they have been in close to a century. In the second half of the twentieth century every major effort to reconstitute the international monetary order was undertaken by the United States and its political allies and military dependencies. This is no longer the case. For the first time in memory, the major players in the international monetary game have diverse, and often conflicting, political interests. This suggests a very bumpy ride ahead for global macroeconomic affairs.

The global financial crisis will also have an effect on the international balance of power, as well as on US power and influence in world politics. The United States will remain, indefinitely, a military competitor without peer, and its economy will remain enormous, advanced, and robust. But, from the perspective of international relations, power is a fundamentally *relative* concept, and US *relative* power and influence are eroding. The differential costs visited by the crisis on national economies, along with variations in national economic growth in the immediate aftermath of the crisis, have accelerated a process already under way: the diffusion of economic power, which in turn translates into political influence.[22] To take the most prominent example, in 1999 China was the world's ninth-largest importer, taking in about $180 billion worth of other countries' products. In 2009, China's imports were worth more than $1 trillion (second only to the United States), and they have only continued to grow. Many countries find their economies increasingly dependent on the large and growing Chinese market, which affects the way that they calculate their interests in world politics, to China's advantage.[23] (Once again, it is important to note that although China is the most prominent example of this phenomenon, it is but one part of a larger story. China's economic surge might ebb, but global tides are shifting more generally.)

The diffusion of economic activity is also taking place within the context of the delegitimization of the second US order. Thus, not only are American capabilities eroding, but the crisis has been a blow to American "soft power," defined as that "intangible attraction that persuades . . . without any explicit threat or exchange taking place."[24] Reassessments of the American model place new emphasis on vulnerabilities already visible in the US economy that were exacerbated by the crisis, which also raised new alarms. Particularly notable—and consequential—is the one novel attribute of the global financial crisis: the United States was at its epicenter and suffered severely. Financial crises are common occurrences, but not, since the Great Depression, in the United States. For three-quarters of a century financial crises were things that happened to other countries. If anything, they further empowered the United States, which served as a safe haven for investors seeking cover from shocks abroad. Even in the most recent crisis, panicking actors ran *toward* the US economy even though it was the source of the disturbance. But that is an illusory respite, and the crisis suggests a new and unfamiliar (though actually more "normal") level of exposure of the US economy to external financial pressures.

One challenge to US power concerns the long-run trajectory of the dollar as an international currency. Again, underlying trends, even before the crisis, made it highly probable that the international role of the dollar would modestly diminish over time.[25] And again, the driver is one of *relative* change; the greenback is very unlikely to be overtaken by a competing international money. But its global reach will almost certainly be encroached on. In addition to the RMB, the euro, despite its current struggles, is also on track to play a greater global role in the future. The World Bank, for example, is among the many that anticipate a multipolar world economy with a multipolar currency order.[26]

This matters, because managing a currency in decline, even one simply in *relative* decline remaining predominant in international use, is a very tricky business involving the loss of old (and accustomed) benefits and the introduction of new (and unfamiliar) vulnerabilities. Since World War II, for example, the United States has taken for granted that the dollar as the world's currency has afforded it macroeconomic policy autonomy and balance-of-payments flexibility unlike any other country—perks that have made it much easier to finance ambitious foreign policies. The central role of the dollar has also made it easier for the United States to shake off (that is, pass on to others) the burdens of adjustment that are generated by the normal processes of international monetary and financial relations. And the special role of the dollar, simply by serving as the axis around which monetary affairs are organized, has provided the United States with what political scientists call structural power. Choices, frameworks, and relations are implicitly shaped by the dollar's international role, and, as with the pattern of international trade, generate incentives that subtly influence the way actors go about calculating what is in their best political interest.[27]

Relative diminution of the dollar's role implies the erosion of these perks, and also the emergence of new costs and dangers. A key challenge comes from a jujitsu-like reversal in market behavior. From its commanding heights a key currency is essentially given the benefit of the doubt, treated as if it is as good as gold. But once it is under stress, perhaps even easing toward retirement, its previous widespread use and vast foreign holdings suddenly make it look overextended and suspect. Instead of a free ride, international currencies perceived to be in decline are subject to the discipline of skeptical market forces at the first hint of trouble. And what does it take to reassure markets? Demonstrations of a commitment to proper—that is, conservative—economic policies, which means austerity, everywhere—pressures from which military budgets will not be immune.[28] The potential exists that in the future financial crises, especially those that once again implicate US financial institutions, will be associated with pressure on the dollar rather than rallies toward it. And, as it is generally the case that countries face negative pressure from markets when they are confronted with an international political crisis or seem to be approaching the possibility of war, the new international macroeconomic constraints faced by the United States will encourage it to be more cautious on the world stage. As a rule of thumb, suspect currencies make for timid states.[29] Finally, even well short of crisis, given the volume of dollar assets held abroad, in an environment where actors are not eager to increase their holdings, the dollar could be vulnerable to politically motivated currency manipulation by political adversaries.

In addition to these new, material challenges that derive from dollar diminution, there is also the question of how these constraints *feel*, that is, how they will be processed by the American political system. For over seventy years—arguably for one hundred years—the United States has simply not faced external macroeconomic constraints in ways routinely experienced by other states. The unfamiliarity of these irritants, especially given the bitterly gridlocked and polarized domestic political setting, will likely serve to magnify the real economic effects of dollar diminution. This book will conclude with a discussion of this and other speculations about how my expectations regarding world politics and the future of American power might be affected by other wild cards and discontinuities. Such a discussion is essential because my objective is not to place bets on the future; it is to understand and anticipate what is likely to happen, and why. The heart of the book is not in its predictions but in its interpretation of history and political economy. The future is contingent and therefore necessarily unwritten. The argument's the thing.

2

Learning from the Great Depression

It might seem odd to begin a discussion of the international political implications of a twenty-first-century financial crisis by looking back at events from the 1930s. But there are good, even compelling reasons to do so. First-year undergraduate students of world politics still study World War I, because, as one legendary professor of international relations explained, World War I is "the great teacher," a virtual laboratory of the causes of war and handily summarized as a "don't let this happen to you" booklet distributed to future generations of leaders so that they might not be so naïve, headstrong, or foolish as to repeat the mistakes that contributed to the Great War. (President Kennedy was reportedly influenced by Barbara Tuchman's *The Guns of August* as he sought to prevent the Cuban missile crisis from spiraling out of control.)

The Great Depression is not only similarly invaluable as a "great teacher," it also demands attention as the most appropriate referent for today's problems as it is eerily, alarmingly similar in its origins and initial manifestations to the current crisis. But by good fortune did the financial crisis of 2007–8 and its aftershocks "only" bring about a severe, protracted recession and not (so far at least) economic suffering and toxic political contagion of the magnitude associated with the Great Depression. But that luck need not hold. Three crucial areas of difference between then and now—ideas, learning, and international politics—provided the safety net that limited the fall this time. In the interwar years, bad public policy made a terrible situation much worse, as states' dismal monetary and fiscal policies resulted in suffocating illiquidity and atrophied aggregate demand. This time around, actors had the mistakes of the Depression as a ready guide of exactly what *not* to do. (In the Great Depression, the Federal Reserve shot the economy in the foot, at best, but in 2007 the chairman of the Fed, Ben Bernanke, had made his academic reputation as a student of those blunders.)[1] As a result, although policy responses during the current crisis were not ideal (and unwinding them will present problems of their own in the future, as I discuss in chapters 7 and 8), the two basic levers reached for—flooding the system with liquidity and new programs of public spending—were crucially necessary and pushed in the right direction.

Just as important in making the Great Depression great was international politics. In particular, the corrosive geopolitical environment of the time meant that cooperative measures that might have been taken to ameliorate the crisis were not forthcoming, as states pursued individually selfish and collectively dysfunctional international agendas. The most infamous of these in historical memory were the rounds of protectionism that contracted global markets, such as America's self-mutilating Smoot-Hawley Tariff Act. (US imports collapsed, but exports fell even further.) And this hurt. But it was the geopolitically rooted failure of macroeconomic cooperation that sealed the fate of the world economy. Especially in Europe, the security situation, still unresolved after the epochal, equilibrium-shattering Great War, left countries eyeing one another with enormous, and at times well-justified, suspicion. In this context, the already compromised international financial system sputtered in disrepair, an accident waiting to happen. Thus, although financial crises are an all-too-common feature of economic history and to be expected, in 1931, during the Creditanstalt crisis—the uncontained failure of one of the biggest banks in Central Europe—steps that could have ameliorated that crisis were halting, inadequate, and soon abandoned. Instead, the crisis spun out of control, spreading from Austria to Germany and then Britain and even Japan, with devastating consequences.

During the Great Depression, then, bad ideas, such as a commitment to the orthodoxy of the gold standard, and an intense international security dilemma were crucial accelerants of the catastrophe. At the onset of the recent crisis, by contrast, the most obvious policy blunders were avoided, and the security setting was comparatively benign. But the strands of to-day's safety net might still fray. Especially as financial systems pulled back from the brink of a complete meltdown, which was a real possibility, and economic activity stabilized, however sluggishly, after an initial free fall that tracked closely with the trajectory of the interwar collapse, less-terrified participants crawled out of their foxholes and felt safe to resume the normal politics of distributional conflict. Ironically, the early successes of the responses this time has left the door open for bad ideas and poor public policy to slip back into the room (and deterioration in international relations is always a possibility)—all the more reason to revisit the lessons of the great teacher.

In this chapter I revisit the interwar period to illustrate the crucial role of ideas and international politics in explaining both the contours of the Great Depression, in particular, and the management of the global finan-cial system, generally. By drawing on the experiences of the 1930s, I also demonstrate how power, security, and ideology shape the possibilities of international monetary cooperation. And in a brief concluding discussion I flip those causal arrows and show that, not only do politics affect the management of financial crises, but such crises can influence both domestic and international politics in very dangerous ways—another warning from the past of great importance today. But to be warned is not always to be wise. As I discuss in chapter 3, the lessons of the Great Depression were the essential building blocks of the financial order constructed after World War II, lessons that were unlearned in the 1980s and 1990s, thus setting the stage for the most recent crisis.

In this chapter I thus establish three important points for the arguments of this book as a whole. First, the similarities between then and now un-derscore that during the recent crisis the global economy was actually very close to the brink of catastrophic disaster. This should serve as a reminder of the stakes still on the table, because there is no guarantee that short-sighted politics, bad ideas, poor public policy, or a turn for the worse in relations between great powers might not still occur. That the crisis was, and potentially is, *that* epochal and dangerous also explains why it will lead to rethinking; as the saying goes, there is something about facing the gallows that focuses the mind. A second, and related theme is that various states will reach different conclusions about what the lessons of the crisis are, a diversity that will contribute to the new heterogeneity in macroeconomic thinking. Third, I demonstrate the importance of "high politics" in explaining the contours of global monetary and financial relations. This matters because it speaks to my expectation of emerging and chronic macroeconomic discord, especially, but not exclusively, between the United States and China. As I will explain here and reprise in chapter 6, macroeconomic cooperation is inherently difficult to achieve and (especially) to sustain. Therefore, even though the lack of an intense security competition between the United States and China, and the great powers more generally, allowed for a nondysfunctional response to the initial crisis, the absence of a shared security vision between the United States and China will raise problems in the future.

The Fire Last Time

In the United States, 1929 is the year associated with the start of the Great Depression, and for good reason. The stock market crash of October 1929 brought the Twenties to a close. It had been a decade, like the first decade of the 2000s, that roared with a dramatically expanding, scandalously under-regulated, irresponsibly leveraged financial sector that was besotted with the expectation that the good times would indefinitely roll. On the eve of the stock market crash, leading American economist Irving Fisher famously proclaimed that "stock prices have reached what looks like a permanently high plateau." Instead, the market suddenly shed about a third of its value in three tumultuous weeks, throwing the US economy into a deep recession.[2] (It would go down much further from there.) Nevertheless, as Harold James has argued, for most of the world "the really severe jolt, the *annus terribilis*, came in 1931."[3] (And the already limping US economy was kneecapped in 1931 as well: the unemployment rate, already high in 1930 at 8.7%, rose to 15.9% in 1931 and 23.6% in 1932. It would peak at 24.9% in 1933 but remain very high for the balance of the decade.)

It was the failure to contain banking panics that made the Great Depression "great." The United States suffered a major banking panic in 1930, two in 1931, and one more in 1933. As noted, from a global perspective, 1931 was the year the bottom fell out, heralded by the failure of the Creditanstalt, which was the point of no return. Banking panics are just that—panics—and they are virulently contagious, as actors scrambling to cover their positions and protect their assets can torch solvent as well as insolvent institutions, which, in the heat of the moment, can be indistinguishable from one another. On May 8, the bank informed the Austrian government that it was on the brink of failure. Understanding immediately that the Creditanstalt was a "too big to fail" institution—it was the largest bank in Austria, indeed, the largest European bank east of Germany—the normally conservative, noninterventionist government immediately went to work on a rescue package. Three days later, both the troubles of the bank and the rescue plans were announced to the public. Despite the efforts of the government, runs on banks throughout Austria occurred. The subsequent failure of the Creditanstalt did not quell the riot; hordes of investors picked up their torches and headed to Germany, whose banks were implicated, or at least suspect, for their ties to Austrian finance. After leaving German finance in ruins, the crisis spread to London, where, in September, a hemorrhaging of reserves forced the pound off the gold standard for the first time (outside of wartime suspensions) in two hundred years. Major aftershocks from the British break with gold were felt in the United States and as far away as Japan.[4]

Why did the global financial system collapse? As one scholar observed with regard to the crisis, "on the single occasion when it was most desperately required, international cooperation was not forthcoming."[5] The reason, in a word, was politics. The European security situation was unsettled in the 1920s and 1930s, and political disputes commonly touched off or exacerbated financial distress. Worse, the great powers in the interwar years were typically rowing in divergent directions, complicating efforts at cooperation toward common ends, even when all parties would obviously suffer in the absence of a common plan. The ambivalent Americans, decisive in determining the outcome of the Great War, had returned home. Germany sought to shed the burdens of the Versailles treaty that had been imposed on it at the point of a gun and the brink of starvation. France, nominally victorious in the war but hollowed out and exhausted by the fight, saw everything through the lens of a future German threat. Britain, sympathetic to France's concerns, nevertheless instinctively placed great value on assuring system-wide economic stability and understood that economic prospects in Europe depended on Germany's recovery and reintegration into the fabric of the Continent.[6] But a thriving Germany was not high on France's list of priorities, to say the least, nor was systemic stability to be purchased at the expense of national security. And France could see to this since a rare area of its relative strength was financial. It was determined to take full advantage of one of the few high cards it held. In relation to Germany and eastern Europe more generally, France sought to use the financial system as a lever of influence. With regard to Britain, Paris resorted to boat rocking, expressing its preferences by exposing the precarious nature of British finances. As Paul Einzig noted, whenever Britain and France came into conflict, gold flowed from Britain to France.[7] Those conflicts were invariably over some aspect of the German question, such as a proposed Austro-German customs union or reparations policy.

In 1931, these politics haunted the crisis at every step. Once the troubles of the Creditanstalt were made public, there was concern that, not just Austria, but Germany as well would be "at once exposed to the danger of panic withdrawal of capital." Britain, hoping to prevent a generalized European banking crisis, favored finding a way to support the rescue efforts of the Austrian government. France, in contrast, saw a political opportunity. Austria and Germany had been moving toward a customs union, a move that made much economic sense and was favored by both potential participants. But France had argued, cogently, that such an agreement was forbidden by the Versailles treaty. Now France could do more than argue; it made any assistance to Austria contingent on the abandonment of the customs union scheme, which it presented as an ultimatum on June 16.[8]

The Americans and the British, who had in May backed an initial loan to Austria through the Bank for International Settlements (more help was now needed), were displeased by what internal US documents described as "blackmail." Secretary of State Henry Stimson personally told the French ambassador in Washington that such behavior was not "the proper way to meet a financial crisis." (Actually, France's efforts went beyond blackmail; with the banking crisis there was a flight from the Austrian shilling, and France withdrew funds from Austria in an effort to pour gasoline on that fire.) Faced with France's demand, the Austrian government announced its resignation, which threatened such chaos that the next day the Bank of England, which previously had preferred to play a small, supportive behind-the-scenes role, stepped in with a large emergency short-term loan of its own. This temporarily saved the Austrian government, but it weakened the position of sterling.[9]

The British credit provided a respite from the storm but could not restore the Continent's fragile finances, and soon enough Germany found itself tested—and wanting—by the financial pressures unleashed by the Austrian crisis. On June 25 the situation was adequately dire that even France joined in with the Bank of England, the Bank for International Settlements, and the US Federal Reserve Banks to collectively provide a $100 million loan to Germany. But when that proved insufficient, and it was clear that Germany would need more help from abroad, France introduced a range of political conditions on any new loans, including concessions on naval disarmament, reparations, the customs union issue (once again), and recognition of French interests in Central Europe and the Balkans. Instead, Germany retreated behind a protective wall of exchange controls, essentially divorcing itself from global financial markets. With the German avenue effectively dammed, the crisis floodwaters were diverted to Britain, and the stage was set for the crisis that would be visited upon sterling in September.[10]

The Unique Power of Ideas about Money

It was not just politics that doomed the interwar economy; ideas—bad ideas—played a crucial role as well. Like medieval bloodletters, many pre-Keynesian economists and policymakers prescribed deflation, liquidation, orthodoxy, and devotion to the gold standard as ritual practices for combating economic depression—cures akin to starving an anorexic that were at least as bad as the disease itself. These faiths were interdependent; as Barry Eichengreen illustrated in his classic book *Golden Fetters*, the gold standard was at the rotten heart of the Great Depression and crucially contributed to why it was so deep and went on for so long. Only by abandoning the gold standard could states dispense with deflation and orthodoxy and revive their economies.[11] But this required shattering two taboos: voluntarily breaking with gold (sometimes helped by a very hard shove, in the case of Britain) and purposefully encouraging economic activity (akin to diving into a pond where schoolmarms had long warned it was forbidden to swim).

Eichengreen argued that the gold standard was the mechanism through which destabilizing impulses were magnified and transmitted through the fragile international financial system, tightening further in response to escape attempts like a Chinese finger puzzle. As he wrote, "central banks starved of gold restricted credit availability and raised domestic interest rates in a futile effort to obtain scarce reserves from one to another. To the extent that all countries engaged in the practice, they frustrated one another's efforts and only intensified the deflationary pressure operating in the world economy." The operation of the gold standard essentially prevented leaders from taking the steps necessary to contain bank failures and prevent the spread of financial panic, or, were they so inclined, to pursue relatively reflationary policies. Such policies would signal a lack of commitment to the gold standard and put pressure on the currency. If the gold standard was to be retained, expansionary measures would have to be withdrawn as the currency came under pressure, and thus attempts at expansion would do little more than drain reserves and compel retrenchment. Similarly, states were unable to prevent the collapse of their domestic banking systems, since containing a bank run requires generous injections of liquidity; but, in response, the new funds would leak out of the country as holders abandoned the currency to avoid the losses associated with anticipated depreciation. Thus, the defense of the gold standard parity required "authorities to sit idly by as the banking system crumbled, as the Fed Reserve System did at the end of 1931 and again at the beginning of 1933"[12]

Recovery from the Depression required the abandonment of the gold standard and the rejection of orthodoxy. Depreciation stimulated the economy, stabilizing prices and causing output, employment, investment, and exports to rise more quickly than in states that remained on the gold standard. It should be noted that depreciation was not the solution in and of itself; the key mechanism of recovery was not, for example, a new competitive advantage in international markets derived from a reduction in the value of the currency, which would have presented a new set of collective action problems, but rather it was that unconcern for maintaining parity freed up monetary and fiscal policies. The recovery itself still depended on the adoption of expansionary policies, which states embraced with different levels of reluctance and enthusiasm.

That embrace was uneven because there remained strong voices of orthodoxy and liquidation in every quarter. But nowhere did they hang on as long, or as consequentially, as they did in France. This compounded the world's problems in two different ways: first, by undermining prospects for much-needed mutually beneficial international cooperation; and second, by asphyxiating the French economy, with negative international political and economic consequences.[13] In France, support for the gold standard and for defending the value of the franc was widespread and ingrained; it even held sway with many actors whose individual economic interests would have been much better served by breaking with gold. Instead, successive French governments chose deflation and, when that failed, "super-deflation." From 1932 to 1936, the money supply contracted, and government spending was cut by 20 percent. But, over the same period, government debt nevertheless increased markedly, as deflation and austerity choked off economic activity and tax revenues. The French economy was chasing its tail in a downward spiral. As the Nazis rearmed, France's commitment to monetary orthodoxy slowed its own economy, eroded its industrial base, and forced reductions in defense spending.[14]

Ideas about money mattered during the Great Depression. But the catastrophe of the Depression and the dismal policies that followed in the name of those ideas are only an extreme, and thus more easily observable, illustration of a universal and powerful truth: when it comes to money, ideas *always* matter. Macroeconomic policymaking—then and now—is unique in that in order for it to work, people must *believe* it will work. This is different than, say, air travel. The collective fear of one hundred frightened passengers convinced that their plane will crash can't cause the jet to go down. But macroeconomic policies require that the majority of the passengers, especially the ones in business class, are not afraid—or those policies simply will not fly. This is not a radical position. Milton Friedman made the same argument about the advantages of abandoning the gold standard in the 1890s, which, in his estimation, might have been the wisest course of action. But in a "fascinating example of how important what people think about money can sometimes be," that potentially optimal policy choice was not possible. Instead, "the fear that silver would produce an inflation sufficient to force the United States off the gold standard made it necessary to have a severe deflation in order to stay on the gold standard."[15]

Simply put, beliefs about money define the possible. As Benjamin Cohen explained, because the value of money is utterly dependent on the willingness of others to accept it—that is what gives money its meaning—policymakers must pursue "credible strategies" that "make considerable concessions to market sentiment." But ideas about money come and go, and that credibility, and those sentiments, need not be singular, timeless, uniquely correct, or even, to some extent, correct. They only need to be *believed*, assuming of course that the attendant policies fall within a range of possibilities plausible from the standpoint of abstract economic theory. And so, as I have argued elsewhere, some (but not all) macroeconomic policies are sustainable—or unsustainable—solely because of the shared belief, unrelated to the economic "facts" regarding their merits, that such policies can or cannot be sustained.[16]

A key tenet of the second US postwar order (discussed further in chapter 3) was the assumption that even modest levels of inflation carry real economic costs and that the principal goal of macroeconomic policy should be vigilance to assure the maintenance of low inflation. In fact, however, there is very little science behind this ideology. The costs of moderate inflation are very hard to find. As one inflation hawk admitted, economists "have not presented very convincing arguments to explain these costs." Nor are they easily shown: it turns out that "for inflation rates below twenty percent a year . . . the relation between growth and inflation is not statistically significant." Study after study confirmed that essential conclusion—the economic costs of moderate inflation are not to be found—yet the belief in those costs and a policy orientation of hypervigilance against inflation remained a pillar of the second US order.[17]

The power ideas have over money matters. One of the "laws" of economic theory, for example, holds that states can choose two, but not three, of the following menu items: free capital flows, fixed exchange rates, and macroeconomic policy autonomy. An implication of this is that if a country chooses to have a floating exchange rate, it should be able to pursue the monetary policies of its choice. Because if a country chooses policies that result in an inflation rate above the average of its trading partners—say 6 percent at home as opposed to 3 percent abroad—with the free flow of capital and exchange rate flexibility, a depreciation of 3 percent should mediate the difference, and that would be that. But if capital mobility is accompanied by a consensus that "correct" macroeconomic policy does not permit higher-than-average inflation rates, capital movements will be more than equilibrating; they will be punitive, punishing the state for pursuing policies perceived to be illegitimate. Here the depreciation would not stop at 3 percent; indeed it might not stop until the offending policies were reversed, and were they not, in the face of such capital flight, it might build a momentum of its own, creating a crisis. In the context of one dominant set of beliefs, macroeconomic policy autonomy is harder to achieve than the economic laws would lead us to believe. Such ambition might require a floating exchange rate *and* restrictions on capital flows, allowing for only one item from the menu, rather than two. But (as subsequent chapters will elaborate) the architects of the second US order also insisted that states abandon their capital controls, and in that context, two of three choices begin to look like no choices at all. For better or worse, ideas about the new American model reinforced its practice. For better and worse (more space for various macroeconomic policy postures; greater discord over the management of international money), the ideational shift from a singularly legitimate American model will have a telling effect on world politics and the international economy.

Explaining Monetary Cooperation

Monetary cooperation—efforts by states to manage their exchange rate and macroeconomic policies so that measures taken by one might not undermine the efforts of another—is, as Bette Davis might say, not for wimps. International cooperation is never easy (cooperation, changing behavior in anticipation of mutual gains, is distinct from harmony, in which good things go together naturally), and it is especially problematic when it comes to macroeconomic issues. Coordinated or not, the normal functioning of the international economy routinely generates problems, pressures, and disequilibria that require resolution. But those "macroeconomic adjustments," as they are called, are costly and invariably become more intense in troubled times, when cooperation is most needed. Some of these adjustments are compulsory, and they can be more or less intense, but states instinctively do their best to shift these burdens abroad. This is what global financial politics are largely about: games of tug of war over who will bear what burdens of adjustment. This is less obvious in the contemporary United States, which, for a number of reasons, including its role as issuer of the world's "key currency," has been, for generations, uniquely *unconstrained* by such pressures and has found it easy, often effortless, to shrug off the burdens of adjustment onto others. (Or as Nixon's Treasury secretary John Connolly put it to his international peers, with characteristic subtly, "the dollar is our currency but it is your problem.") But the inescapable "adjustment problem" is the dilemma at the heart of any monetary order and is the stuffing of global financial politics. It also explains why even when states can agree about the contours of the functioning of the global financial order, those understandings will tend to come under pressure exactly when they are most needed.

The relative complexity of international monetary arrangements also presents unique challenges. Even if all parties sincerely believe that some sort of exchange rate cooperation is appealing in theory, they may still disagree over a wide range of practical issues regarding the "rules of the game," given distinct preferences based on national dispositions (such as small versus large economies) and theoretical disagreements over how to achieve desired ends. Unlike trade, about which there is a robust economic logic (liberalization is globally efficient), monetary theory is more ambiguous; there is no decisive empirical evidence as to which type of exchange rate regime, level and style of capital control, or the rules of the game more generally, is most efficient or appropriate.[18] And, even when agreed on, cooperation is often difficult to execute and monitor. With international trade, law is decisive: states can reduce tariffs and eliminate quotas by fiat. But pledges of macroeconomic cooperation often involve commitments to intervene (or to *not* intervene) in markets; such behaviors are harder to see and evaluate, given that market forces may generate countervailing pressures.

Leaders will also face often intense pressure to abandon macroeconomic understandings that have been reached. This is because monetary cooperation, at bottom, involves the sacrifice of national macroeconomic policy autonomy. Keynes wrote extensively about the difficulty states face in balancing their preferences for domestic policy autonomy and external economic stability, which he identified as the basic "dilemma of an international monetary system," the challenge of mediating international and domestic macroeconomic pressures.[19] To stick with international agreements, states are often called on to bear burdens: cut budgets, tighten money supply, and engage in costly interventions—measures that are routinely unpopular and often at odds with what seems right for the domestic economy, such as during a recession. And because of the particular salience of monetary politics, leaders will feel the greatest pressure to break monetary agreements just when they are most needed—during periods of economic distress.

International macroeconomic comity, then, is hard to establish, and, perhaps just as important, it is particularly difficult to sustain. Both of these problems are exacerbated by the public nature of macroeconomic externalities.[20] "Externalities" in international relations result when states adopt domestic policies that have "spillover" effects, consequences that are felt beyond a state's borders. If injured states push back against the producer of a negative spillover, that is, take measures designed to force that state to rein in its offending policy, those policies will be perceived as more costly than anticipated and they will be somewhat curtailed. (Just as taxing pollution will force a factory owner to consider the cost of negative externalities generated during the production process.) But while states can be discriminatory in their trade policies, macroeconomic policies, such as those regarding interest and exchange rates, are almost inherently uniform in their manifestation abroad. Thus, producers of macroeconomic "bads" (e.g., very high interest rates) will tend to go underpunished because injured states face a collective-action dilemma: all will benefit from the elimination of the public bad, no matter who bears the cost. Due to the free-rider problem (private costs and public benefits), negative externalities in this case will not be significantly reduced.

In sum, although the inability of states to amicably settle their differences about international money and finance can be costly, inefficient, and embittering, disputes between states over international macroeconomic matters ought not to surprise. On the contrary, it is the success stories in these areas that require explanation. Monetary cooperation is possible only when certain special conditions hold; not surprisingly, those conditions are rooted in power and ideas.

One factor, power, suggests that international macroeconomic cooperation will be easier to achieve when it is orchestrated by one clear leader. Such leadership is attractive because of the advantages associated with the natural tendency of monetary systems to be hierarchically organized and follows the logic that a single key currency can provide a focal point around which actors can base their expectations.[21] A leading state is also more likely to overcome collective-action problems; as such a large stakeholder, it may see its own interests as in accord with global financial stability in general, and thus it may be willing to bear the costs of supervising and maintaining systemic stability, such as those associated with efforts to suppress the generation of negative macroeconomic externalities by states. Similarly, a monetary "hegemon" can also help overcome the inevitable, irresistible, and ill-timed adjustment problems generated by the routine functioning of the international macroeconomy by bearing a disproportionate share of those costs or supervising a system designed to mollify and adjudicate them.

Changes to the concentration of power, for example, help explain both the emergence and collapse of the first US postwar monetary order. After the end of World War II, the United States initially took a relatively hard line on monetary issues with Britain, which it still viewed as a potential financial rival, as seen in the conditions imposed by the US during the negotiations for the postwar loan, in particular, the demand for the prompt restoration of convertibility. But it soon became all too clear that Britain especially (but also Western Europe more generally) was much weaker, and the United States relatively stronger, than had been understood. The US disposition changed, and it became less assertive and more supportive in the monetary realm. It switched gears and allowed for widespread deviations from the rules of the IMF, most obviously in the postponement of generalized convertibility until 1958.[22]

But by 1970, US relative economic power had declined considerably, along with its willingness to make sacrifices to sustain international monetary stability. And, as increasing pressure on the dollar emerged in the late 1960s, the United States was staring down considerable adjustment pressures within the context of the rules of the Bretton Woods monetary system. Ultimately, rather than bear those costs, the United States chose the luxury afforded to great powers: it changed the rules of the game and shifted the burden of adjustment to now more capacious and less fragile others. Thus, in 1971, when the dollar come under the sort of pressure that would have forced others to impose bitter deflationary economic medicine, Nixon decided to take his marbles and go home: he closed the gold window, putting an effective end to the Bretton Woods system.[23]

But the concentration of power is neither necessary nor sufficient to assure macroeconomic cooperation. The empirical support for hegemonic stability theory as applied to money is mixed, and, it should be noted, historically speaking, monetary hegemons are often likely to be the source of instability rather than stability.[24] All states, including hegemons, need either a compelling reason to bear the costs of adjustment, or they need to convince themselves that those burdens are just. This is where security and the legitimacy of economic ideas enter the picture. With regard to security, states will be more willing to bear the economic costs of monetary cooperation if concerns about those costs are trumped by more pressing motivations of "high politics." When states have shared salient security concerns, they are more willing to settle, or at least set aside, conflicts over the burdens of adjustment. Thus, concerns about the Soviet threat were essential in forging the first US order. In 1947, it was not simply the shock of British bankruptcy but of its collapse as a great power in the context of the emerging Cold War that fundamentally changed US attitudes about monetary cooperation. In this new, dangerous security environment, the United States became willing to bear a disproportionate share of the burdens of reconstructing and nurturing the international financial system.[25] But, by 1970, it was unwilling even to carry its fair share; again, this was not simply a function of its reduced relative capacity but, crucially, of changes in the saliency of and consensus regarding shared security threats among the Western allies. In the mid-1960s, with the economic recovery of Europe and the easing of Cold War tensions, France felt comfortable enough to pull out of NATO's unified military command; the US diverted military units from Europe to fight in Vietnam. The Vietnam war both underscored the perceived unlikelihood of a Soviet invasion of Western Europe and reflected a growing divergence in attitudes between the United States and its European allies about international security matters. The tightrope of international monetary cooperation lost its high-political safety net and came crashing down.

In addition to a shared, motivated vision of national security, ideological homogeneity, which inhibits deviations from those behaviors commonly understood to be legitimate, can serve as another backstop that sustains cooperation. If shirking the burdens of adjustment is coded as *wrong*— violating a norm all agree is proper—and not just an opportunistic response to changed conditions, a state tends to be inhibited from doing it. The grand bargains of international monetary order were all achieved in the context of relative ideological homogeneity among participants. Thus, although American power saw to it that the establishment of Bretton Woods institutions and the rules of the International Monetary Fund were in accord with US preferences and interests, that order nevertheless reflected a broad intellectual consensus on what a monetary order *should* look like. And, while power and interest are clearly an important part of any explanation of the establishment of the European Monetary Union, as Kathleen McNamara has argued, unification only became possible when policymakers in different states came to share the same ideational framework about the management of money. A "neoliberal policy consensus" emerged and "redefined state interests in cooperation . . . and induced leaders to accept the domestic policy adjustments needed to stay within the system."[26]

Cooperation and Catastrophe during the Great Depression

Power, security, and ideology determine the prospects for monetary cooperation, as (once again) events from the Great Depression plainly illustrate. After the 1931 crisis forced Britain from the gold standard, global economic relations only deteriorated. Subsequent devaluations (including the dollar's break with gold in 1933) and other unilateral measures caused world trade and payments relationships to compartmentalize; efforts to dig out of the world crisis, such as the 1933 London Economic Conference in which representatives from dozens of nations met for weeks on end, collapsed in failure. France, committed unceasingly to gold, deflation, and the franc, lectured the others on their decadent monetary experiments. The British were bitter over the American devaluation, and Britain in turn was accused of using the Exchange Equalization Account to manipulate the value of the pound.[27] Yet, on September 25, 1936, Britain, France, and the United States were able to announce a "tripartite monetary agreement" that allowed for the coordinated devaluation of the franc—there would be no retaliatory measures—and a promise of continued consultation between the three powers over monetary affairs.

What changed in but a few short years? Convergence on both security and ideology. The year 1936 saw the remilitarization of the Rhineland, the Italian conquest of Ethiopia, and the beginning of the Spanish Civil War, an alarming pattern of increasing assertiveness of the fascist powers. The United States and Britain thus tacked toward the French position on the danger presented by Germany and were eager to buttress French power as a counterweight on the Continent. In this context, the economic implications of a devaluation of the franc (such as a competitive advantage in international trade) took a backseat to geopolitical concerns (that France have the capacity to reflate and rearm with the support, as opposed to the resistance, of the Anglo-Americans). At the same time, France moved markedly toward the ideological position of its Western partners on economic policy. With the election of its first socialist prime minister, and with belated awareness that its economic policies were undermining national security, France moved toward the Anglo-American position on money and gave ground on two "unthinkables": abandoning monetary orthodoxy and devaluing the franc. Without these changes, there would have been no tripartite agreement.[28]

With security ascendant, the United States and Britain were willing to bear a disproportionate share of the burdens of adjustment in an effort to strengthen France and signal Western unity. Indeed, the franc depreciated much more than had been hoped—or would have been previously tolerated—losing more than 40 percent of its value during the first two years of the agreement. But the agreement remained in force, because, as one analyst noted, "the US and the UK were prepared to swallow almost any French action rather than announce the agreement was dead." US treasury secretary Henry Morgenthau saw the agreement not as an economic pact but as a way to use monetary policy "to build a united, democratic front to resist Hitler."[29]

International macroeconomic cooperation finally helped the allies address the growing fascist menace. But not to be overlooked is that the preceding years of political-financial machinations and seething monetary conflicts had made it more likely that such a threat would arise—an underappreciated danger then and now. The future of domestic politics within states and the foreign policies that those countries ultimately choose are not random, but neither are they predetermined. Political contestation and policy choice are shaped by the opportunities and constraints presented by the facts on the ground, and the collapse of the global financial system in 1931 cultivated the environment in which dangerous political forces were able to win domestic political struggles and exploit the global economic wreckage.

In Germany, global financial closure strengthened the hand of the expansionists. In September 1934, in response to new exchange difficulties, Germany announced its New Plan, an elaborate scheme designed to insulate itself behind a wall of exchange controls from the international financial system. Those measures allowed Germany to pursue uninhibited rearmament, unencumbered by concerns for inflation or international market pressures, and to enmesh eastern European states, also on shaky financial stilts, within a web of politically motivated exchange-clearing schemes. But the Nazis did not simply abandon the international economy and impose exchange controls. The new measures were rooted in, and an extension of, steps taken in the defensive financial retreat (engineered by a centrist government) of August 1931 in response to the irresistible forces unleashed by the Creditanstalt crisis. At the time, Paul Einzig had predicted that a "collapse of the reichmark is certain to bring about a complete political upheaval in Germany. It is highly probable that the extreme Nationalists or the Communists will then acquire power." It was a prescient warning, which is not to claim that the financial crisis of 1931 caused the Nazis to come to power. But it did contribute to the conditions inside and outside of Germany that enhanced the prospects for the party's political success and economic disposition.[30]

In Japan, the collapse of 1931 was even more tragic. During the 1920s, liberal internationally oriented bankers in Japan were able to access international financial markets and, importantly, international allies in the United States and Britain, and this helped them achieve considerable influence in shaping Japanese foreign policy. International bankers in the United States, eager to support their Japanese counterparts and encourage liberalism and openness in Japan, not only extended credit to the Japanese government, but used their influence to help assure that Japan's political concerns would be reflected in international negotiations, such as those that led to the Washington Naval Treaty of 1922. But in the wake of the failed international response to the global financial crisis of the early 1930s, Japanese financiers lost their markets, their allies, their influence, and the greatest among them their lives; Japan's grand strategy in the 1930s looked very different from its grand strategy in the 1920s. It need not have been so.[31]

These experiences are directly relevant for contemporary international politics. If global economic conditions deteriorate markedly, especially if opportunities for international trade diminish or a new international financial crisis upends normal patterns of economic activity, those twin effects will likely recur: victory in domestic political conflicts within states by relatively unsavory actors; and geopolitical exploitation by aggressive states of opportunities presented to them by the ruins of economic disintegration. Even well short of full-blown crisis and closure, the stakes involved in the continued smooth functioning of the international economy are high. Nowhere are they presently higher than with regard to China. There is a voluminous debate over the future of China and the international political implications of its rise.[32] That debate will continue, because we simply do not know. That future is contested and unwritten. But one lesson from the "great teacher" stands out: those actors and interests within China that prefer that it rise as a responsible player within a thriving, open international order will face dim prospects of success if the opportunities presented in the global arena are inhibited or foreclosed.

3

FROM THE FIRST TO THE SECOND US POSTWAR ORDER

The United States has been the dominant power in world politics since World War II and the leading influence on the nuts and bolts of how global economic relations are organized. That hegemony, however, found expression in the orchestration and supervision of two very different postwar international economic orders: the Bretton Woods system of 1948–73, and what can be called the "globalization project" of 1994–2007. Crucially, these orders were ideationally distinct. The first was a Keynesian-influenced *embedded liberal* order that encouraged orientation toward an expanding international economy while nevertheless seeking to "embed" market forces in the context of varied national management of domestic economies. The second was more classical, or *market fundamentalist*, based on an assumption that markets (even markets for financial assets) always know best and that one economic model, defined and disciplined by those markets, fits all. Not coincidentally, each order also reflected the geopolitical assessments of its creator. During the Bretton Woods era, the United States was concerned with strengthening its allies in Western Europe and

Japan and supporting a Cold War coalition against the Soviet Union. The second, post Cold War order coincided with the widely shared assumption within the US foreign policy establishment that US power and interests would be advanced by globalization.

The Bretton Woods system, named after the town in New Hampshire where the international conferences that led to the foundation of institutions such as the International Monetary Fund and the World Bank took place, was built on the ruins of the Great Depression and the lessons from that experience that architects of a new order were determined to heed. Of those lessons, two simple ones stood out. First, the collapse of the world economy, rooted in the uncoordinated, selfish, and ultimately self-defeating efforts of individual states to spare themselves the worst of the Depression, was singularly catastrophic. It was essential that new institutional arrangements prevent this from recurring and to encourage states to embrace an open, expanding international economy. Second, as expressed most obviously in the ruinous adherence to the gold standard, it was also understood that unmediated market forces, especially macroeconomic pressures, were dangerous, disruptive, and debilitating. Market forces needed to be embraced but harnessed. In particular, Keynes and subsequent managers of the Bretton Woods system assumed that states would deploy capital controls, as well as other regulations, to mitigate some of the costs and dangers of unmediated global market forces, and also to create breathing room for varied domestic economic policies. The resulting American system was successful beyond its most optimistic hopes, ushering in a quarter-century known as the golden age of capitalism, of unprecedented global economic growth and prosperity.

This first postwar order collapsed when the United States had enough. Given economic recovery in Western Europe and Japan and the easing of Cold War tensions, when slower growth and inflationary pressures threatened the viability of the dollar's link with gold (the monetary lynchpin of the Bretton Woods system), President Nixon, with his re-election approaching, was unwilling to bear the domestic political costs of the deflationary measures that would be required to defend the dollar. Instead of playing the game, he changed the rules, and unilaterally "closed the gold window," pulling the curtain down on the first US postwar order. Efforts to patch and reform the system ultimately failed and gave way to a "nonsystem" of generalized floating exchange rates. Abandoning the fixed–exchange rate system had an unintended effect: with floating rates, the most pressing and obvious motivation for capital controls—to defend exchange rates as promised—disappeared. Thus, from the 1970s, states began to relax their capital controls, which generated its own momentum. (If one financial center deregulated, there was competitive pressure on others to follow suit.)[1]

During the dismal 1970s (sluggish growth and high inflation) and the new Cold War of the 1980s, the United States placed less emphasis on international economic leadership and prioritized domestic concerns. But a confluence of unanticipated events—the collapse of the Soviet Union and the end of the Cold War, the economic resurgence of the US economy, and the unanticipated, irretrievable stall of the Japanese economy, which, with its state-led capitalism, was in the 1980s deemed inevitably poised to overtake the United States—put the United States back in the world order business. The common discourse of American decline that characterized the 1970s and 1980s gave way to resurgence, not just of US hegemony, but of unprecedented unipolarity. And, coinciding with an apparent academic delegitimization of "Keynesianism" and a heady dose of American triumphalism, a new narrative was imagined: the victory of the West in the Cold War was now attributed to the magic of the unfettered free market. For the United States, now absent a peer military competitor, ideology and power went hand in hand, and a new American order was forged, rooted in the liberation of finance at home and abroad. Thus the 1990s saw a dramatic acceleration of the domestic financial deregulation that had been initiated in the 1980s. At home, the Clinton administration led a bipartisan charge to dismantle the Depression-era firewalls that had been designed to contain instability in the domestic financial sector; abroad (as discussed in chapter 4), it pushed to eliminate international capital controls.

In this chapter I consider the two US-led international economic orders. I show how the first post–World War II order was built on the anxious desire to not repeat the mistakes of the Great Depression, and how it was shaped by the profound intellectual influence of Keynes, who was present at the creation but died young, in 1946. His absence from the scene accelerated the trip from Keynes to Keynesianism; a central argument of this book is that the subsequent discrediting and reconstitution of the latter obscured the rich, invaluable lessons of the former and directly contributed to the policy mistakes that led to the global financial crisis. The subsequent rise of new economic theories, especially rational expectations and the efficient markets hypothesis, provided the intellectual foundation for the second US postwar order of domestic and international financial deregulation—an order that was arguably constructed in a fit of anti-Keynesianism.

Lessons Learned: Keynes and the First US Postwar Order

Some of the lessons of the Great Depression were learned even in the 1930s. The New Deal in the United States represented a final rejection of the completely unregulated, socially ruinous Dickensian style of capitalism of the 1890s. More narrowly and of particular interest here, President Roosevelt signed into law a series of banking acts that fundamentally reformed the US financial system, the fragility and unsoundness of which had contributed mightily to the Depression and lay in ruins in its wake. Among other things, this legislation created the Federal Deposit Insurance Corporation (FDIC) and the Securities and Exchange Commission (SEC), imposed interest rate ceilings on savings deposits (Regulation Q), and established new margin requirements (leveraged speculation having contributed to the stock market bubble and crash). Most famously, the Banking Act of 1933, which became known as the Glass-Steagall Act, reordered and compartmentalized the entire financial system. In particular, commercial and investment banking functions were segregated; the former were to offer loans to businesses, while the latter would underwrite and distribute corporate debt and equity. Neither was to be in the insurance business. Because of Glass-Steagall, the mighty House of Morgan was broken up (over the bitter and unrepentant opposition of its leadership), its remnants becoming a distinct commercial bank and an investment house.[2]

It needs to be acknowledged that the regulated, firewalled post–New Deal financial sector of the US economy—the industry of the 1940s, 1950s, 1960s, and 1970s—was not maximally efficient. Banking was, to a large extent, a profitable but boring business. But it was also a period of unprecedented financial stability in US history, which is just what the survivors of the Great Depression were looking for. Risk is an essential part of capitalism, and of banking, and it cannot be simply excised: from risk comes opportunity. But banks are uniquely vulnerable; even responsible, solvent banks could not suddenly meet a call on most of their liabilities at once.

And they are uniquely interdependent; engaging in business with industry counterparties means that the failure of one bank can threaten the positions of others, which is the opposite of most other business enterprises in which the failure of a competitor is good for business. Because finance is risky and, much more important, because the collective behavior of individual firms can easily and inadvertently generate *systemic* risk, oversight and regulation are essential. Systemic risk is the unstable, radioactive toxic waste of the financial sector. Just as the government regulates how industry must handle known carcinogens and dispose of the toxic waste its production processes generate, so the public needs government protection from the extreme dangers that would be inevitably produced by unregulated finance. Safe and solid banking is a public good.

Keynes did not inspire the New Deal banking legislation. But he was the singular, formative influence on the economic philosophy of the first US postwar order. The Depression-era US banking regulations were in accord with Keynes's ideal of a "middle way" between laissez-faire and collectivism, a capitalist economy in which some market forces would be managed and contained.[3] Keynes is a controversial figure, and he should be—brilliant, bold, and influential, he invites spirited debate. But, unfortunately, "Keynes" is all too often controversial for the wrong reasons: as a name invoked to condemn those who would engage in deficit spending or inflationary finance. (In fact, Keynes was quite wary of inflation and believed that most of the time government budgets should be balanced or in surplus.)

The 2007–8 financial crisis and ensuing "great recession" rekindled interest in Keynes.[4] This is to be welcomed, as his vast trove of original writings still has much to offer, now more than ever. But tapping this reservoir requires a disciplined hand: to work through decades of voluminous writing requires an alertness to the historical context of specific missives and to the evolution of his thought over time. And pitching a middle way will necessarily yield nuggets that lean more in one direction than another; collecting some but not others is an exercise in cherry-picking. But a consistent core can be distilled. Keynes thought that most markets work well most of the time and that there is no economically viable substitute (or attractive philosophical alternative) to undirected individuals pursuing their idiosyncratic interests, guided by a well-functioning price mechanism. But Keynes also knew that some markets don't work some of the time, and a few markets, in particular circumstances, perform dismally. He devoted much of his career to addressing these dysfunctions. Three main concerns stand out: First, that an economy, once stuck in a rut, often will be unable to right itself on its own; second, that financial markets, driven, for better and worse, by herd behavior, uncertainty, and unpredictable shifts in the attitudes and emotions that he called "animal spirits," are inherently prone to destructive cycles and panics; and third, that an unregulated international monetary system tends to veer toward unsustainable disequilibria, tends to magnify deflationary shocks, and always presents inescapable dilemmas for balancing domestic and international monetary stability.

Keynes's middle way was thus a hybrid that attempted to integrate dissatisfaction with unregulated capitalism with a great respect for market mechanisms. The first element—the rejection of laissez-faire economics—was a watershed. In 1926, in his midforties, Keynes became an apostate when he renounced his membership in the church of classical economics. "The World is *not* so governed from above that private and social interest always coincide," he declared. Into the 1930s, Keynes focused his attention increasingly on the "outstanding faults of the economic society in which we live." Unmediated capitalism, he wrote, "is not intelligent, it is not beautiful, it is not just, it is not virtuous—and it doesn't deliver the goods." Nevertheless, even in the depths of the Depression, Keynes was motivated to save capitalism, not bury it. He was especially concerned that in the absence of needed reforms, the risk was great that unreasonable alternatives would be pursued instead; this was not an idle concern for someone with a ringside seat at European politics in the 1930s.[5]

The second element, the importance of market mechanisms, is not to be underestimated. Once again, a key phrase is the mantra "Most markets work well most of the time." This was certainly Keynes's position, and it is what makes his approach the *middle* way. "A large part of the established body of economic doctrine I cannot but accept as broadly correct," he wrote. "I do not doubt it." On microeconomic questions, "the advantage to efficiency of the decentralization of decisions and of individual responsibilities is even greater, perhaps, than the nineteenth century supposed." In addition, decentralized individualism encourages vital experimentation, assures the liberty of choice, and protects society from totalitarianism. Keynes was utterly dismissive of Marxism and rejected socialism as well, which "offers no middle course." His allergy to economic collectivism was based not only on his assessment of the economic incoherence of such approaches but also because they cut against the grain of the individualism that was at the core of his personal philosophy. As his contemporary and first biographer Roy Harrod observed, Keynes was "an individualist to the finger tips." This was the Keynes who could write to Friedrich von Hayek that *The Road to Serfdom* was "a grand book" and that "morally and philosophically I find myself in agreement with virtually the whole of it; and not only in agreement with it, but in a deeply moved agreement."[6]

Keynes's interventionism was reserved, then, for the macroeconomic sphere and especially for areas that pertained to the maintenance of aggregate demand, incentives to invest and consume, and the stability of the financial sector—places where the market, left to its own devices, would too often stumble and fail to self-correct. But one of the lessons of the Great Depression was that the practice of the middle way at home might be undermined by international market forces spilling across borders. Thus the middle way required either erecting formidable barriers that would reduce engagement with the international economy (a disastrously inefficient choice) or an international economic order designed to accommodate diverse national pursuits of varied middle ways.

This became the basis of the first US postwar order, what John Ruggie dubbed "the compromise of embedded liberalism," which he defined as the consensus that "multilateralism would be predicated upon domestic interventionism."[7] This meant that the postwar institutions of the American system would feature mechanisms, safeguards, and escape clauses to assure that domestic economic management would not be incompatible with exposure to the international economy. The General Agreement on Tariffs and Trade (GATT), therefore, which was designed to encourage liberalization and nondiscrimination, was also designed to include such shock absorbers. It was, after all, the result of the "International Conference on Trade and *Employment*," and in the wake of the Depression, it was employment that mattered, with trade understood as a means to that end.

Similarly, and as an even more pressing matter, the international monetary system, designed to facilitate exchange in an open, expanding global economy, must not be permitted (as it would if left to its own devices) to undermine varieties of domestic economic practice, impose a deflationary bias, and disproportionately throw the burdens of adjustment solely on states running deficits in their external accounts. Keynes strongly favored a system that accommodated controls on short-term capital flows, as he understood that such circuit breakers were essential to the practice of the middle way. As he wrote in his earliest wartime memos on a postwar monetary system, "nothing is more certain than that the movement of capital funds must be regulated."[8] Keynes had hoped for an even more capacious IMF that would place greater pressure on surplus countries to make adjustments. The Americans, holding most of the cards, resisted these points and generally got their way. But the articles of agreement of the IMF explicitly accommodated capital controls.

The Long Good-bye: From Keynes to Keynesianism

"Keynesianism," the most influential economic doctrine of the 1950s and 1960s, stumbled in the 1970s and was declared dead and buried by the 1980s. Reports of its death turned out to be exaggerated, but Keynes's own economics—a very different animal—had been fading away for decades. Keynes himself was gone by 1946, and he had little control over his legacy, a fate he anticipated when he famously joked after one wartime meeting with American economists, "I was the only non-Keynesian in the room." User-friendly postwar Keynesianism was much less than simply a pale copy of the original. From his vast writings, a select few of Keynes's ideas were distilled into what became known as "Keynesianism." The postwar interpretation of this took the form of the so-called hydraulic Keynesianism, which originated in John Hicks's 1937 interpretation of *The General Theory* and was developed in the "neoclassical synthesis" first articulated by Paul Samuelson and refined in the decades that followed.[9]

Keynesianism was not without its opponents. Many of Keynes's own students had little patience for what they saw as the "bastardization" of his ideas, but they were quickly escorted to the fringes of the economics discipline.[10] More formidable were the monetarists, led by Milton Friedman. The postwar debates between Keynesians and monetarists engaged a number of issues, but crucial among them was the extent to which government policy could "fine tune" the economy. In 1958, A. W. Phillips published a paper that showed a stable negative relationship between wage rates and unemployment in Britain from 1861 to 1957. Many economists argued in the 1960s that governments could choose their preferred spot on this "Phillips curve": depending on circumstances, some might be willing to tolerate more inflation for less unemployment, others the reverse. The management of the Phillips curve was debated in the early 1960s, while at the policy level, fine tuning was in vogue.[11]

This was the Keynesianism whose floorboards collapsed under the weight of academic critiques of the 1960s and the real-world circumstances of the 1970s. Advancing similar arguments, Friedman and Edmund Phelps argued that government expansionary monetary policies designed to increase inflation would only reduce unemployment in the short run, as actors in the system confuse the general price increase in the economy with a relative price increase for their product, and increase output. Also, inflation reduces the real wage bill faced by firms in the short run, which encourages an expansion of production. After a short period (which Friedman argued could be two to five years) production would return to its previous level, as all parties' expectations adapted to the new inflation level. Thus, according to the Friedman/Phelps critique, fine tuning that increased inflation would only increase output in the short run, with the result that, after adjustment, output would be the same but inflation higher. This became known as the natural rate hypothesis: that there was a "natural rate" of unemployment in an economy, from which short-term reductions could only be purchased by increasing inflation—and ever more inflation at that. Phillips curves were thus said to be vertical in the long run.[12]

In the 1970s, inflation and unemployment increased simultaneously, lending back-of-the-envelope support to the natural rate hypothesis and delegitimizing fine tuning, and government stewardship of the economy more generally. In retrospect, the 1970s stagflation exposed different problems with hydraulic Keynesianism: the economic difficulties of the period were rooted in supply shocks, which existing Keynesian theories were simply not equipped to address, and generated outcomes that did not easily fit the expectations of their models. In any event, these events were transformative: the very high 1970s inflation was wrung from the system only through a severe recession orchestrated by new Federal Reserve chairman Paul Volcker; and as a matter of theory, the natural rate hypothesis was integrated into the mainstream consensus of economic theory. (Those lessons were actually overlearned: the trauma of the costly Volcker disinflation and wariness about politically motivated bursts of inflation contributed to the unrelated, unsupported new conventional wisdom that all inflation was costly and that macroeconomic policy needed to be designed to vigilantly guard against its potential emergence.) The debate between chastened Keynesians and their opponents shifted to what, if any, productive role the government could play in macroeconomic policy management. For the next two decades, the Keynesians retreated too hastily, while their opponents over-reached.[13]

A new, much more extreme critique of Keynesianism emerged in the form of new classical macroeconomics, at the heart of which was the theory of rational expectations. As the name implies, new classical macroeconomics was self-consciously designed to build a new approach to macroeconomics on pre-Keynesian foundations. Championed by economists such as Robert Lucas and Thomas Sargent, rational expectations theory implied "policy ineffectiveness," that is, that there was very little the government can do to influence the economy at all, even in the short run, other than inefficiently get in the way. Rational expectations theory holds that economic agents, collectively, cannot be systematically fooled. Instead of the passive "adaptive expectations" modeled by old school Keynesians and monetarists, whereby actors make guesses about future outcomes based on readings of past experience, agents under rational expectations are assumed to gather all relevant currently available information and apply that information to the single, shared, best-available (and essentially correct) model of how the economy works. Individual actors can make errors; but, collectively, those errors will be randomly distributed around the correct model.[14]

The crucial component of rational expectations theory is that actors must share knowledge of that singular, largely correct economic theory. As its founding father John Muth explained, "expectations, since they are informed predictions of future events, are essentially the same as the predictions of the relevant economic theory." In 2005, Sargent, in response to a question about "differences among people's models," explained patiently that in the context of rational expectations, "you simply cannot talk about" such differences. "All agents inside the model, the econometrician, and God share the same model."[15] Rational expectations theory captured the imagination of the economics discipline (just as the Keynesian upheaval had done generations earlier), and in the heady days of the new classical revolution it was widely held, if not crowed, that the Keynesian brand was in irretrievable disrepute and would soon be out of business. In the

1980s and 1990s, however, a school of thought called new Keynesianism emerged. It integrated rational expectations into its models while pushing back against the more extreme positions of the new classicals.[16] But new Keynesianism—a convergence of hydraulic Keynesianism with some elements of monetarism and aspects of the rational expectations revolution—was still further removed from the actual Keynes.[17]

Most fundamentally, contra the broad consensus that emerged in the 1990s among mainstream macroeconomists of all stripes, Keynes did *not* assume any kind of rational expectations nor, crucially, its fellow traveler, the efficient markets hypothesis, which holds that current market prices accurately express the underlying value of an asset because they reflect the sum of a collective, rational calculus. On the contrary, Keynes held that investors more often grope in the dark than calculate risk; they can't assign precise probabilities to all potential eventualities because too many factors are unknowable. Faced with this uncertainty, investors inevitably place great weight on the apparent expectations of others. Thus, as Keynes famously argued, investors need to make their best guesses, not simply about the likely business environment, but also about the guesses of other investors regarding that environment. The resulting herd-like behavior can at times generate dysfunctional consequences, such as self-fulfilling prognostications of financial crisis.[18]

Unlike the world described by rational expectations, with its efficient, dispassionate, richly informed, and theoretically confident optimizers, Keynes emphasized instead the central role of "animal spirits," of daring and ambitious entrepreneurs placing bets in an environment characterized by uncertainty, that is, by crucial unknowns and unknowables. As virtually every close student of Keynes has insisted, uncertainty (as opposed to risk),[19] is a "guiding insight at the heart of Keynes's intellectual revolution."[20] This is present in *The General Theory* but stated most plainly in his 1937 *Quarterly Journal of Economics* paper, the only academic paper Keynes published attendant to the book, and which was designed to distill the essential contributions of his magnum opus. There he identified the two "main grounds of my departure" from orthodoxy, one of which makes this central point about uncertainty. (The second relates to the possibility of inadequate demand, the more familiar Keynesian "departure.") He wrote: "The orthodox theory assumes that we have a knowledge of the future of a kind quite different from that which we actually possess. . . .

This hypothesis of a calculable future leads to a wrong interpretation of the principles of behavior which the need for action compels us to adopt, and to an underestimation of the concealed factors of utter doubt, precariousness, hope and fear."[21]

Rational expectations was remarkably successful—as a rhetorical device. It implies that the alternative is to assume people somehow hold "irrational expectations." But Keynes (and others) did not argue that actors were irrational. Rather, he assumed agents were essentially rational, purposeful, and motivated—but not hyperrationalist automatons who always have the right information, know the proper underlying model of how the economy will work, and as such can predict future outcomes with canny precision (leaving space for randomly distributed errors that cancel each other out). Economic players as seen by Keynes will thoughtfully process information, but they will often guess; they will fall back on personal experiences, received "conventional wisdom," and various rules of thumb to help guide them through the cacophony of economic activity and irreducible uncertainty.

It is important to appreciate that one need not embrace Keynes to reject rational expectations. Some of the greatest and most celebrated anti-Keynesian economists have explicitly rejected the utility of assuming such hyper-rationality and eagle-eye omniscience. Hayek insisted that in the study of such complex phenomena as markets, economists could expect to offer no more than "only very general predictions of the *kind* of events which we must expect in a given situation." And he was fine with that. In fact, he was rather insistent about it since his purpose was to chastise the hubris of his fellow economists: "I confess that I prefer true but imperfect knowledge, even if it leaves much in-determined and unpredictable, to a pretence of exact knowledge that is likely to be false." Frank Knight also stressed "true uncertainty," which is "unmeasurable" and which "must be taken in a sense radically different" from risk. Knight not only insisted on the fundamental distinction between risk and uncertainty (a distinction incompatible with rational expectations) but saw uncertainty as the very engine of capitalism, from which entrepreneurs find their opportunities for profit. Uncertainty brings about the "necessity of acting upon opinion rather than knowledge" and of following one's own instincts while trying to gauge the opinions of others for additional clues and insights.[22]

Lessons Unlearned: Finance Risen and the
Second US Postwar Order

This might all seem like academic trivializing but for two things: first, rational expectations theory is wrong—that is, outcomes in the real world are inconsistent with *its* expectations (which should be of little surprise given the shaky deductive foundations of the approach); and second, the broad acceptance of rational expectations by otherwise disparate branches of mainstream economic theory offered intellectual gravitas to financial deregulation.

New classical models, in particular, although they took the economics profession by storm, soon revealed themselves to be "a triumph of ingenuity and technical virtuosity over observation," generating testable hypotheses that "yielded mainly negative results." A similar fate met tests of rational expectations, and even leading anti-Keynesians concluded that "the strong rational expectations hypothesis cannot be accepted as a serious empirical hypothesis." Other mainstream economists concluded that "the weight of the empirical evidence is sufficiently strong to compel us to suspend belief in the hypothesis of rational expectations."[23] By 1999, even Thomas Sargent was forced to throw in the empirical towel. In *The Conquest of American Inflation* he evaluated two competing macroeconomic models designed to explain the pattern of inflation in the United States, one a modified version of the old-fashioned adaptive-expectations model and the other based on the rational expectations challenge that discredited the former. It turns out, Sargent concludes, that the old-fashioned model, "which seems to defend discredited methods," is more successful than the rational expectations version of the natural rate model, which is "more popular among modern macroeconomists." Subsequent critics have spoken even more plainly, concluding that rational expectations models "have turned out to be grossly inconsistent with actual behavior in real world markets, particularly in financial markets."[24]

The failure of rational expectations theory roots back to its extreme (and implausible) assumptions about individual behavior and economic theory. In practice, rational individuals reach different conclusions when presented with the same facts. Knight attributed this to the "inherent, absolute unpredictability of things" and expected that actors would display "diversity in conduct," rather than uniformity.[25] More dubious still is the assumption that all actors are aware of the "true" (and unchanging) underlying model of the macroeconomy. As one critic notes, rational expectations assumes that "the representative individual, hence everyone in the economy, behaves as if he had *a complete understanding of the economic mechanisms governing the world*." But people don't. "No economist can point to a particular model, and honestly say 'this is how the world works,'" explains Mervyn King, governor of the Bank of England from 2003 to 2013. "Our understanding of the economy is incomplete and constantly evolving."[26]

Nevertheless, although the wave of new classical macroeconomics crested and receded, the residue of rational expectations changed the terrain and stuck across all brands of mainstream macroeconomic thought, including new Keynesianism, which was a far cry from Keynesianism, which was a far cry from Keynes. And from the consensus about rational expectations flowed the efficient markets hypothesis, which held that a free market "always produces fundamentally correct prices." Following rational expectations, prices continuously and efficiently reflect all available information, and the price of financial assets, for example, should therefore be relatively stable, accurate, and fluctuating randomly around their intrinsic values; that is, asset prices represent true, underlying, fundamental values. But, not surprisingly, there is a considerable body of evidence that raised doubts about whether this is true in practice.[27]

It is now clear that two foundations of anti-Keynesianism—rational expectations and the efficient markets hypothesis, both of which are embraced by mainstream economics despite the absence of empirical support—are simply wrong. But these beliefs were critical in shaping ideas about financial markets in the 1990s. A Keynesian perspective holds that although a capacious financial sector is an essential, irreplaceable element in the functioning of a capitalist economy, it is nevertheless *dangerous*; that is, the financial sector is inherently prone to failure—failures that wreak havoc with the rest of the economy. (This perspective, it should be noted, is consistent with the tumultuous regularity of banking crises throughout much of US history, from its founding until the decades following the New Deal regulations, and then again after those regulations were repealed.) From a Keynesian perspective, then, finance, however crucial, nevertheless involves as normal practice the moral equivalent of juggling vials of nitroglycerine on a moving (and crowded) train. Regulation and oversight of practice is essential. Letting "the market rule" in finance makes as much sense as letting the market decide where and how nuclear waste will be disposed of.

But from the anti-Keynesian perspective, financial markets always know best and should be left to supervise themselves. The efficient markets hypothesis "justified, and indeed demanded, financial deregulation." To get ahead of the story, discussed in greater detail in chapter 5 (spoiler alert), this turned out to be wrong. The origin of the current crisis "lies in the operation of free (unregulated) financial markets," leading post-Keynesian Paul Davidson is quick to point out. "Liberalized financial markets . . . could not heal the bloodletting catastrophe that they had caused."[28] And those financial markets, of course, did not liberalize themselves. Especially from the 1990s, a bipartisan project of financial deregulation characterized US public policy. Key figures in the deregulatory crusade include Larry Summers of the Clinton Treasury department, Phil Gramm, chairman of the Senate banking committee, and Federal Reserve chairman Alan Greenspan. Abetted by widely held but dangerously misguided assumptions about the stability and self-correcting hyper-rationality of financial markets, fueled by the fortune of a massive lobbying effort by the financial sector, and reinforced by a revolving door culture in which regulators and politicians could anticipate holding future, lucrative positions on Wall Street, the White House, Congress, and the Federal Reserve pushed through legislation that deregulated finance, steamrolling those few who got in the way.

The antecedents of the unleashing of finance in the 1990s can be traced to the 1970s, when a number of factors nudged policymakers into loosening some of the Depression-era protective strictures. The deregulatory ball, once pushed, developed a momentum of its own. Factors that contributed to the initial reforms of the 1970s included increasing complaints about the visible inefficiencies of the banking sector coupled with innovations that made circumventing rules easier; forgetting the lessons of the past after three decades of safe and boring banking had created a false sense of confidence in financial stability; and, more than anything, the rise of inflation. Rising prices put pressure on usury laws that restricted the imposition of high interest rates, especially on credit cards, which were becoming much more widely used. And Regulation Q, which was part of the Banking Act of 1933, capped the rates of interest that banks could offer on various forms of deposit accounts to prevent banks from being pressured by competition to take imprudent risks.[29] That old joke about banking's 3–6–3 model (offer depositors 3 percent interest, lend at 6 percent, and be on the golf course at 3) described a system that only worked when inflation was low; with double-digit inflation, capping nominal interest rates meant that real interest rates were negative.

Deregulations in the late Carter and early Reagan administrations eliminated interest rate restrictions, solving one set of problems while unleashing others (such as putting smaller institutions under pressure to find more lucrative rates of return); embedded in the legislation were provisions that lifted numerous Depression-era prohibitions against a variety of financial practices. In the Carter and especially Reagan era deregulation in general was in vogue (think airlines, trucking, and telephones), and in that context, lobbying from the banking sector and complacency about financial stability hitched a ride on that deregulatory zeal.[30] But liberated banking invited and even demanded greater risk taking. In the search for new profits, banks began to engage in the trading of securities, activities that became increasingly complex, enmeshed, and more and more important as a source of income. Banking became exciting again; so exciting it inevitably led to crisis, in this instance, the savings-and-loan crisis, which marked the end of fifty years of banking stability in the United States. (Thousands of banks failed, compared with 234 bank failures from 1934 to 1980.) The excitement cost the government over $200 billion, the bailout necessary to prevent the crisis from spreading further.[31]

Regulation Q, which undoubtedly was in need of revision and reform, was but the tip of the iceberg. Into the 1990s momentum gathered to repeal the Glass-Steagall Act in its entirety, and in particular to dismantle the firewalls between commercial and investment banking. From the Clinton White House, the effort was led by treasury secretary and former Goldman Sachs cochair Robert Rubin, in close partnership with Senate banking committee chair Gramm, and with the blessing of Federal Reserve board chair Greenspan. An Ayn Rand acolyte, Greenspan was so enthralled with the magic of the free market that he even thought it would prevent, unaided by government, financial fraud. He succeeded the much more cautious and skeptical Paul Volcker in 1987, and the new Fed chief held the view "that liberalization in these markets was long overdue." Greenspan pushed for the repeal of Glass-Steagall, helping matters along by loosening the Fed's interpretation of its prohibitions.

Those with differing opinions were promptly dispatched. John Moscow, deputy general counsel of the Federal Reserve Bank of New York, published an op-ed in the *New York Times* ("Bigger Banks, Bigger Problems") in which he argued that "the results could be catastrophic" if Glass-Steagall were repealed. He suggested that policy should be decided on the basis of "the public interest" as opposed to "the personal interests of the bankers." He was gone from the New York Fed within weeks. In those heady days, confidence was such that in 1998, Citibank merged with Travelers Group to form CitiGroup in *anticipation* of the repeal, which became official on November 12, 1999, with the passage of the Gramm-Leach-Bliley Act. Writing on the eve of the financial crisis, Greenspan called it "a milestone of business legislation" from which "we dare not go back."[32]

There are some ethical issues here that need to be acknowledged. Greenspan was on the board of directors of J.P. Morgan at the time of his appointment to be Fed chair. When Gramm left the Senate, he immediately joined the Swiss banking giant UBS, where he served as an investment banker and lobbyist. Rubin joined Citigroup after leaving the Clinton administration, drawing nine-figure compensation and serving as its chairman from 2007 to 2009. This will be worth remembering when I later discuss how US officials routinely criticized "crony capitalism," to which they attributed the 1997–8 Asian financial crisis. But more to the point here, repealing Glass-Steagall allowed for the creation of CitiGroup, the world's largest financial services company and archetypical too-big-to-fail institution. Citigroup, not surprisingly, was also a major underwriter of Enron, Global Crossing, and WorldCom, companies that collapsed under the weight of shady accounting gimmicks, before suffering its own enormous losses and requiring a massive government bailout during the financial crisis.[33]

Dismantling existing regulations was only one half of the story of the great 1990s financial liberalization project. The other half was the fight *not* to supervise and regulate new and fantastically expanding sectors of the financial economy, which produced massive wealth, fueled the rapid growth of industry, and were inherent carriers of systemic risk. The interrelated phenomena of routine securitization (the repackaging, blending, and resale of bundles of financial assets such as mortgages) and the aston-ishing growth of trading in derivatives (any asset whose value "derived" from another asset, from simple futures and options to extremely com-plex, enmeshed, counterparty risk and insurance dispersal exotica) forged the financialization of the US economy. These activities were enormously profitable for their issuers and traders and were largely unsupervised by an oversight and regulatory apparatus that was designed long before such products came on the scene.

As Greenspan observed, "the extraordinary development and expan-sion of financial derivatives," growing at a compound rate of 20 percent annually and reaching a notional value of $70 trillion in 1999 (it would surpass $600 trillion in 2008), was "by far the most significant event in fi-nance" during the 1990s. Greenspan lauded the instruments as improving risk management, a major factor in bank earnings, and the source of the growth of the financial sector's share of corporate output, and he saw little reason to be concerned.[34] These attitudes reflected a new, ebullient conven-tional wisdom rooted in the ascendant logic of the rational expectations/efficient markets hypothesis. From this sanguine perspective, the prices of all of these assets reflect their underlying fundamental values, determined by the collective wisdom of savvy, well-informed market players drawing on sophisticated understandings of the underlying logic of those markets.

A few voices were raised in concern, however. As early as 1992, the otherwise invariably market-friendly *Economist* enumerated, with consid-erable alarm, the risks that were emerging from this new and uncertain quarter. Warning that "a derivatives disaster could overwhelm the world's financial system," it was somewhat reassured to report that "tighter control of derivatives seems inevitable." In May 1994, the US Government Ac-countability Office (GAO) issued a report describing the very rapid growth of "largely unregulated" derivatives markets. In sober, balanced language that called attention to the benefits of these products and the need to pre-serve market efficiency and competitiveness, it nevertheless emphasized "the weaknesses and gaps that impede regulatory preparedness" in these risky, opaque markets. (The conclusion phrased it more bluntly: "Federal regulatory authority over the derivatives-dealing affiliates of major securi-ties firms and insurance companies is limited or nonexistent.") The report raised some questions about the simple and, especially in retrospect, plainly obvious dangers about how "the size and concentration of derivatives activity, combined with derivatives-related linkages, could cause any financial disruption to spread faster and be harder to contain." Another risk was that, given that a few of the market participants were very large, "the abrupt failure or withdrawal from trading of one of these dealers could undermine stability in several markets simultaneously. This could lead to a chain of market withdrawals, or possibly firm failures, and a systemic crisis." The report concluded with the recommendation that "Congress begin systematically addressing the need to revamp and modernize the entire US financial regulatory system," which "has not kept pace with the dramatic and rapid changes in the domestic and global financial markets."[35]

At the time of the report, momentum was arguably moving toward some limited regulatory action regarding derivatives. Six bills were introduced in Congress in 1994 that proposed new requirements about disclosures of derivatives activity, ordered the GAO to study the speculative uses of derivatives, and sought to prohibit federally insured depository institutions from using derivatives for speculative purposes. Events suggested some urgency for action: in December 1994, Orange County, California, one of the largest counties in the country, lost a fortune through derivatives trading and was forced to file for bankruptcy; its bond rating fell overnight from AA to CCC. Other municipalities lost big on similar bets; "perhaps, because the returns were so good, there was not enough attention to risk" one participant admitted. In 1995, losses from derivatives trading brought down Barings Bank. The oldest investment bank in Britain (it helped finance the Louisiana Purchase), it was ruined, and it sold for a one-pound coin. In 1996, four new derivatives-related bills were introduced in Congress. But none of these bills became law, and the GAO's follow-up report of November 1996 was forced to concede that none of its recommendations had been implemented. "Accounting standards for derivatives continue to be insufficient," which was "a major unresolved problem," the report warned. "Derivatives dealing activities of securities firm and insurance company affiliates, which are still growing, continue to be largely unregulated."[36]

But financial regulation, however modest, however cautious, however market friendly, was anathema to the new American model of efficient markets and the expansion and ascendency of the financial sector. The GAO reports accomplished nothing but provoked a fierce push-back in the form of an overwhelming, countervailing effort by the industry and their like-minded allies. From 1989 to 2002, for example, Gramm was showered with campaign contributions from commercial banks and Wall Street firms, which also sponsored speaking events at which he appeared. Finance was playing offense, not defense: its efforts were designed not simply to resist any new regulation or oversight but to banish, through law, the possibility of such things. In the two crucial years leading up to the final victory for liberated finance, the industry spent almost $400 million in lobbying efforts and campaign contributions.[37]

The Clinton administration, in particular Summers, who became secretary of the treasury in 1999, fiercely resisted any attempt to regulate derivatives. According to the lead author of the GAO reports, administration officials lobbied against them even as they were being written. They were even more aggressive in policing their own, chasing Brooksley Born, head of the Commodity Futures Trading Commission, from office. Born repeatedly raised concerns about the potential risks she saw emanating from unregulated derivatives markets. During testimony before Congress, she was contradicted by other members of the administration; in private, she was castigated by Rubin and by Summers, who had a reputation for screaming at subordinates over the phone. Born resigned in mid–1999.[38]

A crucial ally in these efforts was Alan Greenspan, whose voice carried enormous weight. The powerful Fed chair was a passionate opponent of any government interference in the market, which, as a matter of evangelical faith, he viewed as optimally and uniquely self-regulating and self-correcting. Greenspan testified repeatedly and forcefully against the need to mediate any systemic risks that derivatives might present. "Professional counterparties to privately negotiated contracts," he assured, "have demonstrated their ability to protect themselves from losses from fraud and counterparty insolvencies." Famous for being cryptic in his commentaries, on this issue he spoke plainly: "Regulation of derivatives transactions that are privately negotiated are unnecessary." Expressing confidence in the self-interest of private actors, he saw "no reason to question the underlying stability" of derivatives markets.[39]

In November 1999 the President's Working Group on Financial Markets issued a report on derivatives markets under the signatures of Summers, Greenspan, Arthur Levitt (chairman of the Securities and Exchange Commission), and William Rainer (the Wall Street insider who replaced

Born at the CFTC). The report called on Congress to address the "dangers of continued legal uncertainty" that might "discourage innovation and growth of these important markets and damage US leadership in these areas" by making clear to market participants that derivatives markets in the United States would not be regulated.[40] Gramm took this ball and ran with it, championing the Commodity Futures Modernization Act, which prevented the regulation of derivatives, including the credit-default swaps that would play a central role in the 2007–8 financial crisis. (Gramm also slipped in what became known as the "Enron loophole," which gave additional special exceptions for trading in energy derivatives.)[41] The act passed in the lame-duck days of the Clinton administration (actually the day after the Supreme Court issued its *Bush v. Gore* decision), and in its wake the derivatives markets shot ahead even faster.[42] The value of trades leapt from $100 trillion to $500 trillion in nominal value. It is not surprising that in these frenzied, lucrative, and competitive markets, individual firms were not always certain of exactly which counterparties owed what to whom; and with the government determined to get out of the way, the radar screens that might have been attuned to systemic risk were unattended.

The second US postwar order was built on the faith that financial markets, left to themselves, were efficient, self-regulating, and self-correcting. The repeal of Glass-Steagall and the passage of the Commodity Futures Modernization Act completed the process of transition from a Keynesian order, with a financial sector regulated, supervised, and embedded firmly as the handmaiden of real economic activity, to an economy characterized by unbound finance as an end and a virtue in and of itself. It was to be welcomed and encouraged that the financial sector should become the most important sector in the US economy. (And, as discussed in the next chapter, it was also understood as geopolitically and economically advantageous to the US to have global financial markets as open and unregulated as possible.) The lessons of history and the logic of economic theory suggested otherwise, but these were both superciliously brushed aside as obsolete, even as those lessons kept coming (Orange County, Barings, Enron). In 1998, Long Term Capital Management, arguably the poster child of liberated finance, composed of really smart guys building very fancy models and making billions on Wall Street, took some big leveraged risks and lost a fortune. Its failure was so dangerous that the New York Fed saw the need to coordinate a multibillion dollar bailout provided by LTCM's private creditors. (The creditors were paid back, but LTCM folded in 2000.)[43] Greenspan, for one, brushed off the LTCM affair in his 2007 memoirs, repeating his mantra, Bankers know better than regulators. The apostles of high finance, like Citizen Kane, would need more than one lesson, and they would get more than one lesson.[44]

4

SEEDS OF DISCORD: THE ASIAN
FINANCIAL CRISIS

Liberated finance was the American vision—at home, as seen in the previous chapter—and abroad as well. As Lawrence Summers, who, first as right-hand man to Treasury Secretary Robert Rubin and then as Rubin's successor was one of the principal architects and orchestrators of implementing this vision, which he stated plainly at the time: "Financial liberalization, both domestically and internationally, is a critical part of the US agenda." Country by country, meeting by meeting, and institution by institution, in the 1990s the United States pressed countries to dismantle their capital controls and to create opportunities and access for the giants of the American financial services sector. Not coincidentally, at the same time, the International Monetary Fund, an institution constitutionally incapable of taking bold action against the wind of American opposition (and indeed, in this case, with the strong support of the American executive director of the Fund's board), in a radical and ambitious power play, moved to force its member states to completely eliminate their capital controls. This, despite the fact that there was a lack of empirical evidence to support the contention that capital unbound was appropriate economic policy or to show that an absence of capital controls was associated with improved real economic performance, and despite the fact that periods of high capital mobility *are* clearly associated with an increased likelihood of financial crisis. Nevertheless, the IMF decided to abandon its Keynesian charter (which was written with the presumption that states would rely on some capital controls) and embark on an ambitious project to revise its articles of agreement, a project described by one account as designed "to make unrestricted capital flows a condition of membership in the global economy."[1]

The confluence of ideas, interests, and power that led the United States and the IMF to push hard for universal, uninhibited capital deregulation, is, like so many questions about monetary affairs, not easily disentangled.[2] As with domestic deregulation, the rejection of a Keynesian perspective on expectations and the behavior of the financial sector (and, more broadly, of embedded liberalism), in favor of rational expectations, the efficient markets hypothesis, and the idea that financial markets are always right and always know best, certainly played a crucial role in supporting, or at least permitting, this push. The convergence of forces moving toward this intellectual position in the academy, in Washington, and among the professional staff at the IMF, not to mention within that revolving door traversed by Wall Street denizens and their would-be regulators, was a crucial building block of the second US postwar order.[3] But interests, and power, are not to be underestimated. The ascendant US financial services sector was pushing its friends and patrons in Washington to fight to make the world more hospitable to its business; and those friends, commonly former and future colleagues, needed little pushing. And the stewards of the American economy could not fail to see the comparative advantages on the table: the giant and growing US financial sector was world class and a world beater. Thinking even more broadly, in a post–Cold War world of American unipolarity, the promotion of globalization, financial and otherwise, was recognized as even further enhancing the US geopolitical position.[4]

But the US push, and especially the IMF project, was ill-timed. (And it's not like they weren't warned. The Mexican financial crisis of 1995 unfolded as if its sole purpose was to wave a red flag warning of the dangers ahead.)[5] Just as the IMF was setting the type on its new amendment, the Asian financial crisis began to unfold. A sobering reminder—or at least it should have been—of the perils of finance unbound, the Asian financial crisis of 1997–98, and, just as important, the responses to it by the United States and the IMF, planted the seeds that would grow to *delegitimize* the second US postwar order, especially in Asia. To be clear, the Asian crisis did not undermine US power—in the short run, it enhanced it, and suggested that the American way was the only way. But the *ideational* implications were profound, and they were magnified after the 2007–8 crisis. On the eve of the Asian crisis the United States and the IMF insisted that deregulated finance was the only plausible and permissible public policy choice. And with the surprising emergence and spread of the crisis, an ideological fissure was exposed. Many in Asia saw the crisis for what it was: a classic international financial crisis, something common throughout history and especially common during periods of particularly high capital mobility. The IMF/US perspective saw it differently. According to Fed chairman Greenspan, testifying before Congress, the "root" causes of the crisis could be found in the "poor public policy" within the Asian states themselves.[6] IMF accounts were similarly myopic, not to mention amnesic, with blame for the crisis placed exclusively on the domestic economic policies of states whose economies and macroeconomic management the Fund had only recently been touting.

Japan's vice minister of finance Eisuke Sakakibara, on the other hand, was among those who saw it quite differently and tended to emphasize the role of the "inherent instability of liberalized international capital markets" in contributing to the disaster.[7] Sakakibara and others in Asia were also very alert to, if powerless to do anything about, the nakedly opportunistic US response to the crisis and the gratuitously deflationary measures imposed by the IMF that made a bad situation worse. This bullying was not lost on others, including China, which was spared, like most Asian states that had retained their capital controls, from the worst of the crisis. But it did not spare them, however, from constant (and continued) American lectures on the pressing need for financial liberalization. China's resistance to that advice helped to spare it (once again) from the worst of the crisis of 2007–8 and reinforced attitudes about the soundness of that advice and the underlying American model. The failure of the new American financial model, at home and abroad, at least as perceived by others, will contribute to the new heterogeneity of thinking about how to best manage the world's money and finance.

This chapter begins with the parallel pushes of the United States and the IMF. I then review the astonishing academic facts: that the rush to unleash finance was more of a leap of faith than a sober policy grounded in good economic theory. From there I turn to the unanticipated Asian financial crisis and how this gave some parties pause about the wisdom of the great capital liberalization project, though it did not change its evangelists, who saw in the crisis an opportunity to double down on their preferences. Ultimately, the Asian financial crisis and crises that would soon follow in Russia and elsewhere weakened and discredited the IMF and put an end to the idea of reforming its charter. But the underlying ideology at the IMF, and the ideology (and ambitions) of the United States, continued uninterrupted into the first decade of the new century.

The Great Capital-Deregulation Project

Support for financial deregulation was part of the general ambiance of the Republican 1980s, with advances visible but tempered by its second-rank status on the list of Reagan-Bush policy priorities; the cautious skepticism of Paul Volcker, chairman of the Federal Reserve Board until 1987, who tended to throw cold water on such schemes as his position allowed; and resistance from Democrats in Congress. The prudent Volcker was replaced by libertarian evangelist Greenspan, but it was the Clinton administration that was responsible for reversing the crucial first and third of these impediments to finance unbound. The new administration did not invent the new ideology of financial deregulation that had been gaining momentum in the 1980s.[8] But its embrace of the new orthodoxy represented a decisive shift in the political balance of power that would open the floodgates of unbridled liberalization.

With the Democratic Party in the political wilderness—only Jimmy Carter's dispiriting one term had interrupted twenty years of Republican control of the White House—Clinton ran for president as a "new" and centrist Democrat. Clinton was quick to embrace free trade, an item that had been slipping from the Democratic column, and even quicker to embrace Wall Street, wooing the mandarins of lower Manhattan from early in his campaign. In June 1991, the young governor of Arkansas impressed an assembled gathering of Wall Street executives, as he met for the first time Robert Rubin, the cochair of Goldman Sachs.[9] Clinton later appointed Rubin as the first director of his newly created National Economic Council, and then as treasury secretary in 1995.

In the new administration's partnership with Wall Street it was a very short step from supporting free trade to supporting free trade in finance, buttressed by the calculation that the Untied States was well positioned to see its economic and strategic interests advanced in a world where capital flowed as freely across borders as conceivably possible. And the administration was of one mind on this issue, pushing hard around the globe, but especially in Asia, to expand opportunities for US banks, insurance companies, and brokerage houses. "Our financial services industry wanted into these markets," the head of Clinton's Council of Economic Advisers explained. Wall Street was soon "delighted" as, across the board, the administration's Commerce department and trade representatives pressed their counterparts abroad to lift capital restrictions to the benefit of US companies such as Fidelity, Citibank, and (the ultimately notorious) insurance giant AIG.[10]

Clinton's first treasury secretary, Lloyd Bentsen, was initially the most visible public face of this new and assertive brand of US diplomacy. The Texan was plain spoken in elucidating the logic of the new priority: finance was becoming an ever more important part of the US economy, and "service exports are a major counterbalance to our imports of manufactured products." "Disappointed" at the pace of global financial liberalization, he repeatedly pressed Asian leaders on the issue. It was not, at least initially, an easy sell. At one two-day conference in Hawaii in March 1994, hosted by Bentsen's Treasury department, finance ministers from Japan, Thailand, Malaysia, and Indonesia all expressed reluctance to engage in swift liberalization and raised concerns about the possibility of destabilizing financial flows and the dangers of "hot" money and speculation. They were even more uniform in their agreement that they had little desire to be summoned to Honolulu to be lectured to by the Americans about liberalization.[11]

With the transition to Rubin as treasury secretary, and his essential partnership with Deputy Secretary Summers, US efforts only intensified. At a 1995 Asia-Pacific Economic Cooperation (APEC) forum meeting in Bali, Rubin pressed the case for financial deregulation, dismissing concerns about the disruptive effects of sudden, sharp movements of capital and the dangers of destabilizing speculation. Invoking a mantra that was echoed by the IMF, "investor confidence," Rubin argued that such confidence was the best protection against financial instability, whereas any actions taken to inhibit the free flow of capital "could do major damage to investor confidence." Or, as the IMF put it at the same meeting, "the best insurance against a sudden reversal of flows is a high degree of credibility and clear market oriented policies."[12]

Bilaterally, the United States, and especially the Treasury department, was even more aggressive. In 1995, during negotiations for a free trade agreement with Chile, Treasury representatives insisted that elimination of Chile's modest, innovative market-friendly controls on short-term capital inflows must be included as a condition of the deal. In 1996, as Korea sought membership in the Organization for Economic Cooperation and Development (OECD), the United States insisted that Korea speed up the pace of financial deregulation and provide increased access for American firms. "These areas are all of interest to the US financial services community," the Treasury's internal negotiating memo explained. Summers considered that opening up the world's financial systems was in the "strong national interest" of the United States. "Negotiations" were permissible, he said, but the United States was "not prepared to compromise" on market access and had a "rock-solid commitment to the end goal of liberalization." From the mid-1990s, as one account described, "Working through the IMF or directly with other countries," Summers and Rubin, with the encouragement and support of Greenspan, "pushed tirelessly for . . . free capital flows."[13]

At the same time, the IMF was also pushing hard for the rapid dismantling of capital controls by its member states. Recent scholarship by Rawi Abdelal and others has emphasized that the Fund came to this position independently, and it would indeed be a mistake to dismiss the influence of its managing director Michel Camdessus and first deputy managing director Stanley Fischer. Camdessus and Fischer, who took up his post in September 1994, marking the date of the decisive shift in the IMF's policies, were high priests in the evangelical church of free capital. Jeffrey Chwieroth also emphasizes the ideational shift within the Fund's staff of professional economists, which reflected the broader trend in the discipline away from Keynes and toward an unquestioning faith in the efficient markets hypothesis.[14]

No doubt, then, that the IMF bought the rhetoric it was peddling. Nevertheless, to suggest that the Fund had somehow gone off the reservation or was acting on its own with little regard for the interests of the United States (or the financial community) is equally incorrect. To begin with, no action taken by the Fund, to say nothing of a fundamental change to its charter, could be undertaken without the support of Karin Lissakers, the US executive director. (And Lissakers, more than permissive, was a strong and enthusiastic proponent.) More generally, as Barry Eichengreen and Harold James have argued, "The Fund's actions were consonant with the preferences of its principal shareholder. The mid-1990s may have been the peak of US Treasury influence over the IMF, matched only by the first fragile decade of the Fund's existence." Seasoned insiders and observers such as Jagdish Bhagwati, Paul Volcker, and Alan Blinder all share this perspective. "During the Asian crises, the IMF saw open capital accounts as part of the solution," Blinder recalled, "and it pains me to admit that the US government was a primary pusher of this bad advice."[15]

It need not be the case that the United States was pulling the strings of its IMF marionette. Rather, the Fund, the mainstream of the economics profession, Wall Street, and the US government were so much of one mind that the more appropriate metaphor is of a highly polished barbershop quartet. At the IMF's annual meeting in Madrid in October 1994, John Lipsky, then chief economist and managing director at Salomon Brothers, was among the first to publicly call for the Fund to "legally codify" a commitment that its members dismantle their capital controls. In April 1997, the finance ministers of the G7, emerging from their summit meeting in Washington hosted by Treasury Secretary Rubin, issued a statement in favor of "promoting freedom of capital flows" and "amending the IMF articles." It was within the context of such bookends that the IMF engaged in its long march toward capital freedom. In the pivotal year of 1995, the IMF more pointedly called for "increased freedom of capital movements"; in late 1996, Britain's chancellor of the exchequer Kenneth Clarke "unveiled" a plan that would give the IMF new authority over the international flow of capital and a new mission to press for its liberalization. Such "wholesale reform" would require a "major amendment" of the IMF's charter. The plan was immediately embraced by Managing Director Camdessus, who one suspects was not caught off guard by the unveiling. The race to the finish line was on.[16]

The IMF moved swiftly. In May 1997 it announced its intention to amend its articles of agreement. Instead of expecting and accommodating the judicious use of capital controls by its members, the Fund resolved "to make the promotion of capital account liberalization a specific purpose of the IMF and give it jurisdiction over capital movements." If the point was not clear enough, a fortnight later a banner headline of the *IMF Survey* proclaimed "Forces of Globalization Must Be Embraced." In September at its annual meeting in Hong Kong, the Fund issued its statement "The Liberalization of Capital Movements under an Amendment of the IMF's Articles," which instructed the executive board to complete its work on amending the articles. "Capital liberalization," the IMF now officially held, was "essential to an efficient international monetary system." It was important that the Fund move "decisively toward this new worldwide regime of liberalized capital movements." There was scant opposition.[17] Few on hand seemed concerned that the currency crisis in nearby Thailand might spread or what that crisis might say about the dangers associated with capital decontrol. Fewer still had bothered to take the time to find out that the economic theory supporting the notion of abolishing any mediation of capital flows across borders was a good thing that was tissue thin.

A Leap of Faith

Ideas, interests, and power combined to propel the charge behind the drive to dismantle all the world's capital controls and leave financial flows completely unfettered. What is most remarkable about this is that ideas, which were central to this story, were rooted in untested beliefs and faiths rather than economic science, which tends to suggest the opposite, that completely unregulated capital is suboptimal from the perspective of economic efficiency. This seems counterintuitive: every student in Econ 101 is taught to recite (and understand why) free trade is globally optimal from an economic perspective.[18] Why then would the case for free trade in capital be any less compelling than for free trade in goods?

Well, first off, as an empirical matter, the evidence is simply not there. As the IMF was gearing up to impose free capital upon the world, Jagdish Bhagwati, a noted economist who made his career as a champion of free trade, made just this observation. The case for free capital, he argued, had been little more than inferred from the case for free trade. But the proponents of free trade, in addition to articulating deductive arguments about market efficiency, had done their spade work. There were library shelves buckling under the weight of all of the studies that demonstrated the relationship between free trade and good outcomes such as greater economic growth. But the supporters of free capital, like the Wizard of Oz, had nothing behind their pronouncements but bluster, if in algebraic form. In fact, Bhagwati concluded, "the weight of evidence and the force of logic point in the opposite direction, toward restraints on capital flows."[19]

Furthermore, as I have argued previously in other work, there are good deductive reasons to believe that some positive level of capital control is optimal from the perspective of economic efficiency. In a world of uninhibited capital mobility, the ease with which capital can seek its greatest return creates pressures for conformity across states' macroeconomic policies. In practice, however, countries face diverse economic circumstances and problems, and what makes sense here might not make sense there. But all too often, in a world of footloose capital, governments that deviate from perceived policy norms (even with measures that are well suited to address local problems) are punished by capital flight, not only forcing those policies to be abandoned, but, worse, substituting inappropriately deflationary ones in their place. Perhaps even worse, and certainly more pervasive as a problem, flows of capital differ from flows of goods in that financial assets like currencies are worth, ultimately, what people think they are worth. (Most products, e.g., automobiles, have some comparatively stable value and practical end use.) The ephemeral element of the value of financial assets is especially problematic because the technology of financial markets allows investors to move enormous amounts of money in the blink of an eye and at very little cost. As a result of these two factors, financial markets are vulnerable to collectively catastrophic, if individually rational, herding behavior, unleashing financial stampedes with economic consequences that veer far from the path suggested by the relevant underlying economic "fundamentals."[20]

This is, of course, as discussed in chapter 2, a Keynesian perspective. In addition to the "beauty contest" aspect of financial markets and the way that actors' reliance on rules of thumb, conventional wisdom, and guesses about the guesses of others (all in contrast to the efficient markets hypothesis) contribute to potential instability, Keynes also saw completely uncontrolled capital as suboptimal because it took away the space for monetary policy autonomy, which was essential. "The dilemma of [any] international monetary system," he explained, was to promote a vibrant, thriving global economy and yet "to preserve at the same time an adequate local autonomy for each member over its domestic rate of interest." As he wrote to one colleague, "freedom of capital movements assumes that it is right and desirable to have an equalization of interest rates in all parts of the world." Thus, the wartime Keynes sought to design a postwar system—and many of his ideas found their expression in the original articles of agreement of the International Monetary Fund, which bore their stamp as tempered by the demands of US power and American politics—that would promote a growing, outward-oriented international order that nevertheless inhibited the pathologies associated with free capital. The Keynesian position could not be clearer: "Control of capital movements, both inward and outward, should be a permanent feature of the post-war system." This was not to discourage the flow of productive capital across borders, which was to be welcomed, but to allow states to retain some discretion over their own economic policies and provide the tools that might distinguish between sober investment and destabilizing speculation.[21]

From a Keynesian perspective, then, the problem is not capital mobility but *too much* capital mobility, which essentially amounts to financial pollution, or what economists would call a *negative externality*: a noxious social consequence of an output of the financial services industry whose costs are not counted as a factor of production by its creators. Negative externalities are a form of "market failure," a situation (like many collective-action problems) in which the workings of the invisible hand or "the market"—that is, uncoordinated individuals pursuing their self-interests—do not produce collectively efficient outcomes. The traditional economist's response to negative externalities, such as factory soot that is dumped on neighbors, is to impose a mediating tax on the production of the "bad." The goal of such a tax is not to eliminate the production of the bad but to assure that the costs of the harm to society as a whole are considered in the costs of production, which encourages a firm to do less harm. Thinking along these lines, some economists have proposed market-friendly measures, such as a Tobin tax (a tiny tax on financial transitions that would inherently distinguish between shot-run speculative and longer-term productive capital flows, with the costs overwhelmingly borne by the purveyors of the former) to help mitigate the costs to society from the production of too much capital movement.[22]

This assumes, of course, that the externality does exist and that capital mobility can indeed be inefficiently high. The deductive argument on this is compelling, but what is the actual evidence? Bhagwati's challenge on this point—that economists have not shown the case for free capital—and related academic debates that followed on the carnage of the Asian financial crisis sent economists racing to pick up the gauntlet he had thrown down. A raft of empirical studies were initiated, many inspired to demonstrate the association between the free flow of capital and enhanced economic performance, following the logic that market forces would guide financial flows to their most efficient uses and that market discipline as reflected in the cultivated, chastising movement of capital would rein in wayward policies and force governments to abandon inefficient, misguided, and profligate policies.

It turns out, as they say, "not so much." An initial study drawing on a sample of one hundred countries found "no evidence that countries without capital controls have grown faster, invested more, or experienced lower inflation."[23] And, from there, even scholars who stood out as passionate supporters of capital deregulation were unable to find empirical support for their urgently proselytized policy proposals in favor of free capital.[24] What new studies did reveal, on the other hand, were reasons to tread cautiously. For example, while instances of "market discipline" dispensed by corrective capital flows can be observed, in practice, the market is not up to this job; it tends to wait too long and then punish too hard, an inefficiency well captured by the phrase "too much too late."[25]

Bhagwati, testifying before Congress in 2003, a time during which financial sector dominance of US politics was unrivaled (and unchecked), and the efficient markets hypothesis philosophy was pervasive, again distinguished the case for free trade from the case for free capital and provided illustrations of when "good policymaking requires" that countries "must be allowed the freedom to exercise their discretion and use capital controls." The evidence, or lack of evidence, has only continued to pile up. In 2009, after the heady days when it seemed naïve to challenge the wisdom of financial markets left to their own devices, yet another comprehensive survey delivered the same news: study after study revealed "the absence of any apparent relationship between financial globalization and growth." Even setting aside the issue of financial crises, "the benefits of financial globalization are hard to find. Financial globalization has not generated increased investment or higher growth in emerging markets."[26]

But the situation is even worse than that, because financial crises are in no position to be set aside in any discussion of the regulation of capital. Individual countries liberalizing their capital accounts *are* more likely to experience a financial crisis, even when the government is pursuing policies that seem sound by the dictates of market orthodoxy. And, for the global economy as a whole, as noted, periods of high capital mobility *are* associated with an increased number of financial crises. As Kindleberger convincingly demonstrated long ago and as more recent, comprehensive scholarship has reconfirmed, financial crises are the rule of history, not the exception—they are a "hardy perennial." As such, the Keynesians have it right, as history has proved again and (unfortunately) again.[27] Good public policy, then, should not be designed to *increase* the dangers inherent to the heady flow of capital. Rather, even as it recognizes that robust capital flows are an essential element of a healthy, functional global economy, it should err on the side of reducing the risks and costs attendant to that vital process, the same way that responsible governments insist on the safest possible handling of radioactive material or toxic waste resulting from productive economic activities. Handle them with care.

Into the Asian Financial Crisis

The ill-advised move by the IMF to impose uninhibited capital mobility on all its members was also singularly ill timed. In July 1997, just two months before the "Hong Kong statement" celebrated the final, essentially pro forma push to revise its articles of agreement, Thailand, having lost a fortune, abandoned its efforts to defend the value of its besieged currency, the baht. This, in retrospect, was understood to be the moment that heralded the full-blown emergence of the Asian financial crisis. The crisis quickly and unexpectedly spread throughout the region and engulfed the Philippines, Malaysia, Indonesia, Hong Kong, and, astonishingly, South Korea, which announced on November 21 that it had no choice but to turn to the IMF for a rescue package or it would face national bankruptcy.

The crisis was, to say the least, unanticipated. Before the crisis, the performance of the affected economies was routinely declared a "miracle," and one that was commonly attributed to sound macroeconomic policies. One retrospective account calls the Fund "surprised" and "ill prepared" for the crisis, which puts it more than kindly. In September 1996, the IMF pronounced that "international capital markets appear to have become more resilient and are less likely to be a source of disturbances." (As if the point was not clear enough, the Fund continued, with what can be seen in retrospect as an unintended ironic nod to the global financial crisis that would emerge a decade later: "Although the scale of financial activity continues to grow, market participants—including high-risk high-return investment funds—are more disciplined, cautious, and sensitive to market fundamentals.") In late November 1996, a banner headline of the *IMF Survey* declared "ASEAN's Sound Fundamentals Bode Well for Sustained Growth." And just seven weeks before the crisis broke out, the Fund was particularly bullish in its assessment of the economies about to be overwhelmed by an international financial crisis: economic prospects were "bright," and "overheating pressures have abated in many emerging market economies, especially in Asia—where growth has stayed strong for several years." At the opening press conference of an IMF meeting in Washington of finance ministers and central bank governors, Managing Director Camdessus declared that global economic prospects called for "rational exuberance," and, the Fund reported, "in their official communiqués, ministers echoed this optimism."[28]

The initial tremors of the crisis elicited some murmurs of discontent,[29] but it did little to shake the confidence of the high priests of free capital. Summers was among those who were dismissive of the idea that the Thai crisis, its aftershocks increasingly visible and growing, might be a harbinger of dangers from unleashed free capital. To the contrary, he said, "Recent events in Southeast Asia have only increased our desire to strengthen the world's financial systems—and make them more open." But when the crisis reached the shores of Korea, it forced some to consider slowing down the IMF's deregulatory locomotive. An IMF mission visited the country in October—*October*—and concluded that "Korea would avoid being seriously affected by the crisis then spreading through Southeast Asia." That the crisis would come to Korea, and that it would need a massive IMF bailout, did not easily fit the narrative that the crisis was simply the result of weaknesses within the affected states themselves and very much *not* a rather easily recognizable international financial panic.[30]

But that narrative remained very much in vogue at the IMF, in Washington, and on Wall Street. "I emphatically reject the view," First Deputy Managing Director Fischer argued, "that recent market turbulence in the region" suggests caution with capital account liberalization. Challenged by some ministers at the IMF who were getting cold feet about pressing ahead with the amendment to the articles, Secretary Rubin insisted that "the turbulence which can occur during a crisis should not cause us to reverse" course. John Lipsky, who had moved on to Chase Manhattan Bank, testified before Congress that blaming "runaway capital markets" for the Asian financial crisis was "exactly the wrong approach." There was no alternative to the discipline imposed by the free flow of capital. Both current and former Clinton administration officials (such as Jeffrey Garten, one-time managing director at Lehman Brothers and recent Clinton undersecretary of commerce for international trade) echoed this view.[31]

With member enthusiasm eroding steadily for the IMF amendment, the Fund hoped to rally flagging support by holding a two-day high-level public conference, or "seminar," on capital account liberalization on March 9–10, 1998. Setting the tone at the meeting, Camdessus offered renewed support for pushing ahead, a position captured in the headline of the *IMF Survey*'s account of the event: "Irreversible Trend." In addition to commentary from IMF elites, invited Wall Street executives took turns stressing the importance of "sound and consistent" domestic economic policies as the key to avoiding international financial crises. British representatives remained staunchly in favor the amendment, as did Summers, who, in a forceful address, defended the measure as something "we need." If anything, he insisted, the IMF should "accelerate" rather than "slow the pace of capital account liberalization." But the Korean crisis had changed the political calculation, on several fronts. Within the IMF, opposition from Brazil, Japan, and other countries became more pronounced. Issues of international economic governance, quite uncharacteristically, also became a topic of popular public debate, especially as, in the wake of repeated crises (and the IMF's standard-issue deflationary medicine), an anti-IMF, anti-globalization backlash emerged. In was in this context that members of Congress, holding hostage a bill to increase member contributions to the IMF, expressed opposition to the amendment of the IMF's articles. Making the obvious political calculation, the Treasury department ordered its representative within the Fund to quietly withdraw its support. Without US support, of course, any change in IMF policy was dead in the water.[32]

Interpreting the Asian Financial Crisis and Its Aftermath

The ruinous nature of the Asian financial crisis, and the contrasting experiences of states that followed IMF-approved (or imposed) deflationary medicine that exacerbated their economic distress and states that had retained their capital controls and were thus spared the worst of it, led, not surprisingly, to a renewed public policy debate over the benefits of completely unfettered global capital (and the wisdom of trying to impose it universally).[33] And in the wake of the crisis, the self-evident failure of an absolutist perspective—thou shalt never interfere with the flow of capital—a number of reputable experts came out in favor of one scheme or another that involved market-friendly capital controls.[34] Everywhere, it seemed, scholars and policymakers were newly interested in reevaluating the case for capital deregulation or, at the very least, debating and entertaining ideas about how best to "throw some sand in the wheels of finance" to slow the most frenzied and disruptive flows of capital.

Everywhere, that is, except in places like the United States and the IMF. It was certainly necessary, and tactically wise, to bend to reality and abandon the drive to amend the Fund's articles of agreement. But the underlying ideology—not to mention the interests and the power—that had motivated that push yielded not an inch.[35] The normative context and the policy preference—uninhibited capital liberation—remained unchanged, if somewhat less-aggressively pursued in practice. For many, especially but not exclusively in Asia, the 1997 crisis was easily recognized and largely understood as a classic international financial crisis. But for market fundamentalists, following an efficient markets perspective, the very idea that there could even be international sources of financial crisis was an alien concept. (Similarly, the standard macroeconomic models widely in vogue before the global financial crisis that happened ten years later simply could not account for the events that unfolded.) For Greenspan, giving talks such as "Do Efficient Financial Markets Mitigate Financial Crises?," the causes of the financial crises of the 1990s were exclusively domestic: weak financial infrastructures in Asia and inadequate transparency in Russia, to name two examples. He offered eight reform measures to help avoid future financial crisis, all of them domestic-policy reforms in the affected states. Most fundamentally, Greenspan testified before Congress, "One consequence of this Asian crisis is an increasing awareness in the region that market capitalism, as practiced in the West, especially in the United States, is the superior model."[36]

The leadership at the IMF sang similar tunes. Camdessus never wavered in his faith that completely unfettered capital markets were optimal from an economic perspective; he saw it as an issue not even worthy of debate. More generally, the IMF's retrospective analyses of the crisis remained deeply skeptical of any form of capital control and focused on the domestic factors that contributed to the crisis. Fischer, vigorous in his defense of the Fund's approach, also homed in on (now) apparent structural flaws in the economies hit by the crisis; conspicuously absent from his own postmortems were any international factors that might have contributed to it. Instead, "weak financial institutions, inadequate bank regulation and supervision, and the complicated and non-transparent relations among governments, banks and corporations were central to the economic crisis."[37] Once again, there is an irony here, as ten years later this could be viewed as a particularly potent indictment of the *American* financial model. (And many Asian states could then also count themselves lucky that, in response to Western pressure after the Asian crisis, they only undertook what Andrew Walter dubbed "mock compliance" with many of the demands put on to them to converge toward the American model.)[38]

In the US government and in those international institutions where the United States wielded enormous influence, and in the American economics profession (which staffed both), market fundamentalism remained in vogue. If anything, faith in the superior American model and the efficient markets hypothesis grew after the Asian crisis. But these attitudes were not universally held abroad, and skepticism about them increased in the context of the assertive US diplomacy that accompanied the crisis. Both the crisis, and the (not-unreasonable) perception that the United States exploited the crisis to advance its interests, undermined the legitimacy of the second US order and unwittingly primed the path for the future march away from that vision.[39]

The heavy hand of American power was seen, and felt, most clearly and acutely in the Korean case. Once again, *no one*, least of all the IMF, thought the crisis would spread to Korea. But it did, and the Korean economy— "an economy to envy" as Martin Feldstein would describe it in his critique of the IMF policies that followed—was overtaken by a crisis of "temporary illiquidity," which Feldstein distinguished from "fundamental insolvency." Feldstein urged that the Fund "should eschew the temptation to use currency crises as an opportunity to force fundamental and structural reforms on countries." But that is exactly what the Fund did, along with a heap of deflationary medicine that added to Korea's distress, when it arrived, hat in hand, in need of exactly the kind of emergency help such as bridge loans and coordination with creditors that the Fund was, in theory, designed to provide. But Rubin and Summers shared Greenspan's view that the crisis demonstrated the failure of the Korean economic model, and structural reforms—especially, it turned out, those that would open up a reluctant Korea to US financial firms—were deemed essential. It was an IMF operation, but in this case, the United States was calling the shots. It was the Americans at the IMF who insisted on the quid pro quos imposed on the Koreans in exchange for the Fund's support, and US officials arrived in Seoul to press the same demands.[40]

With little choice, Korea agreed to a raft of IMF conditions that had little or nothing to do with solving their current financial crisis or preventing a future one; these included not only eliminating barriers to foreign direct investment and opening up its markets in insurance and securities dealings but also measures that arguably contributed to the current crisis and made a future one *more* likely, such as accelerating the liberalization of foreign exchange transactions and relaxing restrictions on corporate borrowing from international sources. (High levels of short-term private international borrowing had been one of the proximate causes of the Korean crisis.) The entire affair was easily recognized as a "crude power play" or, more angrily from within Korea, "egregious imperialistic meddling." As Robert Gilpin observed, the IMF letter of intent signed by Korea "included specific items that the United States had long demanded of Asian governments, and that the latter had rejected." It is not surprising to learn, then, that "many Koreans consider" the day the letter was signed to be "Korea's 'Second National Humiliation Day' the first being that of its colonization by the Japanese."[41]

Another hint of nascent fissures in the foundations of the second US order could be found in the contrasting reactions to and interpretations of Malaysia's deployment of capital controls during the Asian crisis. Unlike most of its neighbors, Malaysia didn't go to the IMF and sign on for an austerity program; rather, after experimenting unhappily with some home-cooked deflationary measures, the government abruptly changed course and introduced capital controls on September 1, 1998. This allowed Malaysia to pursue pro-growth policies, which would have been otherwise unsustainable due to the punishing capital flight that would have been touched off in response to its departure from orthodoxy.[42] In this instance, one might think the IMF would have done well to hold its tongue before confidently dispensing unsolicited advice. After all, just a few weeks before the Asian crisis broke, Camdessus singled out Malaysia for the savvy of its economic stewardship. "Malaysia is a good example of a country where the authorities are well aware of the challenges of managing the pressures that result from high growth and of maintaining a sound financial system amid substantial capital flows," he explained. In addition to its reassuringly low inflation, admirable government budget surplus, and laudable outward orientation, "Malaysian authorities have also emphasized maintaining high standards of bank soundness."[43] But he was quick to denounce the Malaysian experiment in capital controls, calling it "dangerous and even harmful." The vehemence of the Western condemnation of any introduction of capital controls, even temporary measures introduced in an emergency, suggested that the protestations reflected something more deep seated than a technical disagreement about optimal economic policy. IMF economists predicted the controls might "be an important setback . . . to that country's recovery and potentially to its future development." Greenspan offered a stern (if implausible) public rebuke, equating capital controls with "borders closed to foreign investment" that would lead states that deployed them "mired at a sub-optimal standard of living and slow growth rate." (He also felt the need to add, as if a requirement of some union membership, "Market pricing and counterparty surveillance can be expected to do most of the job of sustaining safety and soundness.") Summers was more revealing, stating that it "would be a catastrophe" if other countries followed the Malaysian example, which raises the question, a catastrophe for whom?[44]

As it turned out, however, despite the "unanimous condemnation" from the West, the IMF, and the credit-ratings agencies, the Malaysian economy performed well after the imposition of controls. A year later, journalistic accounts could observe that "critics were aghast . . . but now many admit the move succeeded in helping to lift Malaysia out of its worst recession ever." Critical academic market fundamentalists were reduced to arguing that Malaysia would have recovered anyway, conveniently forgetting the contrast between the heady performance of the Malaysian economy and the avalanche of apocalyptic predictions about its implosion as a consequence of the introduction of controls. Rather, the measures did what their advocates hoped they would; they served as a circuit breaker in the midst of a crisis, allowed for otherwise unsustainable stimulus policies, and discriminated between hot money flows of speculative or panicked capital and productive foreign direct investment, which, contra Greenspan's caricature, continued to flow in. As Bhagwati assessed years later, there "seems to be a sound body of opinion that Malaysia did well to use capital controls."[45]

Largely unnoticed by the United States at the time, or, more accurately, largely ignored (with one notable exception) was the fact that not everybody shared the American position that capital controls were an unspeakable taboo practice. Although Wall Street's Solomon Brothers joined the chorus formed by leading officials like Rubin and Fischer, calling Malaysia's controls "regressive" and "ultimately destined to failure," many voices in Asia were strongly supportive. One Chinese official observed with approval that "Malaysia is returning to the route which China has been taking." Japan also explicitly endorsed the controls, and, pointedly, tapped Malaysian prime minister Mahathir to be the keynote speaker at a conference on development held in Tokyo the following month. Japanese finance minister Kiichi Miyazawa spoke out in favor of "market friendly controls," and, as Western credit agencies downgraded Malaysia's sovereign debt to junk bond status, the Japanese government put its money where its mouth was, providing the country with $1.5 billion in new financial support. And on the first anniversary of its successful experimentation with capital controls, Malaysia "received cheers" from the Japanese government, an ovation joined by others in the region.[46]

An indication of the East/West split over the management of international finance (and a suggestion that behind the velvet glove of economic ideology lay the iron fist of American interest) was the stillborn Japanese Asian Monetary Fund initiative. The purpose of the envisioned AMF was to provide emergency liquidity to Asian states facing a financial crisis, without the invasive strings that the IMF was increasingly attaching to its assistance. Japan offered $50 billion to stake the new fund, which would be further endowed by contributions from other regional states. Motivated by its disenchantment with the IMF's response to the Asian financial crisis, in particular the "excessively severe deflationary conditionality" it was demanding, the proposal also raised the possibility that Japan might seek a greater international role for the yen. Such ambitious expectations had emerged in the late 1980s but faded, along with the Japanese economy, during the "lost decade" that followed.[47]

The United States did not look kindly on the proposed Asian fund, to say the least. Japanese officials, no doubt anticipating Western opposition, since an Asian monetary fund would surely step on the toes of the IMF and implicitly reduce US political influence, first consulted quietly and exclusively with other states in the region. Caught by surprise, the United States was swift, vehement, and definitive in its response. Summers placed a midnight call to Sakakibara, known as "Mr. Yen," and by all accounts treated him to a full-force Summers storm. ("I thought you were my friend," the American complained.) More to the point, Rubin and Greenspan wrote their foreign counterparts throughout Asia in opposition to the AMF and sent subordinates abroad to press the message. Rubin, traveling in Southeast Asia and meeting with officials there, went out of his way to inform reporters that he had secured an important diplomatic victory. "The subtext," one journalist wrote, was that "America is back in the middle of the game; the steam is out of the Japanese bailout plan."[48]

The AMF proposal mattered not for what it was but for what it represented: it was the manifestation of a basic ideological disagreement about the management of the world's money, one that would become dormant but never really disappear. These disagreements, which also had important elements of interest-group competition and exposed the geopolitical stakes that great powers quietly attributed to holding the reins of monetary order, were thus primed to resurface ten years later with the onset of the global financial crisis. In 1997–98 that disagreement was about whether or not the crisis demonstrated the failure of the East Asian model of development and the success of the American Way. Greenspan was of the opinion that in the region, after the Asian financial crisis, there was a new realization, "bordering in some cases on shock," that local economic practices had been misguided and that the US economic model, including the embrace of un-inhibited finance, was the singularly correct way to organize an economy.[49]

But this was not the case, neither with regard to the Asian model nor local attitudes toward it. Elites in Asia could recognize an international financial crisis when they saw one, and they could recognize the exercise of power as well. Vice Minister Sakakibara challenged the optimality of completely unregulated capital and the efficient markets hypothesis, stating plainly that "free capital movements do not always bring about optimum allocation of resources." He also spoke of the "inherent instability of liberalized capital markets" and argued that the Asian crisis could not be "explained only by . . . structural problems" within the affected economies. Finance Minister Miyazawa attributed the crisis to "general problems inherent in today's global system" and called for "reforming the international financial architecture." Japanese officials—and, it should be recalled, Japan did not need or seek the assistance of the Fund during the crisis—also held the view that the IMF was over-reaching and was wrong to demand structural reforms not related to solving the crisis as the price of its assistance. This meddling was widely seen as designed to promote American interests.[50]

Contra Greenspan, the crisis did not bring about an ideological consensus on the singular wisdom of the American model, but the attitudes expressed by the Federal Reserve chairman did contribute to an emerging consensus in Asia—one of smoldering resentment toward the arrogance of the American attitude that he was expressing. Other states were weaker now, while the United States was stronger than ever: unipolar, hegemonic. On the surface, American influence seemed almost irresistible, but a sharp ideological divide, and a craving for some insulation from the hyperpower, endured.[51] And with reform of the international monetary system off the table, a world of unregulated capital continued to be characterized by financial crises that began to emerge with regularity, notably in Russia, Brazil, and Argentina. The IMF commonly came under withering criticism during these episodes. The situation in Argentina was particularly embarrassing for the Fund, since Argentina was viewed at the time as the poster child for following the IMF's advice. By the Fund's own assessment, "the severity of the crisis—and the fact that it occurred in a country that had performed reasonably well in a succession of IMF-supported programs—make it particularly important to examine the lessons." In Russia, the lessons would appear to be more easily recognizable: temporary exchange controls might have spared Russia from the worst, but "the IMF and the US Treasury could not accept that option at the time, having drawn a firm line against" such policies.[52]

It is often suggested that the Fund, chastened by all of these experiences, became slightly more tolerant of the idea of capital controls. This risks exaggerating the modest changes that may have occurred. The IMF was still committed to universal capital account liberalization and instinctively hostile to capital controls. But it is fair to say that as it actively directed traffic down a one-way street, it was now willing, occasionally, to let travelers in distress reduce the speed at which they were moving forward. And this modest concession to political reality contrasted with the full-speed-ahead mentality that continued unbridled in the United States. In 2003, the United States pushed hard, against the vociferous objections of its counterparties, to include clauses in its free trade agreements with Chile and Singapore that demanded the renunciation of their right to introduce any form of capital controls. (This also set a precedent for negotiations with other states). What this had to do with free trade, whether it is remotely a wise policy, and that these were rights the states in question did *not* want to give up were of little concern to Bush administration negotiators. The United States wanted what it wanted.[53]

The United States emerged from the 1990s with confidence: triumphant in the Cold War, it was unrivaled both geopolitically and economically. But in embracing the financialization of its own economy, and in designing a second, now post–Cold War economic order to press these advantages, it both erred and overreached. This was more quickly evident abroad, where the collateral damage of liberated finance was first felt. It was not recognized in the United States—or, if noticed, it was untroubling—that its new order was met with skepticism in much of the rest of the world and, in much of Asia, with resentment. China, an increasingly important player in the world economy, was shielded from crises by its own controls (as were other states that were similarly protected), and, looking forward, it hedged its bets. On the one hand, the US financial model did look like the only one left standing, but, on the other, the Chinese Communist Party was not about to change its spots, especially when it came to finance capital. After the Asian crisis, it initially bent toward the American model, if slowly, incrementally, and cautiously.

And the United States, surveying the wreckage of the 1990s—Mexico, Asia, Russia, South America—and blissfully untroubled by the domestic warnings signs of the 1987 crash, Orange County, LTCM, and the like, concluded that financial crises were things that happened to others— others that, for one reason or another, had it coming. But the US financial system, with its size, depth, complexity, sophistication, and, perhaps above all, embrace of the market, was seen by the ideologically enmeshed communities of Wall Street, Washington, and the academy as rock solid, world class, ever growing, and the jewel in the crown of the envied American economy, standing unrivaled at the turn of the century.

5

The New American Model and the Financial Crisis

"As a scholar of the Great Depression, I honestly believe that September and October of 2008 was the worst financial crisis in global history, including the Great Depression," Ben Bernanke, former world-class macroeconomics professor and sitting chairman of the Federal Reserve Board, told a closed-door session of the Financial Crisis Inquiry Commission in November 2009. He estimated that "out of . . . 13 of the most important financial institutions in the United States, 12 were at risk of failure within a period of a week or two."[1]

How did it come to that? In this chapter I argue that the catastrophe was the result of the financialization of the American economy. Big finance and the big money that came with it had political and cultural influence on society as a whole, and the result was a metastasized financial sector irretrievably riddled with systemic risk. That danger was allowed to develop and was left unattended due to an ideological convergence and economic interpenetration of key players across Wall Street, Washington, and attendant academic affiliates, which led the government to voluntarily abdicate its responsibility for supervision and oversight. With a consensus forged by ideology and interest, this new iron triangle overturned an older conventional wisdom that held that unregulated financial systems were inherently prone to crisis. This, from the old school perspective, was the result of a market failure: individually rational behaviors generated a negative externality, systemic risk, that was not accounted for in the cost/benefit analysis of market participants and thus was overproduced.[2]

Despite the crisis—the worst in history—in the United States the new American model remains essentially in place, a tribute to the entrenched political influence of its guardians. But the crisis and its aftermath have weakened the US economy at home and undermined the legitimacy of its model abroad, with consequences for American power and influence that I will consider in chapters 6 and 7. This chapter considers how we got there.

Go-Go Finance and the New American Model

With the deregulations of the 1980s and, especially, the 1990s, it is not surprising that the financial sector grew. But that it would quickly become the largest and fastest growing sector of the economy was nevertheless remarkable, and breathtaking. In broad brush, from 1980 to 2002, as manufacturing's share of GDP fell from 21 percent to 14 percent, that of finance grew from 14 percent to 21 percent. But this understates matters: in 2001 profits from the financial sector accounted for more that 40 percent of the profits in the US economy, which still understates matters, because it does not account for the large financial wings of nonfinancial corporations like General Electric and Ford, which in the 2000s often made more money from loans than from cars. This was all new. From the 1930s through the 1970s, financial sector profits grew at about the same rate as profits in the rest of the economy; but, from 1980 to 2005, financial sector profits rose by 800 percent, as compared with 250 percent in the nonfinancial sector. On the eve of the crisis, finance accounted for 47 percent of all US corporate profits.[3]

Was this a good thing? Although the financial services sector is an essential, crucial, and indispensible element of a mature capitalist society, and while it might even be good to have a large and leading financial sector, at bottom, the role of finance is to *facilitate* economic activity, that is, to allocate capital to efficient and productive use. It is meant to be a hand-maiden (or, if you prefer, the valet) of real activity: moving money around is not valuable for its own sake. But few even thought to ask this question. Prominent Keynesian economist and Nobel laureate James Tobin sounded the alarm in the 1980s, ahead of most, when he suggested the financial sector was becoming suboptimally large. Even then, he observed that such "views run against current tides—not only the general enthusiasm for de-regulation and unfettered competition but also my profession's intellectual admiration for the efficiency of financial markets."[4]

Tobin's concerns, as he anticipated, fell largely on deaf ears, but there were any number of red flags waving for those willing to look up. As the financial sector grew and grew it also became more concentrated and more exposed, with fewer and bigger firms dominating the market and carrying ever larger liabilities. Once again, the story is one of continuity followed by rapid change; in the half-century following World War II, the ten largest banks in the United States typically held between 10 and 20 percent of total bank assets. In 2005, they held 55 percent. And, from 1981 to 2008, finan-cial sector debt increased from 22 to 117 percent of GDP.[5]

Banking, and bankers, also became more powerful, more prestigious, and, most obviously, wealthier. From 1940 to 1980, the average person working in the financial sector made about the same amount of money as someone working elsewhere in the private sector. These stable trend lines then diverged, and by 2007, the average pay for someone working in banking was double that of workers elsewhere. This was most visible at, but by no means limited to, the very high end. In 1990, to the astonishment of many, some Wall Street traders earned bonuses of $10 million. Within twenty years, bonuses were as high as $100 million, and top hedge fund managers could make $1 billion in a single year. (Other than some sort of market failure, the only possible explanation for such increases is that such actors had become exponentially more productive or suddenly much scarcer, two dubious propositions.)[6]

Such things do not easily pass unnoticed, and the rise of finance had social and cultural effects that extended beyond the insular "commu-nity"; seven-, eight-, and nine-figure bonuses tend to focus the mind. It is shocking but not surprising to learn that 40 percent of students graduat-ing from Princeton University from 2000 to 2005 took jobs in the finan-cial services sector. That number approached 50 percent in 2006, and at

Princeton's School of Engineering and Applied Science, something called Operations Research and Financial Engineering became the most popular undergraduate major. In 2007, 57 percent of men who graduated from Harvard took jobs in finance or consulting. This a full two decades after Tobin lamented that "we are throwing more and more of our resources, including the cream of our youth, into financial activities remote from the production of goods and services, into activities that generate high private rewards disproportionate to their social productivity." (After the fall, others saw this dysfunction more clearly. Regarding the physicists and other talented people who had sought fortunes on Wall Street, Richard Posner saw a potential silver lining: that the "depression in finance will channel some of these people into less lucrative but socially more productive jobs.")[7]

At the turn of the twenty-first century, then, finance not only dominated the US economy, it also increasingly dominated its culture, with Wall Street values absorbing Main Street customs, exemplified by pizza joints tuning their TVs to business channels, and sports channels televising celebrity poker. The headlong chase of wealth for its own sake, of course, reduces "the whole conduct of life . . . into sort of a parody of an accountant's nightmare," where every potential course of action is judged solely by its financial results.[8] The United States was arguably veering toward this caricature as the crisis approached. This was accompanied by a national consumption binge that had three faces, visible in government ledgers, external accounts, and personal finances.

The first was a sin against Keynes, who wrote, "the boom, not the slump, is the right time for austerity at the Treasury." Clinton left the government budget in surplus, with more black ink projected into the future. Those funds should have been used to pay down the national debt, but they were instead frittered away by the large Bush tax cuts. Not only did this cause the deficit (and the national debt) to balloon, but by throwing its finances deep into the red, the government was less able to borrow and spend with adequate ease when the crisis hit. Instrumental in this blunder was Alan Greenspan, who recounts in his memoirs that, like others, he initially wanted to use the surplus to pay down the debt rather than grant a tax cut. Yet he came to support the Bush tax cuts, lending his considerable authority and support to them in public congressional testimony—a move that is hard to characterize as anything other than nakedly opportunistic. Looking back, he shares that "within weeks, it turned out I'd been wrong to abandon my skepticism" and that he found the abandonment of fiscal discipline that followed "troubling."[9]

The federal government wasn't the only entity living beyond its means. The United States, as a country, was consuming more goods and services than it was producing. This wasn't a new story; the United States hadn't had a trade surplus since its bicentennial. But it was a new problem. The trade deficit soared by 50 percent in 1998, setting a new record of $166 billion. But that was nothing. It reached $375 billion two years later, and then set a new record, both in real terms and as a percentage of GDP, in virtually every year that followed, reaching over $750 billion in 2006.[10] A shift in the philosophy and culture of American capitalism was reflected, statistically, in the steady decline of the personal savings rate (from 10% of GDP in 1985 to 2% in 2005) and more viscerally in the frenzy of the housing bubble and a consumption binge based on leveraged credit. Housing prices increased 156 percent between 1997 and 2006, the largest increase since the 1920s.[11] And, as in the Roaring Twenties, it was generally assumed that prices could only go up.

A New Financial Model

American finance was not just getting bigger, it was changing, and it was becoming riskier. Three interrelated developments transformed the nature of the business. The first was the innovation of securitization—slicing up, repackaging, and selling mortgages and other instruments—that changed the model of banking. Banks used to follow an "originate and hold" model, which meant they would retain the mortgages they issued until maturity. In the new model, "originate and distribute," they would pass along these assets to other investors. This meant that issuing banks no longer would bear the costs of defaults, so their incentive to weigh risk was dramatically decreased.[12]

A second characteristic of the new financial model was complexity. A modern financial instrument could be composed of parts of many individual assets, a blending and reblending of pieces of assets and obligations of various types, with different levels of risk and varying rates of maturity, and enmeshed further with devices of insurance and reinsurance against possible default. An alphabet soup of new, exotic, and unregulated financial products proliferated: structured investment vehicles (SIV), collateralized debt obligations (CDO), and credit default swaps (CDS); the value of outstanding CDS was over $57 trillion in 2007.[13] Assessing the value of these assets was well beyond the reach of the overwhelming majority of investors, and so credit rating agencies were essential for providing some guidance. For the financial engineers, the magic was in adding dollops of risky assets to an otherwise worthy one, right up to the point where their alchemy would still yield an AAA rating that would assure investors that the asset was as safe as it could be. The ratings agencies could have served as guardians against the excesses of such practices. But in one of many astonishing conflicts of interest that riddled the American financial system, the agencies were "being paid by the banks that originated the securities they were asked to rate." Instead of protecting investors, the ratings agencies rubber-stamped the products of their benefactors, always with an eye toward future business and the fear that their competitors might be even more accommodating.[14]

The third element of the new financial model was a shift in individual incentives that heavily valued the present over the future and encouraged ever-greater risk taking. The emergence of a "bonus culture," whereby the ratio of bonuses to base pay in the industry soared, generated pernicious incentives. And as Posner notes, "executive compensation is both very generous and truncated on the down side." These developments strongly encouraged both risk taking and myopia. Karen Ho, in her ethnographic study of Wall Street, found an "obsession with immediate results" and a culture of "high-risk high-reward" in which performance was measured "according to the number of deals executed," with investment bankers "motivated to milk as much money out of the present as possible."[15]

As Ho suggests, drivers of the new model were money and movement. The new exotic financial products were highly leveraged, but they were also *enormously* profitable, and in an "originate and distribute" model there was little incentive to assess the risk of borrowers. There was every incentive to create product, and move product, with profits, and bonuses, tied to origination fees. Compensation structures emphasized sales over quality. And why not? Investment banks charged between $1 million and $8 million to underwrite a mortgage-backed security, and even more to act as the placement agent for a CDO securitization. From 2004 to 2008, US financial institutions issued almost $1.5 trillion of the former and over

$1.4 trillion of the latter. And, because investors needed some shorthand to try and get a handle of the meaning of such fantastically complex assets, Moody's Investors Service saw its annual revenue from assessing CDOs rise from $12 million in 2003 to $93 million in 2006.[16]

It was a financial world awash in a dizzying array of interconnected financial products, glittering with the prospects of creating fantastic, immediate amounts of wealth. Leverage was increased, greater risk was embraced, and fortunes were made. Increasingly, speculators and even many market participants who were experienced and sophisticated investors were trafficking in assets the value of which they didn't fully understand. Deals became "so complicated that in many cases *nobody* understood the risks," and many banks, even with "all the relevant information and data [at their disposal], couldn't figure out their own positions."[17]

The new American model, then, led to individual actors and, more important, large financial institutions routinely taking on greater risk. Why is this important? Because the financial sector is different: all banks carry short-term obligations, but most of their assets are not immediately accessible, and they are routinely deeply enmeshed in business dealings with other similarly situated houses of finance. As a result, it is all too easy for the failure of an insolvent firm to threaten the viability of an otherwise sound outfit. Thus firms can carry levels of risk that are individually reasonable but systemically dangerous. And, obviously, this is doubly true of firms that carry what could be considered excessive risk. It boils down to this: A risk-taking confectioner who makes big bad bets and goes out of business does not threaten the solvency of his peers and competitors in the candy store across town. A wayward bank does.

But the very idea of systemic risk was anathema to the ideology of the new American model. In fact, at the turn of the century, Bush and Greenspan took the Clinton financial model and ran with it. If the 1990s were about the dismantling of regulation, the 2000s were about the abandonment of oversight. Regulation and oversight were fellow travelers, perhaps, but two different things. The chief bank supervisor in the United States, Federal Reserve Board chairman Greenspan, had no interest in that part of his job, and, he recalled, "taking office, I was in for a pleasant surprise . . . being a regulator was not the burden I had feared." Greenspan was passionately opposed to any form of banking regulation ("Why do we wish to inhibit the pollinating bees of Wall Street?") and saw little need for the government to exercise its responsibilities for supervision and oversight. Passivity was be encouraged, as "market stabilizing private regulatory forces" were fully capable of looking after potential untoward behavior by financial firms; and they were much more up to the job than clumsy government. It was well known that "his staff and his colleagues knew where he stood."[18]

The Senate report on the financial crisis observed that "the multi-trillion-dollar US swaps markets operated with virtually no disclosure requirements, no restrictions, and no oversight by any federal agency, including the market for credit default swaps which played a prominent role in the financial crisis." In fact, "federal regulators could not even ask US financial institutions to report on their swaps trades or holdings," and more generally, "no regulator was charged with identifying, preventing, or managing" systemic risk. As suggested by the attitudes of those in charge, *this* was not an oversight. Greenspan, in an attitude widely shared, saw these financial innovations as stabilizing and was dismissive of concerns for systemic risk. "Systemic breakdowns occur, of course, but they are surprisingly rare," he wrote in 2007. "Rising leverage appears to be the result of massive improvements in technology and infrastructure." Credit default swaps and other financial innovations were a tribute to the magic of the market and to be welcomed: "These increasingly complex financial instruments have contributed to the development of a far more flexible, efficient, and hence resilient financial system than the one that existed just a quarter-century ago."[19]

Greenspan was an influential champion of such views about finance (and the role of government), but he was by no means alone in holding them, and he was not the only one caught by utter surprise by the financial crisis. The International Monetary Fund, noting the growth in derivatives contracts (from $4 trillion in 2003 to $17 trillion in 2005, with "the most complex products" accounting for most of recent growth), and cheerfully admitting that "detailed data on structured credit products are not readily available, and relatively few studies have been done so far on the broader financial stability implications of these credit risk transfer markets," was nevertheless another exuberant cheerleader for the new financial order. (There is something of an echo chamber effect here, as the Fund quoted Greenspan as a supporting authority.) In April 2006, the Fund saw little evidence of any threat to systemic stability, offered praise for the "well-regulated" US financial markets, and stressed the positive role of credit rating agencies with their "sophisticated quantitative modeling" and "advanced financial engineering skills." With unintended irony, the Fund added that "for many market participants, the application of such skills may have become more important than fundamental credit analysis." The IMF summarized the stuffing of its report and the state of financial affairs thusly: "The rapid growth of credit derivative and structured credit markets in recent years, particularly among more complex products, has facilitated the dispersion of credit risk by banks to a broader and more diverse group of investors. . . . Credit risk dispersion has helped to make the banking and overall financial system more resilient and stable."[20]

The Fund's batting average was no better in April 2007, on the eve of the crisis. The number of outstanding derivatives had leaped again, more than doubling from mid-2005 to mid-2006, and there was still precious little data about them; and the subprime US housing market was not doing well. But overall, the Fund assessed "global economic risks as having *declined*" over the previous six months, to some extent due to "structural improvements in markets, including the improved risk management made possible by the increasingly sophisticated and liquid derivatives markets."[21]

Also, in that fateful year of 2007, Eugene Fama, the intellectual father of the efficient markets hypothesis, articulated what can be called "the four nos" in a November interview. Is it possible that some CEOs are overcompensated? No. ("If it's a market wage, it's a market wage. I don't know of any solid evidence that the process was corrupted.") Is there a bubble in the housing market? No. ("The word 'bubble' drives me nuts. . . . People are very careful when they buy houses.") Have mortgage-backed securities become so complex that even sophisticated investors who hold them are uncertain of their value and risk? No. ("I'm very skeptical of these stories. . . . Bonds are simpler to evaluate than stocks. . . . Bond products have become more complicated because of the securitization of that market, but still not that big a deal.") Is there reason to believe that CDOs and other new financial instruments increase market risk? No. (There is not enough data "to come to any conclusions on these issues"; it might take as long as "another half century before we really know.")[22]

The views of Fama, Greenspan, and the IMF sound incautious and extreme, and perhaps they were, but they were also well within the mainstream of state-of-the-art academic macroeconomics. As discussed in chapter 3, from the 1990s there was a convergence in macroeconomic thinking, as new Keynesians integrated rational expectations into their models and the efficient markets hypothesis into their thinking. (As Fama noted, "Rational expectations stuff is basically efficient markets.") The state of macroeconomic theory was such that new classical economist Robert Lucas, leader of the anti-Keynesian revolution, could articulate without controversy this widely shared view in his 2003 presidential address to the American Economic Association: "[The] central problem of depression prevention has been solved, for all practical purposes, and has in fact been solved for many decades."[23]

Macroeconomic theory had converged around an approach called "dynamic stochastic general equilibrium," or DSGE. There were new Keynesian versions of such models, and new classical versions, but these competing perspectives, at one time characterized by bitter and fundamental opposition, were now characterized by their similarities, their marginal differences attributable to marketing incentives for product differentiation. Academic squabbles are inevitable. But to anyone watching the game, as opposed to playing inside baseball, the scholarly macroeconomic community looked like one big happy, satisfied community.[24]

Dynamic stochastic general equilibrium sounds intimidating, but its basic features are fairly straightforward. Its starting points are familiar, rooted in the microfoundations of individual actors with rational expectations: they understand the underlying model of how the economy works and efficiently process all available information in order to optimally pursue their goals. Markets are always and everywhere efficient, and prices, derived from the sum of collective knowledge, accurately reflect underlying value. From there, DSGE kicks in. It is a "general" model, meaning it accounts for all markets simultaneously, as opposed to "partial" models that account for the behavior of specific markets in isolation, holding other sectors constant. Markets are assumed to tend toward "equilibrium," that is, when disturbed, they self-correct rather than collapsing or spiraling out of control. The analysis is "dynamic," because it looks at an economy as it moves through time (as opposed to a static snapshot). "Stochastic" refers to the expectation that the economy is buffeted by random shocks. Actors can't anticipate for sure what those shocks will be, but they live in a world of risk, not uncertainty; they can assign correct probabilities to every possible change and outcome that might occur.

What DSGE models *can't* do, however, is account for a financial crisis (or for sustained economic downturns that don't self-correct). It is not simply that DSGE models failed to see the crisis coming, though they certainly did not. It was that DSGE models had no way to account for the possibility of such a crisis. (Legend has it that one eminent financial historian had long been dismissive of the approach because "it excludes everything I am interested in.") As the *Economist* explained, DSGE models "do badly in a crisis . . . because their 'dynamic stochastic' element only amounts to minor fluctuations around a state of equilibrium, and there is no equilibrium during crashes." Not surprisingly, after the financial crisis horse had raced out of the barn, DSGE models, and mainstream macroeconomic theory more generally, came under considerable criticism.[25]

Who Knew? The Old School and the Regularity of Financial Crises

There were some voices of dissent from the consensus of complacency. Raghuram Rajan, chief economist of the IMF, in 2005 presented a paper to an eminent gathering of bankers and scholars at Jackson Hole, Wyoming, in which he raised a number of rather modest and cautious concerns about the stability of the system. Rajan, who had just published a book that mounted a rousing defense of free financial markets, nevertheless thought that the rise of the market-dominated system presented new challenges that regulators and supervisors needed to be alert to. Recent changes to the financial sector, he argued, had altered managerial incentives and encouraged taking on of greater risk, and especially hidden risk. Compensation arrangements also encouraged managers to move with the herd, resulting in behavior that "can move asset prices away from fundamentals." More generally, technology, deregulation, financial innovation, and institutional change had created new vulnerabilities, increasing a possibility of systemic risk that should not be ignored. "We should not be lulled into complacency by a long period of calm," he argued. Not only were there new and growing risks in the system, but with a "myriad of complex claims written on the same underlying real asset," small problems could quickly get out of hand and "may create a greater (albeit still small) probability of a catastrophic meltdown." Raising a particular, and prescient, concern, he argued that if some banks became distressed they would require infusions of credit from their more robust counterparts. But if those banks "lose confidence in their liquidity-short brethren . . . one could have a full blown financial crisis." Explicitly setting aside too-big-to-fail questions, Rajan proposed modest reforms designed to tweak incentives, increase transparency, and encourage managers to place greater emphasis on the long-run implications of their investment decisions. The trick, he concluded, was to avoid the extremes of burdensome regulation and "a belief that markets always will get it right."[26]

Other scholars were highly critical of the risk management models in vogue throughout the financial world. Fantastically sophisticated, these models were nevertheless vulnerable to five basic, and to some extent inescapable, problems. First, financial models, like all models, are utterly dependent on (and in fact all of their outputs flow directly from) the basic underlying assumptions used to construct them. Second, many models were road tested on data from a few good and stable years, and they fit that data well (or vice versa). But in the words of one critic, writing before the crisis, the models favored by financial risk professionals were "extremely sensitive to small changes in the assumptions" and were characterized by "almost-arbitrary choices in the use and selection of data." Third, all models assume that the past is a reliable guide to the future, although in periods of innovation and change it is plausible, even likely, that behavioral relationships will change. Fourth, with so much product innovation, there was very little past. As one observer asked, "How could the trajectory of a CDO squared be judged from past data when that 'past' was just two years old?" Finally, and like DSGE, financial models are best in the context of continuity, when things are "normal." But they are prone to "fail badly during times of panic, fear, and limited liquidity." This is why it became common for critics of these models to ridicule their performance during crises. The 1987 stock market crash, for example, would have been predicted to occur once in a billion years, but it was only part of a long list of once-in-a-lifetime disturbances that occurred in the decade that followed.[27]

Yet the impressiveness of the sheer complexity of the models and the intellectual firepower needed to build them, coupled with a long run of crisis-free fat years, left market participants overly confident that the risk of financial crisis had been transcended and somehow squeezed out of the system. And so critics of prevailing risk models and other Cassandras were ignored or, when necessary, as in the case of Rajan, shouted down. At the Jackson Hole conference, his paper was showered with angry criticism. Larry Summers dismissed the paper's basic premise as "misguided" and called Rajan a "Luddite." Summers was reliably supercilious, but his basic position was shared by the overwhelming majority of the commentators. Alan Blinder offered a small respite, volunteering that he'd "like to defend Raghu a little bit against the unremitting attack he is getting here." But that was a minority position.[28]

"Luddite" is an easy term to throw around in a hand-waving dismissal of positions one is not inclined to debate seriously. But there were influential figures who indeed did question whether the new American model of finance was superior to the older model that preceded it. Among the most eminent of these was Paul Volcker, former undersecretary of the treasury for international monetary affairs, head of the Federal Reserve Bank of New York, and, most famously, chairman of the Federal Reserve from 1979 to 1987. Volcker is credited with taming the seemingly intractable inflation of the 1970s (if at controversially high cost), and his commitment to caution in the exercise of monetary policy brought him into chronic public disputes with Reagan administration officials.

Monetary policy was not the only issue area about which the Fed chair and administration officials did not see eye to eye. Volcker, like Tobin, from the early 1980s harbored deep reservations about the changing nature and rapid expansion of the financial sector. Volcker, of course, was no Keynesian. But supervision and regulation of the banking system were responsibilities that fell within the Federal Reserve's portfolio, and his attention to these details was part and parcel of his dyed-in-the-wool instincts with regard to general financial stability. This set the stage for a major conflict between Volcker and the Reagan administration, whose general appetite for deregulation extended to the financial sector. In 1983, a working group headed by Vice President Bush proposed shifting much oversight and regulatory authority from the Fed to the Justice department. The *New York Times* reported that "an angry Mr. Volcker resisted efforts by the Bush staff to strip the Fed of most of its authority to supervise banks." Fighting a pitched battle into 1984, the Fed chief succeeded in keeping "what he called sufficient 'hands-on' supervisory responsibility to properly fulfill [the Fed's] role as a central bank." Volcker won that battle, but he was losing the war, as the tide was shifting in favor of deregulation. He "became the foremost advocate for the reregulation of finance," which "outraged" the financial community and administration officials. In 1985, the chairman was repeatedly testifying before Congress in an effort to preserve the integrity of the Glass-Steagall Act. But Reagan-appointed officials at the Fed, reluctant to challenge Volcker on monetary policy, would vote against him on other issues. In his final months as chairman, the Federal Reserve Board approved the request of three New York banks to expand their business into new areas of securities underwriting. "Bank Curb Eased in Volcker Defeat," summarized the *Times*.[29]

Volcker's replacement as chairman of the Federal Reserve was Greenspan, who immediately used his authority to reinterpret Glass-Steagall in such a way as to undermine its integrity a full decade before its ultimate repeal. But where the ascendant deregulation crowd saw the rise of big finance in terms of sophistication, innovation, and opportunity, Volcker saw paper profits and systemic risk. He attributed the stock market crash of 1987 to volatility-inducing financial innovations, pausing to observe, "I don't think these techniques add much to the sum of human endeavor."[30] Out of power, Volcker consistently resisted the idea that the growing financial community could easily, and optimally, regulate itself via what Greenspan liked to call "counter-party surveillance." To the contrary, for Volcker, big finance meant big risk. In 1995 he observed, "I think it is obvious that if you had a large investment bank aligned with a large [commercial] bank, the possibility of a systemic risk arising is evident." In a comprehensive interview conducted in 2000, he reflected, "I think that financial deregulation has been another big strand of what I've been concerned about." Seeing through the system, he expressed basic doubts about the risk models favored on Wall Street. "The banks want to run a risk management system based upon the idea that we have a normal distribution of outcomes," he explained. "But there ain't no normal distribution when it comes to financial crises."[31]

Volcker continued to express these doubts as the new century opened. In 2007, on the eve of the financial crisis, Volcker surveyed the financial terrain of securitization, derivatives, collateralized debt obligations, and custom-tailored structured investment vehicles, which he called "mysterious conduits of uncertain parentage." He again sounded the alarm: "To those of us of a certain age, perhaps more sensitive to market history and the nature of human behavior than to the attraction of mathematical al-gorithms, it all looks confused and even dangerous, susceptible to excesses and breakdowns." He dissented from the au courant position that "the financial market itself, left free and unfettered by official oversight . . . can reliably be self-stabilizing" and expressed regret at the rejection of an older philosophy of regulation that was designed "to protect the core of the financial system from the recurrent bouts of speculative excesses and frightful contractions that have marked financial markets from time immemorial."[32]

Volcker and other critics were articulating a position on finance and the risk of financial crisis that was at odds with the Wall Street–Washington consensus of the new American model. They were in the minority, mar-ginalized, and routinely dismissed as untutored, or worse. But in fact they were representing a perspective that had a rich tradition (and that on in-spection had history on its side), that I call the KKM perspective, to reflect the influence of John Maynard Keynes, Charles Kindleberger, and Hyman Minsky.

Keynes's perspective was discussed in chapter 3, but it is worth briefly reviewing. Although a capacious financial sector is crucial for the function-ing of a capitalist economy, it is inherently prone to failure, and thus its regulation and oversight is essential. Market failure is a chronic concern in finance because actors do not efficiently and hyper-rationally process all available information in the context of definable, calculable risks by draw-ing on their shared knowledge of the correct underlying model. Rather, market participants do the best they can to process information guided by "animal spirits" and by making guesses about the sentiment of the crowd, drawing on varied, implicit models in an environment characterized by uncertainty. Unable to assign precise probabilities to all potential eventu-alities because too many factors are unknowable, investors rely on rules of thumb, instincts derived from personal experience, and "conventional wisdom." And again, one of Keynes's great insights is that in such an envi-ronment, investors must place great weight on the apparent expectations of others. What matters most, then, is not an assessment of the value of a given asset but a best guess about what value other investors are likely to assign to it. It does not matter if you are right about the asset, it matters that you are right about the crowd. In such an environment, asset prices, of course, are not always and everywhere "accurate" but can gyrate unpredictably, are influenced by the mercurial passions of the herd, and are vulnerable to the emergence of self-fulfilling panics.[33]

Thus, for Keynes, finance is inherently vulnerable to crisis, a perspective that Hyman Minsky spent much of his career attempting to build on and elaborate. Minsky developed the "financial instability hypothesis," the fundamental premise of which was that "financial traumas . . . occur as a normal functioning result in a capitalist economy." Because of the central role of uncertainty in the financial world, financial crises are "systemic, rather than accidental events." That being the case, it is necessary for public policy to be alert to the evolution of the financial sector and to dampen the natural tendency for speculative excesses to develop.[34]

Charles Kindleberger also emphasized the common occurrence of financial crises, which, as he explained in his well-known and aptly titled book, *Manias, Panics, and Crashes*, are a "hardy perennial." Kindleberger laid out "the anatomy of a typical crisis"—speculation, expansion and accommodation, swindles, propagation—and reviewed episodes of financial crises dating back hundreds of years, upheavals that occurred with almost rhythmic regularity. All of them are revealed to be the same beasts in different, period-fashionable disguises. And as his title suggests, greed, excitement, and hubris were common elements in these upheavals—emotional drivers, it should be noted, that are utterly incompatible with rational expectations and the efficient markets hypothesis. If you happen to come across a copy of the first edition of Kindleberger's book, published in 1978, you would be forgiven for thinking in had been written in 2009 and based on the events of the global financial crisis.[35]

Kindleberger's argument and illustrations are given a modern revisitation in Carmen Reinhart and Kenneth Rogoff's comprehensive study, *This Time Is Different: Eight Centuries of Financial Folly*. The book, like Peter Yates's 1973 film, *The Friends of Eddie Coyle*, is summarized by the intended irony of its title. Just as Eddie Coyle had no real friends, this time was *not* different, and it almost never is. Reinhart and Rogoff wrote: "Our basic message is simple: we have all been here before." Financial crises are the rule, not the exception. "Countries, institutions, and financial instruments may change across time, but human nature does not." Despite many claims proffered about the singularly exceptional nature of the current crisis, in fact, "the United States has driven straight down the quantitative track of a typical deep financial crisis." The United States also picked up some familiar passengers along the way, as periods of high international capital mobility and booms in housing prices are common precursors to crises throughout history.[36]

The exceptional phenomenon with regard to American finance was not the crisis but the remarkable period of banking stability the United States enjoyed from the 1940s through the 1970s. The United States has been routinely rocked by major financial crises throughout its history, most notably in 1837, 1857, 1873, 1893, 1907, and 1929. A key element in the exceptional period of banking stability was regulation, at both the domestic and international level. The United States has suffered fifteen major banking crises since 1800—about the same number as Denmark, France, Italy, Britain and Brazil—but only two since World War II; and both of those took place recently, in the age of deregulation. There were no major banking crises in the United States in the 1940s, 1950s, 1960s and 1970s. Such crises only re-emerged in the age of deregulation.[37]

Minsky attributed the tendency toward crisis to the phenomenon that "tranquility and success are not self-sustaining states." Instead, paradoxically, success breeds crisis as investors are lulled into a false sense of security. A long period of stability encourages actors to take on more risk and to drift further from the shores of prudence. Acceptable levels of debt and degrees of leverage are gradually increased, and they are accelerated by new financial innovations. As long as the good times continue, those practices are validated, and everyone is happy—right up until that Wile E. Coyote moment when a disturbance exposes that the ground has disappeared from beneath the frantically spinning feet of the financial system.[38] Put another way, in the context of financial stability, some actors are able to gain by bearing greater risk, and these gains are observed by others, who seek to reap similar rewards. As the last big crisis recedes from memory, regulation and oversight are seen as increasingly antiquated, and new innovations (circumventing the spirit of laws written in a previous era) make regulation and oversight harder anyway. Fortunes are made, and the crowd follows. The first risk takers are essentially free-riding on the underlying stability of the system, but as more and more follow in their footsteps, that underlying stability becomes more fragile.

In the United States, many bankers and public officials have been little shaken by the financial crisis, which, from a rational expectations/efficient markets perspective, was a freak event. As summarized by one critic, from this perspective, "if financial crises are black swans, comparable to plane crashes—horrific but highly improbable and impossible to predict—there's no point in worrying about them." Reinhart and Rogoff dismiss the black swan narrative, recognizing it as a vestige of the "this time is different" thinking that pervaded America on the eve of the crisis, where arguments that financial players were better and smarter than those of the past, that the United States had a new and superior financial system, and the old rules no longer applied were common currency. From a KKM perspective, however, a crisis was anything but unlikely—it was probable—because the old rules always apply. "How we get the advantages of an open competitive flexible financial system and deal with its proclivity toward volatility and crisis has been an unsolved problem, one that has preoccupied me," Volcker explained. "The problem is chronic."[39]

Crisis and Continuity: Politics and the Enduring American Model

The financial crisis flipped over the rock of American finance and exposed the massive dysfunctions that had built up just below the surface.[40] The IMF owned up to these problems in 2009, although it retreated first behind the passive voice—"Prior to the crisis, securitization was almost universally hailed as a financial system stabilizer"—and then to British understatement—"Indeed, it turned out that the degree of risk dispersion fell far short of ideal." The Bank for International Settlements came around to the view that flawed risk management techniques, poor corporate governance that "encouraged managers to forsake long run prospects for short run return," and a failure of the regulatory system that "allowed the entire financial industry to book profits too early, too easily, and without proper risk adjustment" were responsible.[41]

A vivid illustration of the problems of the new American model can be seen in the behavior of the CRAs and their relationship with the issuers of the securities that they do business with. Given the complexities of the assets being created, investors had little choice but to lean heavily on the certifications of CRAs. A triple-A rating essentially represented a Good Housekeeping seal of approval; anything so branded should have an extremely low risk of default. Indeed, in 2007, only six companies could boast of meriting the coveted AAA rating. But thousands upon thousands of

AAA ratings were stamped on the new, exotic securities; in 2006, Moody's assembly line handed out over thirty a day. It was big business. Standard and Poor's charged between $40,000 and $135,000 to rate tranches of mortgage-backed securities; fees for rating CDOs were especially lucrative. Unfortunately, the ratings agencies' risk models were usually based on "strong, recent performance," and, worse, they reflected inherent conflicts of interest: issuers of securities needed AAA ratings for their product, while ratings agencies craved their business and feared if they were too stringent another CRA might be more accommodating. There is little doubt that both sides gamed the system, exchanging information and cajoling each other about just what it would take to achieve those crucial three As.[42]

The junk value of CRA product (over 90% of the AAA ratings issued to mortgage-backed securities in 2006 and 2007 were downgraded to junk bond status during the crisis) did more than feed the speculative mania of the bubble; it added fuel to the fire of the crisis. The sudden, massive, comically belated downgrades—one is reminded of John Belushi's "Sorry about that" apology after seizing and smashing a stranger's guitar in *Animal House*—left investors, already in distress and forced to sell assets, scrambling desperately to try to move paper they thought was investment grade but which turned out to be, in the vernacular of the time, toxic.[43]

But the problem was much broader and more fundamental than the compromise of the CRAs.[44] Too-big-to-fail, and too-interconnected-to-fail financial institutions were leveraged and exposed, and when the music stopped, not only were they set to collapse to the floor, they were certain to drag down their partners with them. Firms individually crawling out on ever thinner limbs endangered their own positions and contributed to collective systemic risk, which went unnoticed by disinterested would-be overseers. When Bear Stearns was on the brink of bankruptcy, it was a party to 750,000 derivatives contracts and had open trades with thousands of other firms. When President Bush asked his advisers why the fortunes of one insurance company, AIG, could present so much systemic danger that there was no choice but to bail it out, Bernanke explained what the new financial system had allowed to happen: AIG wasn't so much an insurance company, it was "more like a hedge fund sitting on top of an insurance company," and there was "no oversight" of its financial products division, which "made huge numbers of irresponsible bets." Again, the problem was that AIG was not the exception, it was the rule. As Bush treasury secretary Henry Paulson later reflected, the financial system "contained far too much leverage," with much of that leverage "in opaque and highly complex financial products." Writing in the present tense in 2010, he argued further that "the largest financial institutions are so big and complex that they pose a dangerously large risk."[45]

The financial crisis was ultimately contained by massive government intervention and bailouts that prevented the entire system from collapsing. Nevertheless, the trauma threw the economy into a deep and persistent downturn, which is what typically happens in the wake of such a crisis. Given these costs, a key question is, have the fundamental causes of the crisis been addressed in the United States? The answer to that question is no. The crisis was caused by financial institutions that were too big to fail and too interconnected to fail pursuing highly leveraged, short-sighted strategies that filled the economic waters with icebergs of systemic risk. Deregulation encouraged dangerous size and high connectivity, and an efficient markets culture that championed the withdrawal of oversight and supervision clipped the wires of early warning systems. And, despite new laws and regulations, the post-crisis US financial system is characterized by more continuity than change.

Actually, in some ways, the structural situation is worse than before the crisis because there are now fewer firms left standing with even greater market share and left largely to conduct business as usual. The current stasis is a testament to the power of the financial community and its enmeshment with political elites. The Wall Street–Washington axis endures, and its narrative is *not* that the crisis revealed (yet again) the essential truths of the KKM perspective: that the financial system, left to its own devices, is highly susceptible to crisis and thus must be regulated and supervised by authorities alert to the possibility of systemic risk. Rather, it retains an efficient markets perspective that sees the crisis as a unique and freak event, a black swan. Much like General Buck Turgidson appealing to President Muffly in *Dr. Strangelove*, they "don't think it's quite fair to condemn a whole program because of a single slip-up."

This position wins for reasons that are taught in Political Science 101: the costs of systemic risk are shared diffusely by the general public, whereas the benefits of uninhibited banking are reaped by a relatively small, concentrated group. Small, highly motivated groups usually win political battles over large diffuse interests, and the power, influence, and interpenetration of finance in politics is difficult to overstate. The financial sector invested $5 billion in the political process from 1998 to 2008, $1.7 billion in campaign contributions and $3.4 billion in lobbying expenses. The chairman of the Senate banking committee always did well: first Alfonse D'Amato, then Phil Gramm, and finally Chris Dodd, who received $2.9 million in contributions from the industry in 2007–8. In the first nine months of 2009, as Congress considered financial reform, the industry spent $344 million on lobbying. Additionally, as noted in the discussion of ideological convergence in chapter 4, to a large extent they were often lobbying themselves. Both Clinton's and Bush's treasury secretaries hailed from Wall Street. Friend-of-finance Phil Gramm left the Senate in 2002 and immediately joined the financial giant UBS. Larry Summers raked in over $5 million for a part-time job at the hedge fund D. E. Shaw and got $135,000 from Goldman Sachs in exchange for a personal appearance a few months before joining the Obama administration. And these were just the most recognizable figures making their way through a revolving door that was spinning at every level of government.[46]

Robert Rubin is perhaps the poster-boy for the cozy relationship between government and finance that, if observed in other countries, Greenspan and other champions of the American model would have labeled "crony capitalism." Rubin left the Clinton administration and immediately joined Citigroup (an institution whose existence was only possible due to the regulatory changes that took place when he was treasury secretary) where he was paid over $125,000,000 between 1999 and 2009 to serve on the board of directors and hold the title of "chairman of the executive committee," a strategic advisory position whose responsibilities were described by the *Wall Street Journal* as "murky." From this perch in 2001, Rubin called the undersecretary of the treasury to ask that the government urge credit rating agencies to delay issuing a downgrade of Enron. (Citibank was a major Enron creditor.) In advising Citigroup, Rubin was also known for urging the company to be more aggressive and take on more risk, and pursuant to that strategy, the firm became a major player in CDOs. In 2003, it issued $6.28 billion in CDOs and then tripled that business to more than $20 billion's worth in 2005. In that year the bank received about $500 million in fees from that activity. Of course, those strategies ultimately led to ruin.

"Mr. Rubin encouraged changes that led Citi to the brink of collapse" was the broadly shared assessment, but he "was reportedly critical to securing" its bailout by the federal government.[47]

The support for business as usual in American finance remains bipartisan. Republicans are hostile to anything that smacks of government intervention in the economy; if anything, members of the Grand Old Party favor repealing the marginal reforms that were put in place after the crisis. As for the Democrats, Obama, coming to the presidency in the midst of the financial crisis, threw his lot in with those who were central to bringing it about. Rubin was an economic adviser on the transition team, and the appointments that followed were "a virtual Rubin constellation." Summers was named to head the White House National Economic Council, avoiding what would have been a bruising confirmation process, and Timothy Geithner, one of Summers's top lieutenants in the Clinton administration, was tapped for Treasury. (Succeeding Geithner as president of the New York Fed was the former chief economist at Goldman Sachs.) Paul Volcker, an early Obama supporter, was appointed head of the newly created President's Economic Recovery Advisory Board. The position, unstaffed and virtually freelance, served as a distant perch from which he routinely clashed with Geithner and Summers. "They considered me an old man," out of touch with the realities of modern finance, Volcker told his biographer. He was, at least, successful in including a version of what came to be known as the "Volcker rule," which was designed to limit high-risk speculation by commercial banks, into the Dodd-Frank financial reforms. But the Volcker rule as adopted included vague exceptions, and its influence is dependent on how it is interpreted and enforced. The same can be said for Dodd-Frank more generally, which certainly has some constructive elements but which is also often vague, and, in the words of Robert Shiller, "only a beginning of a dialogue on how to move our financial system into the twenty-first century."[48]

That dialogue, however, is not taking place—not in the United States, that is. There was no alternative to a massive government intervention and bailout; it was those measures that prevented the equivalent of another Great Depression. But that success—no complete financial meltdown, "only" a deep and stubborn recession—took the wind out of the sails of what would have been a grand debate about what the financial system *should* look like. For critics, this meant that although flames had been extinguished (at great cost), the firetrap remained.[49]

"The fact is, God created the financial sector to help the real economy, not to help itself," Nobel laureate Robert Solow argued. "I suspect," he also mused, "that the financial services sector has grown relatively to the point where it is not even adding value to the real economy. It may be adding compensation to its members but it is not improving the efficiency or productivity of the real economy." Solow acknowledged the obvious, that a strong, capacious, and sophisticated financial sector is a crucial part of an advanced economy. "But I have the feeling," he added, "that we have got to the point where the financial services sector is creating risk rather than allocating it." At what point does the financial sector become too large? At what point does a financial institution become too big? The industry too concentrated? Too interconnected? These were the types of questions that might have been asked in the United States in the wake of the financial crisis, but were not.[50]

The View from Abroad

The United States did not go in for any financial soul searching, but, as I will emphasize in the next chapter, the global financial crisis of 2007–8 stimulated greater reassessment abroad, especially in Asia, where this was the second catastrophe of capital unbound in the last decade, and in other corners of the globe that had similarly unhappy experiences. The United States, from its position of hegemony for much of the post–World War II era, had experienced a long period of financial stability, but many other countries did not. To them the global financial crisis looked less like a black swan and more like yet another bird in a flock that had been released from the pens by financial deregulation. And even though this chapter has obviously reflected my analytical sympathy for the KKM model, to a large extent, as will also be discussed in the chapters that follow, much of the political fallout of the crisis is the result of this new divergence of opinion—a new heterogeneity of thinking about money and finance—and not due to whether one side or the other in the economic debate is correct.

Looking at the United States from the perspective of other countries after the crisis, we find three reassessments now in play. First, there were new questions about the attractiveness of the American model, both the financial model, previously understood as the single template toward which maturing economies must converge, and the general economic model as well. Second there were new (and greater) concerns about the dangers lurking within the American economy. Its largely unreformed financial sector suddenly and uncharacteristically seemed vulnerable to future crises; and the necessary emergency measures taken to contain the crisis, a flood of liquidity and increases in government spending (resulting in large federal deficits and debt), only added to wariness about the long-term economic prospects of the United States. Finally, there were new questions about the wisdom (not to mention the sustainability) of national economic strategies that relied on the presumption of the indefinite growth of very high levels of US demand. In sum, in the wake of the financial crisis, the idea of finding a bit more insulation from the US economy, and some distance from the American model, was taken more seriously.

6

The Crisis and World Politics

The United States emerged from the global financial crisis with its banking model essentially intact or, more precisely, with its system dominated by fewer and larger too-big-to-fail institutions, playing by modified versions of most of the same rules and by all of the same norms. In much of the rest of the world, however, there has been a more consequential reassessment of the management of money and finance. This can be observed in policy choices throughout the developing world and in Asia generally; elements of new thinking can even be seen, if expressed tentatively and cautiously, in some Western international financial institutions. The Bank for International Settlements concluded that banks must become "smaller, simpler, and safer," which is, paradoxically, the opposite of what has happened because crisis response required "the sale of distressed banks to other banks . . . creating financial institutions so big and complex that even their own management may not understand the risk exposures." Despite "nearly universal" concerns about the dangers posed by too-big-to-fail institutions, the Bank observed, "short run government actions are increasing financial sector concentration and adding to systemic risk."[1]

Even the International Monetary Fund has retreated somewhat, if with palpable reluctance, from its position that capital controls are always inappropriate; it now grudgingly concedes that the judicious use of some types of controls can be "justified as part of the policy toolkit." Scholars at the IMF have also begun to question other aspects of previously sacrosanct macroeconomic orthodoxy, even suggesting some relaxation of the single-minded pursuit of very low inflation as the necessary cornerstone of sound macroeconomic policy. Although new thinking at the IMF has been gradual, cautious, and qualified, Ilene Grabel argues that "the IMF's ambiguous and fluid stance" on these issues, which is perhaps to some extent politically inevitable given that the crisis "provoked policymakers around the world to impose capital controls," has created permissive space for states to experiment with new approaches. The Fund's muted response to Brazil's postcrisis imposition of capital controls, which contrasts notably with its vehement condemnation of Malaysia during the Asian financial crisis, "makes it easier for other countries to follow suit." Grabel argues that the IMF's new restraint has allowed for what she calls "productive incoherence" with regard to strategies of economic governance.[2]

That incoherence will contribute to what I dub the new heterogeneity of thinking about money and finance that is emerging in the wake of the delegitimization of the American financial model in many parts of the world. Manifestations of the new heterogeneity can be seen throughout the globe, but they are most visible, and most consequential, in China, the world's second-largest economy, and in Asia more generally. The loss of faith in the American model has transformed China's international economic strategy, changing Beijing's attitude about how to best manage money and finance and dramatically accelerating its strategy of promoting the RMB as an international currency. These changes, in China and elsewhere, will alter the international balance of power and will also affect the nature of international economic relations. I will address balance-of-power questions in chapter 7. In this chapter, I focus on China's new thinking, the politics and economics of the rise of the RMB as an international currency, and how these developments and others, including the trajectory of the euro, will present new challenges to international macroeconomic relations. Much of the discussion here focuses on China for good reason.

But the story and its implications are more general and illustrate well the changes brewing in the post–financial crisis world. The emergence of new thinking, new preferences, and new politics are widespread phenomena that are most immediately visible and consequential in China due to its distinct economic size and political disposition.

The Political Economy of Monetary Ambition

Unless something goes terribly wrong with China's economy, a possibility not to be casually dismissed, even if it is not the most likely outcome, Beijing will look to increase the international use of the yuan and eventually seek to establish its currency as the international money of East Asia. Two core motivations will guide this policy of facilitating and encouraging the emergence of the RMB as a regional currency: China's search for enhanced economic autonomy and increased international political influence. These are the two reasons why great powers have routinely sought to expand the international use of their currencies throughout modern history. And, in the case of contemporary China, each of these motivations is particularly acute. Although the (often implicit) desire to enhance international influence has typically been the primary motive for states seeking to encourage the international use of their currencies, in the case of contemporary China the aspiration for greater autonomy in the wake of the global financial crisis has accelerated this impulse. The crisis, especially understood in the context of the Asian financial crisis just ten years earlier, has undermined the legitimacy of the US-championed, dollar-centric, unregulated financial order. Since the crisis, Beijing prefers to establish some distance from the dollar and to explore distinct approaches to economic governance that offer an alternative to radically unmediated global finance. With regard to political influence, as an emerging great power (with aspirations to regional hegemony) in a crowded geopolitical neighborhood where states tend to pursue internationally oriented growth strategies and are wary of naked power plays, China will find that encouraging the regional use of the yuan is an especially attractive strategy.

To be clear, this is not to suggest that the yuan will displace the US dollar as the preeminent global currency. Rather, I expect it to encroach on the influence of the (still formidable) dollar and eventually emerge as the dominant currency in East Asia.³ But even in this qualified context, such encroachment on the dollar (along with the emergence of other currencies, including the euro, as more important players in economic spaces where the dollar once dominated) will have significant consequences for international politics. The changing geography of money will also affect international economic relations, especially as China, a rising great power, will work for reform within existing international institutions where the status quo does not adequately reflect its growing importance. Because it is likely to meet with limited success on this front, given the entrenched interests of others, Beijing will also pursue its own international arrangements on a parallel track.

Emboldened by its rising status and spurred by the global financial crisis, China's increased monetary ambition follows a pattern, and logic, seen throughout modern history. Simply put, extending their monetary reach is one of the things that great powers tend to do. It is important to recognize that states that pursue leadership of regional (or global) monetary orders are almost always motivated by *political* concerns, in particular, by the desire to gain enhanced influence over other states and for greater autonomy more generally—that is, for the greater freedom of action provided by a buffer from external pressures and constraints. This point needs to be stressed because it is somewhat counterintuitive, given the historical association of international currency areas with colonialism. But currency fiefdoms are typically money losers, and not due to miscalculation or error but because states at the center of monetary orders knowingly and willingly offer perks and otherwise spend cash in an unacknowledged effort to purchase power and influence. Thus, although leadership of a currency area does provide new levers of coercive power, the appeal and pursuit of "structural" power, as I have argued elsewhere, is so coveted that it tends to inhibit the overt or coercive exercise of currency power within zones of monetary influence.⁴ Following logic first articulated by Albert Hirschman with regard to international trade, smaller states can become conditioned upon and vulnerable to the whims of their larger partners in asymmetric economic relations. Hirschman, it should be acknowledged, for the most part emphasized vulnerability: the implicit threat by the larger state to terminate the relationship, the consequences of which would be disproportionately felt by the smaller. But, in practice, it is the *conditioning* rather than the vulnerability that is the more cultivated prize and more consequential outcome for international politics. Within small states, actors that benefit from participation tend to thrive and are empowered. At the aggregate level, although it is true that states may fear offending their larger patrons, much more profoundly, over time, they quite voluntarily come to recalculate their own national interests. Given their external economic associations and shifts to the balance of domestic political power, small states can increasingly see their own interests as progressively more in accord with those of their most intimate economic associates.[5]

With notable consistency, most states that have been in a position to extend their monetary influence have attempted to do so.[6] As early as the 1860s, France's efforts to establish the Latin monetary union reflected an "express desire to see all continental Europe united in a franc area which would exclude and isolate Germany." French leaders made every effort to manage the union and keep it alive; the modest 1930s notion of a "gold bloc" was a coda to those efforts. France also cultivated the use of the franc or franc-based currencies, first in its colonies and later, at considerable expense, in the franc zone of former colonies. (Even critics of participation in the franc zone acknowledged that from an economic perspective the affiliation was beneficial to its members.) Nazi Germany and Imperial Japan extended their monetary influence as part of their interwar grand strategies, and, after spending the first few decades after World War II in the penalty box, by the 1980s each was harboring renewed (if considerably more benign) monetary ambitions. The German mark was the anchor of the European monetary system; the yen, whose experience provides important insights into contemporary Chinese motives, choices, and behavior, seemed for a time on the cusp of mounting a challenge to the dollar. British sterling, of course, served as the world's currency for over a century, before retreating to the sterling area and then the sterling zone, which, even when reduced to a smaller, defensive organization, provided a crucial source of financing during World War II. Finally, the United States, even with an immature and skeletal domestic financial system, during the first third of the twentieth century extended on an ad hoc basis its monetary reach within the western hemisphere and sought to promote New York as an international financial center. In the second half of the century, the Americans bankrolled the dollar-based gold-exchange standard of the Bretton Woods system and spent a decade tolerating exceptions and waiting for its Cold War allies to recover to an extent that would permit them to play by its rules.[7]

The experiences of Britain and the United States also call attention to the potentially extractive, exploitative, and ultimately burdensome attributes of sitting at the center of a monetary order. Britain called on the financial resources of the sterling system during World War II without so much as asking and was saddled with the difficulties of managing the postwar "sterling balances," a significant overhang of liabilities that hampered its economic policymaking for decades. And the United States forced the burden of adjustment on others—and not for the last time—when it suddenly ended the Bretton Woods system by closing the gold window.[8] But these elements and observations, important for a comprehensive accounting of the political economy of international currency use, are of limited or what might be called ironic relevance for China's emerging monetary ambitions. When states embark on the project of extending their monetary influence, then and now, they are usually, as is contemporary China, on the rise and invariably looking to enhance their structural power. Efforts at economic exploitation would undercut, not enhance, such ambitions, and the opportunities and/or headaches of mature or even senescent monetary arrangements are unlikely to factor as significant considerations given the time horizons of the confident leadership present at the creation. But one reaction to the perceived exploitation by the issuer of a currency that is perhaps past the peak of its appeal may be to spur other states into taking on a more ambitious monetary role. In addition, and as a separate matter, the instabilities associated with the age of globalized finance has created an additional incentive for states to increase the supply of regional monetary arrangements; and it has as well increased the demand by smaller states for opportunities to shelter from global financial storms.[9] These concerns have been part of the motivation behind successive phases of European monetary integration and have spurred both Japan and now China into thinking more about monetary leadership in Asia.

The Japanese experience from the late 1980s holds a number of lessons that provide insight into the case of contemporary China. There are some remarkable parallels between the two episodes. As Japan emerged as the second-largest economy in the world, and according to many heady accounts of the day it was poised to become "number one," the sky seemed to be the limit; many Japanese officials imagined an internationalized yen as a major currency that would be a means to further enhance Japan's growing influence. But with the stagnation of the Japanese economy in the 1990s (and the resurgence of growth in the United States) such attitudes fell into remission, only to resurface, in a very different guise, in the wake of the Asian financial crisis. After that crisis, a revived interest in a larger role for the yen was rooted in defensive motivations: the search for greater insulation, autonomy, and greater space from the American vision of global financial order. As William Grimes explained, the revived debate was now "fundamentally about *insulation*" and rooted in disenchantment with the instability associated with (US-championed) uninhibited financial globalization and deregulation, with the US ability to shift macroeconomic burdens of adjustment abroad (and chronic US pressure over ex-rate issues), and with the more general implications of the ideological divergence between the United States and Japan in their respective reactions to the Asian financial crisis. As discussed in chapter 4, throughout Asia in general there was "profound resentment" of the US response to the crisis, which created new incentives for and receptivity to greater regional cooperation that would provide some space from the American model. This was also in part a reaction to US behavior that followed a pattern described by Andrew Walter: when building an international monetary order, system leaders start out with considerable self-restraint; at the height of their power, they are increasingly tempted to exploit the advantages presented by their privileged status; but, over time, the accumulation of such transgressions encourages "the emergence of rival lead currencies and associated financial centers."[10]

The aborted Japanese effort to establish a more capacious, internationalized yen offer crucial lessons for understanding the likely behavior of China in the coming years. Once again, they illustrate the tendency for ambitions plans for a more assertive presence in the international money game to flow naturally from the momentum and confidence of a more general economic rise. They serve as a reminder that such ambitions have important defensive components, those that Japan then shares with China now: the desire for insulation from the instability associated with financial globalization, irritation with the US tendency to use its key currency status to force burdens of adjustment abroad, and ideological alienation from the US vision of a completely unmediated global financial order. Finally, even as China's continued economic and political rise seems like the most likely trajectory, the Japanese experience serves as a reminder of the mistakes analysts can make in casually projecting underlying trends indefinitely into the future. China faces its own formidable challenges moving forward, as I will discuss in chapter 8.

China's Monetary Ambitions and Their Acceleration

Prior to the global financial crisis, RMB internationalization was already a gleam in the eye of elites in China, but it was understood that the yuan was a long way off from serving as an important international currency. The dominant position of the dollar, the emergence of the euro, and the fragility of China's sheltered, murky domestic financial sector (in contrast with the venerable institutions and market powerhouses to be found in the West) tempered expectations about how quickly the yuan might take its place as a currency widely used in international transactions, and beyond that, when it might begin to serve as a reserve asset. Nevertheless, such ambitions, however distant, were clearly harbored, and as China continued its rise to great power status it was natural to assume that a greater international role for a maturing RMB would be part of that process.

On the one hand, before the global financial crisis it was understood that the Anglo-American financial model was the only game in town and that convergence toward that model was the path that China was taking. On the other hand, China had always been wary of exposing itself to international capital markets and understood that its controls had spared it from the Asian financial crisis and other tumult that had characterized global finance in a succession of crises since the mid-1990s. From the early 2000s, then, China embarked on a cautious path that accommodated controlled yuan appreciation and modest movements toward financial liberalization, while being alert to the tendency of the United States to shift the burden of adjustments abroad. The example of Japan, which was pressured by the United States into yen appreciations that were seen as contributing to that country's economic malaise, was routinely invoked by Chinese observers. Pushing further into the decade, China's continued economic growth and its massive and increasing holdings of dollar assets assured that, at the very least, discussions of the country's role as a potential monetary powerhouse would take place. Still, on the eve of the crisis, it would be hard to take issue with the assessment of Chin and Helleiner that China's position as a creditor had increased its autonomy and influence and that it would seek greater financial independence from the United States and look, cautiously, to enhance its regional role, but that it nevertheless faced considerable challenges on this path. In sum, they concluded, "China's power in the international financial system, certainly growing, should not be overestimated."[11]

But the global financial crisis fundamentally changed this. It accelerated the process of RMB internationalization, and it ended the project of converging with the American model. Thus the crisis both provided a new impetus to and urgency regarding the promotion of the yuan and altered the trajectory of its path. By exposing profound flaws in the American model, the crisis elicited what can be called "buyer's remorse" in China with regard to its development model that had bound it so tightly to the (weaker than previously assumed) US economy and made it such a stakeholder in the (even more vulnerable that once thought) US dollar. The crisis also redoubled the already robust wariness of Chinese elites about the risk of exposure to the global financial economy and reinforced demands for insulation.[12] And the relative rates of recovery in the aftermath of the crisis: swift in China, sluggish in the United States (and Europe), magnified the pre-existing trends that were already suggestive of a rising China. Finally, and crucially, the crisis delegitimized the American model that China had been cautiously tacking toward right up until the crisis, if invariably at a rate deemed inadequate by its American tutors. Just months before the crisis, Treasury Secretary Paulson was (again) lecturing that "the risks for China are greater in moving too slowly than in moving too quickly" with financial liberalization. This was revealed to be transparently wrong, and the American black eye from the financial crisis was not just material, it was also ideational. Since the end of the Cold War, the United States had benefitted from what John Ikenberry and Charles Kupchan dubbed "hegemonic socialization," an enhancement of its power that derived from foreign elites buying into its model. But now it was China's turn to lecture, with its bank regulators publicly blaming the crisis on their American counterparts who "tend to overestimate the power of the market and overlook the regulatory role of the government," which they described as a "warped conception." With the American model at the epicenter of the catastrophic global financial crisis, then, one consequence was an unwinding of the hegemonic socialization that had to that point been enjoyed by the United States. This inverse effect—from socialization to disrepute—implies negative consequences for the political power and influence of the United States, as elites, especially in Asia, began to search for alternatives to and distance from that delegitimized approach.[13]

RMB internationalization is seen as a necessary corrective for buyer's remorse. "When we were elated about the rapid growth in foreign reserves, China had unconsciously fallen into a 'dollar trap,'" Yu Yongding, former director of the Institute of World Economics and Politics at the Chinese Academy of Social Sciences, explained in 2011. It was now necessary to hold fewer dollar assets, and, to promote this, "the internationalization of the RMB truly is an important option for China." This conclusion has been reached by a number of elites, academics, and public officials throughout the People's Republic. "As the US's largest official creditor, the Chinese government has discovered that it relies too much on the dollar in international trade, international capital flows, and foreign exchange reserve management," another well-placed observer concluded, "and that this overreliance contained a huge risk."[14]

Buyer's remorse also reflects a greater disenchantment with the US management of the dollar and its role in the international financial system more generally, two things about which Chinese observers are increasingly critical. These reassessments have contributed to a desire for insulation from anticipated future instability caused by American mismanagement and demands for reform of the global macroeconomic order for similar reasons. The United States, from this perspective, is also inadequately attentive to the global implications of its management of the dollar. American policies force others to adjust "in accordance with the needs of the US dollar," argues Li Ruogu, chairman and president of the China Export-Import Bank. "The US used this method to topple Japan's economy, and it wants to use this method to curb China's development." RMB internationalization is necessary to reform and to pluralize the international monetary system. "Only by eliminating the US dollar's monopolistic position" can the system be reformed. Li Yang, vice president of the Chinese Academy of Social Sciences, offers a similar analysis. Attributing the unsatisfactory response of the International Monetary Fund to the Asian financial crisis to the under-representation of Asian voices and interests, he holds that "actively promoting the internationalization of the RMB is not only the necessary choice for China's economic and financial development, but it is also an important step to systematically raise Asia's position within the international financial system." The global financial crisis reveals an obvious need for basic reform of the international system, with a greater emphasis on regional needs and arrangements. Many Chinese academics have stressed that the management of the dollar as the world's currency "lacks necessary constraints" and is an important source of volatility in the world economy. RMB internationalization is seen as a necessary step toward a multiple currency system that would reduce the influence of the dollar, contribute to systemic stability, increase China's voice, and provide some insurance against a dollar crisis.[15]

The crisis has also encouraged a new ambitiousness about the rate at which the RMB might ascend to the world stage, because it reinforced an underlying geopolitical trend that had been much talked about for some time, the astonishing rise of China and the relative decline of the United States. This subtext, often creeping into the text, has informed discussions about the role of the dollar in supporting US power, and whether and how global economic governance ought to better reflect the changing international balance of power. A relatively benign interpretation suggests that China's record of "tiding over two financial crises" and "three decades of growth," as contrasted with "weakened confidence in the dollar" and new skepticism about "the soundness of Washington's macroeconomic policies," offers compelling logic in favor of reform. (Some more nationalistic voices see the dominance of the dollar as a crucial lever of American hegemony.) Others observe that emerging from the crisis, the United States is seen as weaker, and the IMF ineffective, which again, suggests a revisiting of the rules of the game. Most Chinese academics see a troubled US financial order and a vulnerable greenback, and share the assessment of the World Bank that a multiple currency system is likely to emerge in the not-too-distant future. In all cases, the rise of China's economic and political power in the context of the global financial crisis is suggestive of a greater role for the yuan and a distinct regional flavor to global financial organization, leading to a central Chinese role in Asian monetary and financial cooperation.[16]

But to focus solely on power, which, certainly, is an essential variable, risks missing the crucial role of ideology in the recalculation of China's strategy with regard to its management of domestic and global monetary and financial affairs, and how it envisions the future of the RMB. Like Jimmy Carter reassessing the Soviet threat late in his presidency, the scales have fallen from the eyes of Chinese elites, in this case about the true (and dangerous) nature of uninhibited financial deregulation. Chen Siqing, executive vice president of the Bank of China, attributed the financial crisis to "six surface level reasons"—familiar items, including excessive leverage and conflict-of-interest-ridden credit rating agencies. But he also went on to describe "deeper problems" that made the crisis "inevitable," problems that implicate the basic assumptions of the US economic model, including a disregard for systemic risk. His analysis speaks forcefully for creating some space between the Chinese and American economies and for altering the trajectory of China's financial model away from the path of convergence with the Anglo-American approach and toward something different. This perspective was echoed quite explicitly by Li Ruogu of the ExIm Bank: "Blindly believing and even following the models and theories extolled by the west can only result in failure, I'm afraid." This is a widespread assessment among Chinese elites and academics. "The Anglo-Saxon model is not the only one; and it should not be the final model for emulation," one observer insisted. "China cannot simply use Harvard University's teaching materials to guide the development of Chinese finance," opined another.[17] This perspective is not limited to China; many in Korea, for example, have been reaching similar conclusions. And the delegitimization of the American model in Asia has been noted by numerous experts in the West.[18]

When the global financial crisis, in America, of America, and from America, confirmed the worst fears of the skeptics of the American model, actors and critics drew on reservoirs of ideological and political opposition that had been pre-positioned. Among other problems, the West is "still living with the consequences of its decision to call the East Asian crisis a comeuppance for crony capitalism," as John Williamson reflected. "Recognizing it as a panic then would have been much better."[19]

Toward RMB Internationalization

Rejection of the American model, desire for greater space from the US economy, and the acceleration of the rise of China's relative power and influence have all stimulated visions of a more important, international RMB. It remains to be seen how quickly this will come about and the economic template it would follow. But as Benjamin Cohen has argued, "in both words and deeds, the Chinese have appeared to underscore a dissatisfaction with the status quo that goes well beyond anything expressed by earlier newcomers."[20] And, in the wake of the crisis, there was a clear increase in official rhetoric about the RMB, although questions remained about how that talk might be translated into action, especially given potential barriers such as the yuan's limited convertibility and uncertainty about the stability of China's domestic financial sector. But some tangible moves designed to increase the international role of the RMB, especially a series of bilateral swap agreements, are visible signs that, to some extent, official talking up of the RMB is not just talk. After the global financial crisis, there is both an increase on the *supply side*: China's willingness to have the RMB deployed in a greater role internationally, and at the same time a clearly increased *demand*: a greater desire by states to find ways to transact business in ways that do not bind them tightly to, or at least provides some diversification away from, the dollar, the American financial model, and the US economy.[21]

In March 2009, Zhou Xiaochuan, governor of the People's Bank of China, delivered a speech titled "Reform of the International Monetary System." The speech, subsequently published (in a slightly revised form), was seconded by statements from other leading officials and attracted, appropriately, considerable media attention. Nominally a call for a greater role for the SDR,[22] the governor's statement was properly understood as a challenge to the dollar. If not a call for a greater international role for the RMB, which it was not and which would have been counterproductively heavy-handed, it was nevertheless an explicit call to move away from the dollar, which, as a practical matter, amounts to the same thing. "The frequency and increasing intensity of financial crises following the collapse of the Bretton Woods system suggests the costs of such a system to the world may have exceeded its benefits," he argued; more to the point, he attributed the crisis to "the inherent vulnerabilities and systemic risks in the existing international monetary system." And if that was not clear enough, he added, the crisis was "an inevitable outcome of the institutional flaws" of relying on a single national currency to serve as the world's money.[23]

Zhou's speech was also notable for two additional reasons. First, the governor repeatedly invoked Keynes ("The Keynesian approach may have been more farsighted"). This, admittedly, was specifically in defense of a supranational currency, but the recurring appeal to Keynes stands notably in contrast with the fundamental anti-Keynesian ideological underpinnings of the second US postwar order. Second, as Chin and Wang have argued, the speech reflects "the consensus Chinese view . . . that a multi-reserve currency era is coming, even if only gradually, and that it would be in China's strategic interests to promote such a scenario." Publications by Chinese elites and academics increasingly illustrate this perspective by calling attention to the observable facts on the ground ("To mainland Chinese economists, the issue of the international monetary system and the so-called post-dollar era is not only possible but is already showing its first signs") and assessments of government policy ("The aim of this strategy is to promote the RMB on an international scale, and to decrease . . . reliance on the dollar"). And they often include prescriptive support for such measures rooted not only in economics but also politics ("As a major power, China urgently needs to carry out internationalization of the RMB as a national strategic priority").[24]

Despite all this, there remain potential bumps on the road to the emergence of the RMB. To some extent, this remains a question of *pace* and *scope*, that is, the trajectory is clearly there for the yuan to become a much more important currency on the world stage, yet questions remain about how quickly this will occur and just how influential it will become. (And, to repeat, this discussion is about the emergence of the RMB as an important international and potentially dominant regional currency, not about its supplanting the dollar and becoming *the* global key currency.) Helleiner and Malkin, while acknowledging that the government has taken steps to promote the international use of the RMB, argue that the relative dearth of domestic economic interest groups lobbying in favor of internationalization suggests an underappreciated lack of political wind behind the sails of the enterprise. A more treacherous potential disruption of the yuan's trajectory is the extent of the weakness in and discomforting opacity of Chinese banks and of its domestic financial sector more generally. China's sheltered institutions were able to weather the storm of the global financial crisis. But the state holds a major stake in many of China's banks, which rely on government protection, carry considerable loans to state-owned enterprises of uncertain promise, and would likely come under pressure if fully exposed to market pressures and foreign competition.[25]

This matters in and of itself as a barometer of the future of the economy but also because most experts consider rich, deep, and stable financial institutions to be crucial foundations for an international currency. In particular, most Western analysts consider full currency convertibility and completely open capital markets as virtual prerequisites for establishing the international financial centers that would be the platforms for and hubs of international money. Many see this as the rate-limiting factor of the yuan's rise and even suggest a ceiling for its ultimate status. For the RMB "to become a genuine international currency," one such study concluded, "China must . . . lift capital controls completely."[26]

As a matter of practice, this may or may not be the case. China seems poised to act as if it is not and appears set to embark on considerable internationalization of the RMB without pausing to fully liberalize its capital account.[27] (This is, of course, an illustration of new heterogeneity in thinking.) In a very telling essay, Governor Zhou sought to redefine the meaning of capital account convertibility in a way that would accommodate these ambitions. "The definition of capital account convertibility is something that can be discussed, and how standards should be set should have a certain degree of flexibility," he wrote, noting that the IMF charter itself is vague on the definition, which invites national interpretation. Moreover, "capital account convertibility does not equal the abandonment of oversight or controls on transnational financial transactions." In particular, "when international markets experience abnormal volatility or when problems occur with a country's balance of international payments, it is reasonable to apply appropriate controls to short-term, speculative capital flows." And finally, and crucially, Zhou added, "China has to have its own voice in the establishment of international standards." All this may be part of what rejecting the American model of financial governance looks like: putting the infrastructure in place for the yuan to become more internationalized, promoting its use as a vehicle currency, and encouraging other central banks to hold yuan as reserves while retaining some capital controls and other market-inhibiting devices. One way to encourage this would be through bilateral swap agreements, which China has quite actively pursued.[28]

After the global financial crisis, Chinese leaders decided to step up the pace of RMB internationalization, promote regional monetary cooperation, and encourage reform of global monetary management in an effort to begin to reduce its dependence on the US dollar and to a establish some alternative to the American model. Crucially, China's willingness to increase the "supply" of international monetary options coincided, for similar reasons, with greater demand, especially, but not exclusively, in Asia for alternatives to the dollar and to the ideology of unbridled financial globalization.[29] The desire for diversified options, as well as assessments of "credibility" that derive from different sources than the lack of capital controls and adherence to one version of macroeconomic orthodoxy, might further facilitate a distinct path to RMB internationalization. "I would rather bet on China's authorities—who ignored the prediction . . . [of] the US Treasury Secretary, that they risked trillions of dollars in lost economic potential unless they freed their capital markets," explained the former prime minister of Thailand. "That seems wiser than praying to god that the US soon finds a credible model of economic growth and regulation of financial institutions." Similarly, area specialists have noted the crisis has invited "many in Korea [to] question the wisdom of following the Anglo-American model as practiced in the past few decades with such a heedless emphasis on deregulation."[30]

The signature move in China's new "deliberate" and "aggressive" promotion of the use of the yuan has been the bilateral currency swap, which facilitates the utilization of and provides easy access to yuan without requiring multilateral negotiations and without necessitating ambitious or comprehensive commitments to financial liberalization. (Beijing has also pursued agreements that allow China and its trading partners to settle their trading accounts without moving in and out of dollars.) Such pacts are welcomed by China's trading partners, of which there are many; the People's Republic is the world's second-largest importer and the most important trading partner for an increasing number of major economies that share most if not all of China's motives in diversifying away from the dollar. Notable among these many agreements, negotiated throughout Asia, and also in Latin America, the Middle East, and the former Soviet Union, was the one reached with Japan. China recently overtook the United States as that country's largest trading partner, and Japan also requested, and received, the right to purchase yuan-denominated bonds, which will result in Japan including RMB in its foreign-exchange reserves.[31]

In 2011, more than 9 percent of China's total trade was settled in yuan, up from less than 1 percent the year before, a percentage that seems poised to continue to grow. And in addition to its expanding roster of swap agreements, and the increasing (if still very modest) international use of the yuan in some countries' foreign-exchange reserves, China is also taking advantage of the distinct status of Hong Kong, permitting some local banks there (and Chinese banks based in Hong Kong) to issue yuan-denominated bonds. Singapore, boasting new free-trade and currency swap agreements with Beijing, is also jockeying for position to serve as a regional hub for yuan business in Southeast Asia. All of these developments are continuing and generate momentum that encourages further growth.[32] Some scholars have expressed skepticism of the import of these measures, suggesting that they are largely symbolic and that Beijing's appetite for bilateral deals, controls on its currency, and capital account restrictions fundamentally circumscribe the international role that the RMB can hope to play. In contrast, and in accord with my emphasis on the role of economic ideology in shaping China's development model, I argue that China need not fully liberalize in order for the RMB to emerge as an important international currency.[33] In that light, actions taken by both China and its economic partners suggest the pre-positioning of an apparatus for supporting the emergence of the RMB as the key currency in Asia—if cautiously, slowly, and in a form somewhat different than the Anglo-American financial model.

The New Politics of Monetary Discord

Barring a major internal economic setback, then, the RMB will emerge as an important international currency and has the potential to become the money of preference in East Asia. From China's perspective, the logic of international politics, the desire for some insulation from globalized financial markets, and a preference to foster an ideological alternative to the American model all motivate public policy in this direction. The rate at which the RMB will emerge will be most likely determined by politics, regionally, and economics, globally. That is, if China's foreign policy in Asia becomes clumsy and heavy-handed, which it occasionally threatens to become, then, regardless of the eagerness with which China is willing to supply international money, the demand side will atrophy, as regional players seek to avoid becoming more intimately enmeshed with an intimidating regional giant. On the economic side of the equation, if cracks at the foundations of China's economic order visibly widen, that would tend to temper the pace of the RMB's reception abroad; conversely, renewed economic distress elsewhere, such as a new financial crisis that implicates Europe and/or the United States, will further accelerate all of the trends that have encouraged the RMB's emergence. No matter what the rate, however, regional monetary arrangements in Asia, anchored in Beijing, with features, practices, and norms recognizably distinct from the second US postwar model, are very likely to emerge in the coming years.

Similarly, the euro, which is currently down but not out, poses a potential challenge to the position of the dollar. Before the financial crisis exposed its own contradictions and vulnerabilities, most analysts considered the euro on track to becoming a peer competitor to the dollar as an international currency. The encroachment of the euro on the international role of the dollar will be addressed in chapter 7. And the ultimate prospects for the euro, even before the financial crisis, were subject to active debate.[34] But, over the longer run, in one form or another, the euro is likely to take its place as an important international currency, resulting in a multipolar or "leaderless" currency system, which the World Bank projects as the most likely future for the global monetary order.[35]

A growing role for the RMB and the euro, the new heterogeneity of thinking about money and finance, and, not to be underestimated, the international political relationships between those states at the center of the monetary action, all suggest greater and potentially more consequential macroeconomic conflicts between states in the period after the global financial crisis, as compared with the first and second US postwar economic orders. A return to the catastrophic dysfunction of the interwar years is unlikely—both the politics, and the ideas, are better now than then. But, as discussed previously, cooperation between states in international money and finance is inherently and especially difficult; and, thus, default expectations in these areas should be set for discord rather than cooperation. Recall that monetary cooperation is particularly difficult, as compared with, for example, international trade because of the opportunities for technical disagreement over means, the tendency for macroeconomic policies to generate public negative externalities (leading to an overproduction of macroeconomic "bads"), conflicts over the often severe, politically crippling burdens of adjustment, and the tendency for understandings to unravel over time as underlying conditions shift, generating new pressures on established agreements.

The theory of monetary cooperation I elaborated in chapter 2 held that the existence of certain special factors could help overcome the inherent tendency for monetary discord. *Monetary hegemony* can provide a focal point for cooperation around which expectations can converge and a hegemon ameliorate the public-goods problem by taking on a disproportionate share of the burdens of adjustment or by policing agreements that are reached.[36] *Ideological homogeneity* can grease the wheels of cooperation, providing a cloak of legitimacy to the inevitable economic distress associated with the burdens of macroeconomic adjustment. (Thus those burdens look less like the outcomes of political struggles and more like the natural and irresistible functioning of politically neutral market forces.) *Shared, salient security concerns* can foster monetary cooperation, not by reducing the burdens of adjustment, but by increasing the willingness of states to bear those costs, either as a mechanism to support vital allies and/or because concerns about the security situation are seen as of overriding importance. States may also be anxious to avoid letting economic agreements unravel, which might threaten more important security understandings or signal discord to potential adversaries.

In the wake of the global financial crisis, however, all three of the special factors that can overcome the barriers to monetary cooperation—hegemony, ideology, and security—are less likely to come to the rescue. Although the United States remains the world's dominant military power and largest economy, its relative power is nevertheless declining, and the reach of the dollar is eroding, although it is likely to remain the "first among equals" in the realm of internationally used money. The global financial crisis shattered the legitimacy of the American model of financial globalization, leading to a new heterogeneity of thinking about the political governance of money and finance at both the domestic and international levels. (Note that it does not matter which ideas, if any, are "right"; it matters that actors will not share the same set of ideas with regard to these issues.) Finally, the international security situation offers no respite. Again, to be clear, the key variable is *not* the existence of security competition between would-be macroeconomic partners, although this cannot be ruled out as a future concern—and such problems greatly contributed to the interwar collapse—but rather the absence (or diminishment) of shared, salient security concerns between them. The relevant international politics between great powers are actually relatively benign in historical context, and the lack of intense security dilemmas helped prevent the more recent global financial crisis from spiraling out of control. Nevertheless, the diversity of political interest among states with seats at the monetary table has not been greater for nearly a century.

Indeed, what is remarkable about every major monetary conference of the twentieth century is that participants in them were more or less political allies. Recent experience is even more notable in this regard: every major effort to reconstitute the international monetary order in the second half of the century was undertaken by the United States and its political allies and military dependencies. This is simply no longer the case. Major players in the international monetary game now have different and often divergent international political agendas. As for the "big three," the United States and the major states of Europe remain political allies, but they no longer share a salient security threat that binds them. And the United States and China need not be locked in a relationship of hostility to recognize that they will often be in political competition. At a minimum, the US-Japan Cold War macroeconomic relationship, which, it should be noted, had more than its fair share of discord and squabbling, had something that US-China relations do not: a security alliance that served as an emergency brake to prevent squabbles from getting out of hand.

In sum, discord over monetary relations is normal, and an increase in such conflicts will likely be the new normal. The United States and China have already been scuffling over exchange rate issues since the turn of the century. A major factor in this conflict is China's large annual trade surpluses with the United States, coupled with Beijing's practice of maintaining the exchange rate of the yuan through regulation and (often heavy) market intervention. The yuan was set at 8.28 per dollar from 1994 to 2005, by which time few observers doubted the currency was considerably undervalued. But for the following three years, Beijing engineered a gradual appreciation of its currency, which hit 6.83 per dollar in 2008. An additional 6 percent rise took place in 2010–11; and in 2013, the yuan was trading at 6.23 per dollar. Still, many assessments hold that the yuan remains undervalued, and the issue is a politically sensitive one in both Washington and Beijing.[37] Both the Bush and Obama administrations have been critical of China's exchange rate policies. In 2005, before the first appreciation, the US Treasury called the exchange rate "a substantial distortion to world markets," and insisted that China "should move without delay" to remedy the situation. Still, both administrations resisted taking more aggressive steps, such as labeling China a "currency manipulator," that have been demanded by many in Congress and powerful interest groups such as the National Association of Manufacturers.[38] (The 2012 Republican presidential nominee Mitt Romney repeatedly promised that he would label China a currency manipulator on "day one" of his presidency.)

Even without the financial crisis, then, exchange rate conflict between the United States and China was likely to prove intractable. A basic problem is that to some extent both sides are "right." On the one hand, China's exchange rate policies and its massive dollar purchases, which do seem to violate IMF provisions against protracted one-sided interventions in the market, strongly support the contention that the yuan is artificially undervalued. But, on the other hand, even if China revalues the yuan, the motivating problem, China's trade surpluses with the United States, will not go away. For a host of technical reasons,[39] exchange rate realignment will have a disappointing and modest effect on the overall *balance* of trade between the two countries, although price adjustments could affect the composition of trade between the two. And, most important, the US trade deficit is not driven primarily by the exchange rate but rather by its extremely low rate of savings and high rate of consumption compared with the rest of the world, and especially China. As long as these disparities continue, US external accounts will remain unbalanced. This is widely understood. According to one authority, "China's exchange rate policy has only a modest influence on the overall trade deficit." This is not the Chinese position—it is the American position, the conclusion of the Congressional Budget Office.[40]

Cold War–era monetary tensions between the United States and Japan illustrate the types of problems that will surely aggravate future Sino-American exchange rate politics: the failure of exchange rate adjustments to resolve trade imbalances, in this case compounded by absence of a security alliance like the one that helped smooth over (or at least contain) disagreements in the US-Japan case. This history is valuable for the parallels it provides and also because, while Japan's unhappy experiences in dealing with the United States are not much present in the minds of Americans, elites in Beijing are acutely aware of the pattern of Japanese-American relations in this context and are keen to avoid something similar.

During the first two decades of the Cold War, the United States was eager to stimulate the development of the Japanese economy. Pressure built, however, by the end of the 1960s, as the undervalued yen and over-valued dollar produced large sustained trade surpluses with the United States. With détente and the easing of the Cold War, the increasing prominence of Japanese exports, and, crucially, expansionary US policies that eroded the credibility of its commitment to the value of the dollar, overt monetary conflict erupted in the 1970s. In 1971 the Americans unilaterally abandoned the Bretton Woods fixed exchange rate system in an effort to force currency realignment. This was the dramatic opening gambit in the protracted monetary battle of the 1970s, which was driven by trade concerns; the United States would press for yen appreciation in an effort to stem the flood of inexpensive Japanese imports, while Japan desperately resisted, often intervening in foreign exchange markets to limit yen appreciation. In fits and starts, from 1971 to 1978 the yen appreciated from 360 per dollar to 180 per dollar, although trade remained imbalanced. With the resurgence of Cold War tensions at the end of the decade, monetary conflict was put on the back burner, only to reemerge in the late 1980s and early 1990s, with the end of the Cold War and in the context of high-profile debates in the United States about Japanese exports undermining US industry. The yen doubled in value again before finally retreating, again failing to resolve the trade balance but contributing to Japan's economic malaise of the 1990s.[41]

This pattern seems almost certain to repeat itself, as the United States, motivated by concerns for trade and the domestic politics of employment, will routinely call for revaluation of the yuan; moreover, American demands will not be a one-time thing, since there will inevitably be disappointment about the results of any changes that are made. At the same time, China will resist US pressure; if faced with credible threats of significant US protectionism, it will probably make grudging adjustments. But monetary conflict will be chronic and become acute at the worst possible (economic) times. And China will resist more forcefully and successfully than did Japan, for a number of reasons. Most obviously, China is less beholden to the United States than was Japan during the Cold War. Moreover, even when the yuan is revalued, the basic problem will remain the same, creating serial conflicts and irritations, and, unlike the US-Japan relationship, there will be no "emergency brake" of high politics to contain macroeconomic squabbles.

China will not only be more capable of resisting US pressure, it will be more inclined to do so. Authorities in Beijing will view exchange rate policy not simply as a function of its trade with the United States but, as the world's second-largest trading economy, through the lens of its somewhat more balanced global trade accounts. In addition, despite the astonishing performance of China's economy over the decades, and its prompt recovery from the global financial crisis, it is characterized by a number of fragilities, in particular, the challenges of managing massive internal rural-urban labor migration, environmental and logistical bottlenecks, and a fragile and immature domestic financial sector.[42]

Compounding these problems is that the legitimacy of the Chinese Communist Party rests, however ironically, on its ability to continue to deliver high rates of economic growth. Its leaders will be loath to experiment with policies that might pose a risk to that success, especially as some cooling down of the economy (leaving still-high rates of growth) is to be expected, or, at the very least, anticipated. The desire to retain the stability of the yuan as an anchor for its unbridled domestic economy will temper China's appetite for exchange rate variability.[43] Finally, it should be remembered that for years American demands for yuan appreciation went hand in hand with lectures about the need for financial liberalization, especially as a freely floating and fully convertible yuan would have surely appreciated. As such, Beijing will hear future US demands for appreciation through ears newly and acutely sensitive to doubts about American economic advice and assessments more generally. In sum, in an environment of chronic monetary squabbling, crises will arise, and Sino-American currency conflicts will not be easy to resolve. Despite mutual interests encouraging cooler heads to prevail, understandings will be hard to reach, and those agreements that are reached will be brittle—each dustup will raise the possibility that it will evolve into a larger and mutually destructive economic conflict.

Nor should it be forgotten that the dollar/yuan is not the only exchange rate in town. With eroding hegemony, new heterogeneity, and the absence of intense security incentives, exchange rate politics are likely to be fractious more generally. Although relations between the United States and its traditional allies and friends in Europe are certainly much warmer and more robust than they are with China (even assuming an optimistic trajectory for Sino-American relations), nevertheless, in international monetary affairs, the reservoir of goodwill they share is shallower than at any time since World War II.

Politics has always shaped and will continue to shape the monetary order, with outcomes the result of political calculations on the part of states in regard to their preferences and interests. And as David Calleo has argued, since the end of the Cold War, with the Soviets gone and the euro in place, both the strategic and financial imperatives that compelled others to sustain the dollar have faded.[44] This matters, because periodic stress is to be expected in international monetary affairs. But resolving disequilibria that arise requires some determination about how the considerable burdens of adjustments will be distributed. During the Cold War, the unilateral (1971) and coordinated (1985) adjustments involving the dollar reflected considerable deference to American interests by its political and military allies in Western Europe (and Japan). If and when new international discussions take place over the resolution of problems, how to distribute the burdens of adjustment, and the nature of the international monetary order, that political context will be profoundly different. Old friends in Europe, eyeing a greater international role for the euro and sensing less urgent geopolitical harmony with the United States (illustrated, for example, by profound disagreements over the Iraq War), will less instinctively rush to the dollar's defense and be less willing to shoulder the costs of adjustment than in the past.

After the financial crisis, then, there is considerably less space, and less flexibility, on both sides of the Atlantic with regard to the management of money in general and potential disputes over exchange rate issues that might arise. Given economic distress and slow growth in the eurozone, currency appreciation is likely to be especially unwelcome on the Continent. Moreover, despite the current struggles and institutional challenges that inhibit the potential for the euro as an international currency, the European appetite for greater structural monetary power and the ambition for the euro to play a greater international role are certainly there.[45]

Increased and occasionally intense conflicts over global macroeconomic governance and contestation over burdens of adjustment will not simply be a more common feature of international economic relations. From the perspective of America, which is accustomed to setting the agenda and, since 1971, shaking off burdens (and leaving them to others), these challenges will seem *novel* and thus represent an apparent contraction of US power and autonomy in world politics. This exposure to unfamiliar external constraints will be common, and consequential. In the wake of the global financial crisis, the United States will face a number of new challenges to its international position; in addition, many of the effects of those new challenges will be magnified by the reaction of the American political system to such novel difficulties.

7

The Crisis and the International Balance of Power

The global financial crisis will not only affect the nature of world politics and the pattern of international economic relations, it will also have an effect on the balance of power between states, and on the power and capabilities of the United States. To be clear, the US economy will remain the world's foremost, and US military power is unrivaled and will remain so indefinitely.[1] Nevertheless, *relative* power, *changes* to the balance of power over time, and the *equilibrium* between a state's power and its international political ambition and commitments are the crucial metrics for understanding international relations.[2] And from this determining perspective, American power, capabilities, and influence are eroding. The United States is also confronted with new vulnerabilities. Geopolitical shifts and ideological changes have diminished underappreciated political and economic multipliers of American power and weakened its subterranean foundations.

The crisis will have both material *and* ideational consequences, and both will matter. As a material phenomenon, the crisis will create new

American vulnerabilities and accelerate two pre-existing trends: relatively reduced US international political capacity, and the continuing emergence of China as well as other regional powers.[3] This chapter explores these developments. I first briefly review the state of those vulnerabilities, observing those that were visible even before the crisis and how new ones were created as a result, weaknesses that are in turn magnified and exacerbated by the delegitimization of the American model. I then focus on challenges to the international role of the dollar, which I anticipate will result in a *relative* diminution of its role as an international currency. Pressure on the dollar will be a significant drag on American power in the coming years, and it also offers a representative illustration of the types of new challenges faced by the United States on the changing world stage more generally. With regard to international currency diminution, consequences will include pressure on defense spending, reduced macroeconomic autonomy (and thus the ability to finance ambitious foreign policies), vulnerability to currency manipulation, and greater exposure to debilitating financial distress, especially during times of international political crisis. All these difficulties, it should be noted, will be exacerbated by increased disagreement and contestation between states over international monetary relations and global financial governance.

Finance and the Achilles' Heel of American Power

Even at the unquestioned height of US global hegemony, in that halcyon decade leading up to the global financial crisis, there was nevertheless an active debate about the sustainability of the American economic machine. Some scholars and policymakers were raising alarms about the historically unprecedented size of the deficits on US external accounts, the risk of volatility in the international financial system, and prospects for the future of the dollar.[4] Given the large number of dollars held abroad and anxiety about large US budget deficits, a small crisis threatened to mushroom into a large one, implicating the dollar and its role as an international currency. I was among the alarmists, writing in 2004 that "America is . . . at greater risk for a major financial crisis than at any other time since the Second World War," which I thought would be sparked by a "medium sized financial disturbance that emerges in the US [and] work[s] its way through the system via the recently deregulated US financial economy and high flying international capital markets." I argued further that as "a few firms were pulled down by the undertow, a full blown panic would emerge. In the United States, the paper losses would be enormous; the contraction of wealth and instinct for caution would throw the economy into recession. The elements that make this scenario more rather than less likely are in place."[5]

It is especially sobering to realize that after the global financial crisis, those elements remain in place; in fact, by almost any account, they are more alarmingly in place. As noted in chapter 5, the United States has emerged from the crisis with a largely unreformed, but even more concentrated, financial system with fewer, larger too-big-to-fail and too-interconnected-to-fail financial institutions conducting business largely as usual. Worse, the crisis of 2007–8, distinguished by the fact that the United States stood at its epicenter and felt its wrath acutely, is suggestive of the possibility that the nation is entering a new and dangerous phase in its exposure to financial crises. Three other eras can be identified: First, through 1907, financial crises in the United States were common and associated with, and characterized by, the nation's relative financial immaturity. Second, the 1929 crisis stands at the center of an international economic, political, and financial crisis rooted in the dysfunctional interwar international system. Third, the post–World War II era saw financial crises from which the United States was insulated by its financial regulations and superpower status. The financial crises of this era happened to others and tended to relatively empower the United States compared to other states, both in its capacity as a safe haven and from its ability at times to gain concessions from other states in exchange for the provision of emergency assistance.

What is novel, then, about the global financial crisis of 2007–8 is not its novelty; as noted previously, historically speaking, financial crises are not exceptional, they are the norm.[6] Rather, it is the harbinger of a new (actually a return to a very old and more normal) level of exposure of the US economy to external financial pressures. Moreover, the apparent novelty of those pressures, largely absent since the 1930s, will only increase their sting.

In addition, the United States emerges from the crisis more rather than less vulnerable to still another crisis because the policy responses needed to contain the crisis have only added to the underlying burdens and vulnerabilities already apparent in the US economy. And the crisis also exposed unanticipated weaknesses in the economy more generally. Those essential emergency measures: a flood of liquidity and a large injection of government spending, will, in the coming years, present the formidable problem of how to dial them back. Either the United States will fail to adequately do so, which would damage the long-term health of its economy (and thus its global power over time), or it will take bold measures to "put its house in order," which, among many other things, will imply reductions in both military spending and the American appetite for international adventurism. In either event, the United States will emerge from this crisis with relatively inhibited international political standing and capacity.

Real pressures on the economy and the dollar will be magnified by the ideational consequences of the crisis, especially, as discussed previously, from the collapse of the legitimacy of the second US postwar order. For many influential actors in world politics, the crisis has served as a "learning moment," discrediting the culture of American capitalism, especially as it applies to finance, and, as noted, this will affect both state choices and international politics. Yukio Hatoyama, head of the opposition Democratic Party of Japan, attributed the crisis to "a way of economic thinking based on the idea that American-style free-market economics represents a universal and ideal economic order" and the insistence that all counties conform with that model. For Hatoyama, who served briefly as prime minister in 2009–10, "the financial crisis has . . . raised doubts about the permanence of the dollar as the key global currency," and he anticipates that "we are moving towards an era of multipolarity."[7]

The delegitimization of the American model, and the effect of the global financial crisis on the US image abroad, especially in Asia, should not be underestimated. As noted in chapter 6, Ikenberry and Kupchan have argued that "socialization"—the embrace by elites in secondary states of the substantive beliefs of a great power—is an important source of influence for a hegemon. Their work is focused on the establishment of hegemonic socialization and how such legitimacy crucially buttresses its political influence. What we will witness in the coming years is the flip side of that phenomenon, the likely *erosion* of that influence, as others come to reject the ideas that they once embraced or at least tolerated.[8]

Disenchantment with the American way and the erosion of US influence after the crisis stands in marked contrast with the experience of China and its initial rapid recovery from the crisis and continuing (to date) comparatively high rate of economic growth. This will eventually translate into greater military might, as its defense spending will rise commensurately.[9] But the effects on its political power and influence will be even more profound. Differential rates of recovery from the current crisis have accelerated pre-existing trends of China's relative economic rise, and enhanced its status, confidence, and appeal. Most visible with regard to China, the emergence of new nodes of global economic growth, contributing to more assertive political preferences, is occurring more generally.[10] Again, political influence and international power can only be productively understood as relative phenomena. Relative rise implies relative decline, and as power diffuses throughout the international system, especially as regional powers enjoy increased political influence in their own neighborhoods, it is the reach of US power that will find resistance at its frontiers.

One challenge to American power concerns the long-run trajectory of the dollar as an international currency. Although alarmists were correct about the risk of financial crisis and the factors that contributed to it, the 2007–8 meltdown—rooted in the house-of-cards collapse of the US banking system and then transmitted abroad—actually bolstered the dollar in the short run as investors fled in panic to the (comparatively) safest haven. But the long-run implications of the crisis leave the US economy, and the greenback, weaker than before and magnify real concerns about a debt-addled America and a dollar in (relative) decline.

Paradoxically, one legacy of the dollar's historical attractiveness is that it has increased its vulnerability. There are an enormous amount of dollars held abroad. Thus if there was a spark somewhere that touched off a financial crisis that implicated the dollar, given the state of underlying expectations about its future value, a sudden and dramatic reversal of its fortunes could result. Moreover, changes to international politics, and new wariness of the dollar, have frayed the safety nets that in the past prevented potential dollar crises from hurtling out of control.

The Dollar's Diminishing Domain: Pressure from All Sides

Even without the financial crisis, the most likely scenario was for the dollar's international role to modestly diminish over time.[11] It was expected that for the foreseeable future the dollar would remain the world's most widely used international currency. This is still the case. But it also should be clear that the greenback need not be supplanted for there to be a politically consequential contraction in its global role. The dollar's use, and influence, will likely be encroached on by the euro at the frontiers of the eurozone, and possibly the Middle East (despite Europe's current troubles), by the yuan in Asia, and, after the crisis, by a greater *motivation* for diversity on the part of numerous and varied actors. Disenchantment with the American financial model will matter when it comes to choices about money, which is an area where ideas are especially consequential, affecting both state choices and international politics.

China's increased monetary ambitions are significant; I have already discussed these at length, but it is worth recalling the common assessment that it "will not be long before a Chinese RMB bloc emerges in Asia." But China is not the only source of push-back against the range of the dollar's influence—far from it. Russia, a shadow of the world power that it once was, nevertheless has considerable international political capacity; and many there do not smile upon the reach of American power. President Vladimir Putin is typically quick to join the chorus of those critical of the dollar as a reserve currency, and Russia may be one of the few states in the world—perhaps the only state—that holds considerable foreign exchange reserves *and* might not be alarmed for its own position by a crisis of the dollar. The Middle East might also prove a battleground for competing monetary influences. For now, the dollar dominates that region, but the commitment to the dollar by key Gulf states such as Saudi Arabia and Kuwait is linked to an understanding about US security guarantees. These could easily be reevaluated if the United States decides to scale back its international commitments, especially with Europe and China already and increasingly the two most important consumers of Gulf oil. And, even before the financial crisis, it had been suggested that "that the limits of Japan's dollar support capacity have finally been reached." Japan's burgeoning dollar reserve portfolio is surpassed only by that of China. Even without "buyer's remorse" Japan may rethink the extent of its commitment to the dollar.[12]

China, Japan, Saudi Arabia, and Russia: not counting the European Union, those are the nations with the largest official foreign exchange reserves, and most of those reserves are held in dollar obligations, most notably US Treasury bills.[13] Reassessments by some of those actors about how many dollars to hold, or whether they prefer slightly less intimate ties with the dollar and the American financial economy, could prove especially consequential. Even without emphasizing such motivated recalculations, the World Bank, in its 2011 *Global Development Horizons* report, anticipated an increasingly multipolar world economy and, notably, a multipolar currency order. China's importance in international trade, the report observes, is by historical standards already past the threshold at which currency internationalization has commonly taken place (although it does see financial and structural economic reforms as a prerequisite to this). It sees the euro as, even sooner, becoming "the currency with the potential to rival the dollar." The prospects for the euro, and the endurance of the dollar, are still actively debated by specialists in this area. Euro-skeptics tend to emphasize the economic and geopolitical advantages of the dollar, structural limitations to the euro's capacity to serve as an international currency of choice, and the power of inertia and hierarchy in international monetary affairs. Eichengreen and Flandreau, on the other hand, argue in their recent work that incumbency advantages and inertia are not as powerful as traditionally thought and that the euro can serve as an alternative reserve asset.[14]

Much of this, like the debate over the internationalization of the RMB, is really a question of *to what extent* will challengers encroach on the domain of the dollar. And since, as I will elaborate, no challenger need "overtake" or "overthrow" the dollar for such encroachments, especially cumulatively, to have consequences for American power, the specific resolution of many of these controversies need not be of central concern. What matters is the almost certain encroachment, from all shores. The euro is one of the major players in this process, and it will increasingly command greater influence over not just its participants but also the European Union and its immediate neighbors, quite possibly the Middle East, and more generally in public and private reserve portfolios in the future.

This may sound overly bullish, since, to say the least, the euro faces some daunting challenges of its own, as expressed by Europe's sovereign debt crises and deep recession that followed the global financial crisis. But, currently flat on its back, Europe is down but not out, and in the longer run, the euro will resume its encroachment on the dollar's international role. Certainly, Europe's own troubles have exposed the weaknesses of the euro as a potential peer competitor to the dollar, a status that the European currency seemed close to achieving before the global financial crisis exposed its own problems and, not to be underestimated, contradictions.

The euro, it needs to be recognized, was always a *political* project, part of an effort to forge a common European entity and identity. There is no law that forbids this, but to fail to recognize the fact is to misunderstand the problem. In anticipation of the euro, there was an academic literature produced on the efficiency gains to be found and the transactions costs to be reduced from the move to a common currency. But, in the broader scheme of things, those gains were modest, and, considered solely from an economic perspective, the euro project was incoherent. Certainly by the logic of economic theory, which is actually not very good on the question of the geography of money—that is, what money will be used where—the eurozone is not an "optimal currency area." Admittedly, few monetary domains are optimal currency areas, but the eurozone stands out among them. The limits to a common fiscal policy, and to labor mobility, are the most obvious examples of this.

That economic incoherence was papered over by the motivations of the political project, the core political bargains at its foundation, the desire to encourage a common European space and identity, and, importantly, by lack of a major crisis that would expose its contradictions. The global financial crisis was the stress test that did just that.[15] The monetary union had invited problems and allowed pressures to develop, and, when faced with real difficulties, states found themselves disarmed of essential policy defenses. Joining the euro meant the abdication of monetary policy and exchange rate policy without gaining any new policy levers[16]

Moreover, the crisis has exposed and intensified a political conflict within Europe. Paradoxically, as with the United States, the fact that the global financial crisis was contained short of a complete financial meltdown prevented game-changing reforms from taking place, in this case with regard to the management of the European economy. Once they felt more secure, more narrowly defined interest groups had the confidence to return to a "political business as usual" mentality. In the United States, this prevented fundamental reform of the financial sector. In Europe, the return to normal politics inhibited addressing two basic problems: the institutionally codified deflationary bias in the management of the euro, and the axis of conflict over burden sharing still being national in orientation.

The Germans may be wary of "Keynesian" solutions, but they are also wary of "bailing out" Greeks and other southern Europeans; which is to say, the European Union, still composed of individual sovereign states, is witnessing an easily recognizable, if monumental, struggle over the burdens of macroeconomic adjustment, a struggle in which surplus countries usually have the upper hand over deficit countries. The hand of those favoring austerity in those European states that might be called on to engage in countercyclical policies is further strengthened by the fact that debates over political ideology and economic doctrine also take place in a context in which stimulus measures will "leak" across national borders. National identities still hold sway in the eurozone.

To a considerable extent Europe's crisis has handed (yet another) get-out-of-jail-free card to the profligate dollar, leaving it again the only game in town. Indeed, some of the strongest arguments of those most optimistic about the future of the dollar rest not on the inherent attractiveness of the greenback but of its relative appeal, as the shortcomings of alternatives are often exposed on closer scrutiny.[17] But this is a thin rope on which to hitch the future of the dollar, and it is fraying. Europe's troubles do not bode well for the US economy in general or even, potentially, for the dollar. Taken collectively, the European Union is a massive economic space, larger even than the US economy. And, as the US Congressional Research Service reports, "the US and the EU have the largest and most deeply integrated bilateral trade and investment relationship in the world." Stagnation in Europe thus hurts the American economy. And should Europe's sovereign debt crisis worsen, American financial institutions will be exposed to the possibility of very significant losses.[18]

Thus, it is certainly the case that the euro does indeed bear its own political, economic, and institutional burdens, and is still finding its voice. Nevertheless, underlying trends again point away from the dollar. Despite its current difficulties, structurally the euro is positioned to present a genuine alternative to the dollar for many actors.[19] And it is likely that the crisis will force the European Union into a "corner solution"—forward or backward—in which it becomes larger and more capacious or leaner as it sheds some of its members.[20] In the future, either of these scenarios would empower the euro as an international currency. In the first scenario, the range of its authority would be poised to expand. In the latter, a "leaner and meaner" euro might be used as "home" currency for fewer countries, but shedding its most suspect participants might make it even more attractive as an instrument of international money. And, as with the discussion of the RMB, the question of international money is not simply a supply-side phenomenon. There are emerging alternatives to the dollar, but there is also, increasingly, a greater demand on the part of public and private actors throughout the globe for such alternatives: not necessarily to abandon the dollar but for insurance, diversification, and insulation. Such individual behaviors, however, could conceivably have collective consequences that would put even more pressure on the dollar than the sum of individual motives would imply.

Over the coming years then, the dollar's international role is likely to come under pressure from emerging regional competitors from one side and a general preference for diversification on the other. Why does this matter? Three distinct types of consequences of relative dollar diminution follow, each of which implies reductions in American power: the loss of benefits, the challenge of new burdens, and the emergence of new vulnerabilities.

Dollar Diminution: Fading Exorbitant Privileges

What are the benefits of issuing a currency that is used internationally, in particular, of issuing a "key" currency that serves as the monetary foundation for an international economic arrangement or is predominant within a particular region or is the money of choice throughout the world? Essentially there are three: seigniorage, autonomy and balance-of-payments flexibility, and structural power.[21] Estimates of seigniorage vary. Minimalist calculations focus on the equivalent of the interest-free loan provided to the issuer of notes that are held by the public but that do not bear interest. A ballpark figure for the United States would be about $15 billion annually; one study puts the windfall for the euro at $4 billion. Larger (though debated) figures can be established by including an estimate of the gains from an interest rate differential between "home" and "foreign" assets, based on the idea that the issuer of a key currency can fetch greater returns from their investments abroad than what they must offer foreign investors for domestic assets. In any event, from the perspective of international politics and power, seigniorage is the least consequential perk for the issuer of a key currency.[22]

The real political action takes place with the other two benefits, and each is substantial (if much harder to specifically quantify). Autonomy and balance-of-payments flexibility has been enjoyed, and exercised, by the United States for decades and to an extent greatly underappreciated by most actors within the country. The United States has been able to routinely shake off the (often costly) burdens of macroeconomic adjustment and essentially dump them on others.[23] As for the balance of payments, this was an issue of some consternation in the 1960s, when it was understood that the "principal advantage" of the Bretton Woods system for the United States was that its balance-of-payments deficits could "be financed in part through increases in the dollar reserves held by foreign monetary authorities." To the extent that its deficits were financed in this way, the United States could run larger balance-of-payments deficits than other states; moreover, and perhaps with even greater consequences, "it [could] take greater risks in adopting economic policies that might have adverse effects on the balance-of-payments."[24] The rules of Bretton Woods and, in addition, US bullying to force dependent allies to hold more dollars than they wanted, fueled many of the protestations over what the French called America's "exorbitant privilege."[25] The US-engineered collapse of that system in 1971, breaking the dollar's last links with gold, took much of the edge off those politics; but the exorbitant privilege nevertheless remained. For as long the dollar retains its attractiveness abroad, the United States is able to borrow in its own currency, sustain deficits on its international accounts that others cannot, and take risks and adopt economic policies that would, anywhere else, elicit a withering "disciplinary" response from international financial markets. The erosion of these perks will circumscribe US power and autonomy, and fights over the burdens of adjustment—the normal stuffing of international monetary politics—will become a more common and salient feature of foreign policy, at least from an American perspective.

The dollar-centric international system has also rewarded the United States with structural power. Structural power is not easily measured, nor it is obviously "coercive," but, as Susan Strange described, it reflects "the power to decide how things shall be done, the power to shape frameworks within which states relate to each other."[26] Structural power also affects the pattern of economic relations between states and their calculations of political interest. States that use the dollar, and especially those that hold their reserves in dollars, develop a vested interest in the value and stability of the dollar. Once the dollar was in widespread use, its fate became more than just America's problem—it became the problem of all dollar holders.[27]

Thus, while many saw the collapse of the Bretton Woods system as evidence of a general decline in US power, Strange saw through this and observed, "To decide one August morning that dollars can no longer be converted into gold was a progression from exorbitant privilege to super-exorbitant privilege." Freed from any formal constraints, "the US government was exercising the unconstrained right to print money that others could not (save at unacceptable cost) refuse to accept in payment."[28] In fact, the end of Bretton Woods allowed the United States to shed some of the costs of having the dollar serve as the world's currency while retaining most of the benefits.

Strange's conception of structural power owes something to Woody Allen; as for aspiring playwrights, so for the issuers of key currency: ninety percent of structural power is just showing up. Simply by the breadth of its international use, the presence of a dominant currency creates the context in which political interactions take place—often without even active agency or a specific agenda. Since World War II, for example, any discussion of the international monetary system has taken place in the context of dollar primacy. Of course, structural power can also be quite purposeful, but it tends to be expressed not by "relational" power or coercion over specific outcomes but via agenda setting and establishing the context, often implicitly, in which choices about money are made.[29]

Another interpretation of structural power—not so much a competing approach but one reflecting a different mechanism though which such power is manifested—is associated with Albert Hirschman. As noted earlier, Hirschman's approach emphasizes how the pattern of economic relations between states can transform their calculations of political self-interest. In addition to nominal friends and allies, even those countries that simply peg to the dollar as part of a broader international economic strategy can also come to have their interests conditioned by their relationship with the greenback, even without signing on as "stakeholders" the way large holders of dollars (purposefully or unwittingly) have.[30]

The fact that the dollar has long served as the global currency of choice, then, has increased both the "hard power" and the "soft power" of the United States. Not to be underestimated is the extent to which America's coercive capacity, and in particular its ability to wage wars, has been enhanced by its greater autonomy to run deficits and to adopt policies that would otherwise elicit a countervailing market reaction. And the dollar's structural advantages have afforded to the United States what can also be interpreted as enhancing what Joseph Nye dubbed "soft power"—getting others to want what you want them to want.[31] For Strange, the gravitational force of the dollar in the world economy benefits the United States by necessitating that relevant political arenas operate in ways that inevitably if implicitly overrepresent the weight of American interests. From a Hirschmanesque perspective, the participation in a dollar-based international monetary order advantages the United States by shaping the perceived self-interests of states and of many private actors within states, and by creating stakeholders in the fate of the dollar. Structural power is also self-reinforcing; as one study concluded, the "structural power of the US in the international financial system" has in the past served as a barrier to the emergence of rival currencies, such as the yen. This suggests that the erosion of that structural power might produce a positive feedback loop that accelerates the rise of other centers of monetary gravity while accelerating the contraction of the dollar's reach.[32]

In any event, the bottom line is that if significant dollar diminution takes place, the United States will face a reduction in the power-enhancing macroeconomic autonomy and balance-of-payments flexibility it has long enjoyed, along with the erosion of its structural power, and thus its political influence.[33] With regard to the potential decline in American structural power, this will likely also be reinforced by issues that transcend monetary politics, but it will nevertheless influence the future of the dollar. In particular, China's structural power, generally, and unrelated to the internationalization of the RMB, will almost surely rise in the coming years, with potentially profound political consequences.

China's swift recovery from the global financial crisis will only enhance its growing structural power, both as its economic model is seen as attractive and, more concretely, as states come to increasingly depend on the Chinese market. The People's Republic is now one of the three engines of world trade, along with the United States and Germany (or the European Union collectively). The milestones of its achievements are well known, such as when it became the world's second-largest economy or when it surpassed Germany to become the world's largest exporter. But the emphasis on China's aggregate growth, or the seemingly relentless expansion of its exports, obscures its increasing importance as an *importer* of other countries' products; and this is where the political rubber really meets the road. In 2009, China was the world's second-largest importer, behind only the United States. And its imports have soared at an astonishing rate, from $132 billion in 1995 to $561 billion in 2004 to $1.7 trillion in 2011. As early as 2008, it was the biggest export market for, among other countries, Argentina, Chile, Iran, Kazakhstan, Oman, Yemen, Burma, Taiwan, and South Korea (which now exports more than twice as much to China as it does to the United States). By 2010, China had become Japan's largest trading partner, and the number one destination for its exports. This bears repeating: China is now the most important export market for the key US military allies in Asia: Japan, South Korea, and Australia as well. It is also the second-most-important importer of goods from a host of other countries; and its demand for raw materials— it is now the world's number one consumer of copper, tin, zinc, platinum, steel, and iron ore—has boosted the fortunes of primary-product producers throughout the globe. China is also an increasingly important customer of oil-producing countries such as Saudi Arabia and Iran, and its reach is felt keenly even in Latin America, where China's imports from the region have produced large trade surpluses for Brazil, Chile, Argentina, and Peru; its expanding business activities in Latin America, while still relatively modest, are increasingly visible.[34] Moreover, China's value as an export market for the world is likely to only increase in importance in the coming years, given the likely trajectories of relative economic growth.

The result will be to China's political advantage, following the logic articulated by Hirschman, as the pattern of international economic relations affects domestic politics, which in turn shapes national interests. This is always the case but is most significant in asymmetric relations in which the effects on the smaller state can be quite considerable. As Hirschman observed, business groups "will exert a powerful influence in favor of a 'friendly' attitude toward the state" on which their economic interests depend. Moreover, when these relationships are sustained, and especially when they involve expanding sectors of the economy, over time the reshuffling of power, interests, and incentives among firms, sectors, and political coalitions will increasingly reflect these new realities. Those that favor warm relations will be empowered, and the trajectory of the "national interest" will be remolded.[35]

These effects will be most obvious in Asia, where intraregional trade has expanded dramatically and China's role as an engine of growth is most obvious. As one study concluded, "Asian countries thus have a huge stake in China's continued economic growth and stability."[36] In general, China's structural power is increasing, deriving first from the tug of its economic gravity (à la Hirschman) but also from enhanced soft power, if less from cultural appeal and attraction than from the desirability of associating more intimately with the successful Chinese approach (as distinct from the discredited American model). One result of this will be that in international institutions and bilateral relations the United States, to its consternation, will find other states increasingly sensitive to how outcomes and agreements will affect their relations with China. More pointedly, in political disputes in which China and the United States find themselves on opposing sides, increasingly, in many corners of the world, China's case will be heard with more sympathetic ears, and this will come at the expense of American priorities. And, to return to a more narrow focus on international monetary power, China's enhanced importance as a trading partner, and its growing structural power, will reinforce and enhance the potential appeal of the RMB as an international currency. This, necessarily, must come at the expense of the dollar and the benefits that have accrued to the United States as a result of its international use.

Dollar Diminution: New Burdens, New Inhibitions

The relative diminution of the dollar as an international currency to something like first-among-equals status will not only cause the United States to lose privileges it once enjoyed—its coercive power enhanced by greater autonomy and its structural power implicitly shaping the preferences of others—but it will also produce new burdens, which America will be singularly unaccustomed to bearing. These additional burdens come not from the loss of perks but from the costs associated with managing a currency in relative decline. For issuers of once-dominant international money, those new difficulties arise from what can be called the overhang problem, and from a loss of prestige that once protected its currency from potential difficulties.

The overhang problem arises as a function of a currency's onetime greatness. At the height of its attraction, numerous actors are eager to hold a key international currency—governments for reserves and private actors as a store of value (and often as a medium of exchange). But once the key currency is perceived to be in decline, it becomes suspect, and these actors will, over time, look to get out by exchanging it for some other asset. The need to "mop up" all this excess currency creates chronic monetary pressure on the once-great currency, and macroeconomic policy will take place under the shadow of the overhang.[37]

The loss of prestige is also a crucial consequence of managing a currency in decline. Prestige is a very slippery concept, but it finds a home in monetary analysis under the rubric of credibility, which is generally acknowledged to play a crucial role in monetary affairs, even if it, too, is not easily measured. The unparalleled reputation and bedrock credibility of the key currency during its glory days is an essential source of the power it provides. The willingness of markets to implicitly tolerate imbalances in accounts and impertinent macroeconomic politics that would not be tolerated in other states rests on these foundations.

The loss of prestige and reduced credibility (which the challenge of the overhang exacerbates) imposes new costs on the issuer of a currency in relative decline. Whereas, in the past, the key currency country was exempted from the rules of the game—that is, placed on a much longer leash by international financial markets than other states—the opposite becomes true. With eroding prestige and shared expectations of monetary distress, market vigilance is heightened and discipline imposed more swiftly by the collective expectations of more skeptical market actors. A presumption of confidence is replaced with a more jaundiced reading of the same indicators, and the long leash is replaced by an exceptionally tight choker.

Some of these problems can be illustrated by historical analogies. The experience of the British pound in the decades following World War II offers one such example of the challenges faced by an international currency under pressure. In the nineteenth and early twentieth centuries sterling served as the international currency of choice, and its status enhanced British power. But eventually the management of sterling-in-decline became a vexing problem for British authorities, complicating economic management and exacerbating its chronic financial crises in the 1960s. With the pound invariably on the ropes in international financial markets, the demand for a clean bill of macroeconomic health placed British budgets—and British military spending and overseas commitments—under constant pressure.

The limits of British power and the constraints of financial fragility were brought into stark relief with the Suez Crisis in 1956. On October 31 of that year, British and French forces attacked Egypt with the stated goal of seizing the Suez Canal, but with the additional goal of causing the overthrow of Egypt's president Gamal Nasser. But on November 6, just days short of victory, and to the great dismay of the French, Britain called a halt to the operation. Harold Macmillan, chancellor of the exchequer, and up to that point one of the most forceful proponents of the Suez adventure, informed his cabinet colleagues that a run on the pound had become overwhelming and the country did not have adequate reserves to save the currency on its own. Moreover, the Americans, opposed to the invasion, made it clear that they would block Britain's ability to seek help from the IMF. On the other hand, if (and only if) the British agreed to an immediate cease-fire and prompt withdrawal from the Suez Canal zone, the United States would facilitate IMF support and provide additional emergency financial relief of its own.[38]

Britain caved in, and the entire affair was a formative experience for a generation of British politicians, who came away with an instinctive sensitivity to the economic limits of British power. That sensitivity would be reinforced by decades of less spectacular but nevertheless chronic hard knocks. Currency weakness and resulting pressure on government spending—austerity to balance the budget, austerity to shore up confidence in the pound, always and everywhere, austerity—would become a defining problem for British governments in the mid-1960s and beyond, ultimately forcing the country to reluctantly abandon its military role "east of Suez." President Lyndon Johnson considered sterling's weakness a "major foreign policy concern" and was eager to take steps that would take the pressure off the British currency and thus "sharply reduce the danger of sterling devaluation or . . . British military disengagement east of Suez." But economic pressure on sterling, which staggered from crisis to crisis throughout the period, was unrelenting and ultimately decisive.[39]

Sterling crises in autumn 1964 and again in summer 1965 rocked the British economy. Prime Minister Harold Wilson's response was to cut defense spending without addressing the overall military posture, a tightrope that could only be negotiated for so long. With the February 1966 defense review the rope frayed further, with defense cuts eroding British overseas capacities. But the sterling crisis and relentless pressure on budgets continued, and 1967 featured the blows that finally burst the sterling piñata. Yet another defense white paper bowed to the inevitable and finally outlined a phased withdrawal from Singapore, Malaysia, and Aden: British forces were to be cut in half by 1971 and gone completely by 1977. Some pretense was maintained regarding Britain's positions in the Persian Gulf, but these fig leaves were swept aside by the financial crisis that led to sterling's devaluation in November. Chancellor of the Exchequer Roy Jenkins insisted on a fundamental reassessment of defense policy. Not only was military spending cut further, but the timetable for withdrawal from east of Suez was accelerated and was completed by the end of 1971. This met with vigorous opposition from the Tories, but pressure on sterling presented stubborn truths. Returning to power in 1970, faced with sluggish growth and the need to fight inflation, the Conservatives could not escape the same financial constraints that had plagued Labour, and the new posture was retained.[40]

Notably, even with the "east of Suez" question settled, the devaluation of the pound, and the shift to a floating exchange rate, the relationship between Britain's fragile finances and its military capabilities remained. A financial crisis in 1976 forced Britain to seek help from the IMF, which insisted on still further cuts to domestic spending. An additional £300 million was squeezed from the military, despite vociferous protests from the Chiefs of Staff.[41]

There are, of course, fundamental differences between postwar sterling and the contemporary dollar. The British economy then was weaker than the US economy is now, and the pound was confronting a more daunting reduction in its relative role then than the dollar today. But as a more extreme case, it helps to expose and magnify the mechanisms by which currency diminution can affect national security. The politics of austerity will not spare military budgets, especially in peacetime and especially if such budgets appear large. And it will be generally so that a currency in decline faces increased (and more skeptical) market scrutiny, especially during moments of international crisis and wartime. Markets tend to react negatively to a country's currency as it enters crisis and war, anticipating increased prospects for government spending, borrowing, inflation, and hedging against general uncertainty.[42] In that sense, the Suez analogy is not inappropriate. Nor was this an isolated incident: weak currencies make for timid states.

This axiom is well illustrated by the experiences of interwar France, a case that offers something of a laboratory for the national security consequences of currency weakness. In this instance, the franc came under withering pressure somewhat "voluntarily"; that is, domestic politics in France enforced an almost obsessive fixation on "defending the franc," which need not have been the only policy choice. (Indeed, the socialists finally, if very reluctantly, abandoned the cause in 1936.)[43] But the pressure, even if to some extent self-imposed, illustrates again two invariable mechanisms via which monetary distress fuels national (in)security: through the relentless march of austerity and existential anxiety about the power of financial markets.

Monetary orthodoxy, and thus constant pressure to balance the budget, meant that finance was the "soft underbelly" of France's defense posture. These interconnections cannot be overestimated; it was accepted as an article of faith that the franc rested on the foundation of a balanced budget, and defense spending was gutted in an effort to achieve that end. From 1930 to 1933, defense spending was cut by 25 percent; in fact, military spending at the 1930 level would not be reached again until 1937. Between 1933 and 1938, Nazi Germany spent almost three times what France spent on the military, and during roughly the same period, real defense spending in Germany increased by 470 percent, in France, 41 percent. Pressure on the franc routinely provided the major impetus for new rounds of deflation and budget cuts, and repeatedly new weapons programs and modernization were the first, easiest place to find savings in the defense budget.[44]

A commitment to maintaining the convertibility of the franc into gold at the level established in 1928, even more than the budget cuts, circumscribed French foreign policy. In 1933, the Bank of France explained that it was "resolved to consent to no measure whatsoever that could again endanger the stability of the franc." This contributed to France's sluggish response to Germany's rearmament, which was clearly understood in France by the end of 1932.

The constant threat that a financial crisis would force the franc off gold paralyzed French leaders and contributed to a conciliatory bias in French foreign policy. Adherence to orthodoxy in France required, if not appeasement, something very close to it. In 1934, financial journalist Paul Einzig expressed his grave concern that "monetary orthodoxy will be sufficiently influential to delay urgent armament expenditure in order to avoid jeopardizing the stability of the franc."[45]

But this was the course followed by France until September 1936. Each year leading up to that point France recognized new German challenges and remained passive. A dramatic increase in German military spending in March 1934 had no effect on French policy. In March 1935, Germany announced that its army would expand to thirty-six divisions, more than five times the ceiling mandated by the Versailles treaty. Yet France again stood by passively, only raising protests and seeking to stitch together a multilateral response, which came to nothing. The threat of capital flight reinforced the policy of appeasement. In the words of one critic, due to such fears, the "government was condemned to a certain impotence."[46]

This had more severe consequences one year later. On March 7, 1936, Germany remilitarized the Rhineland. Not only was this in direct violation of the Versailles treaty, as well as the 1925 Treaty of Locarno, it also closed the corridor through which France would, in theory, come to the defense of its eastern allies. Yet again, France took no action, a policy that has been called "the first capitulation." Certainly, a number of factors involving both domestic and international politics contributed to this outcome. But financial questions were decisive and essentially ruled out the use of force, or even the threat of force.[47] Worse, mobilization was incompatible with the protection of the franc. It would have required devaluation.

This stark fact guaranteed French inaction. As one student of the crisis observed, "Hitler and the rest of the world knew" that the French government would "above all . . . do nothing that would endanger the franc." This proved to be tragic, because German forces at that time were in no position to resist any challenge from the French army, and the resulting blow to Hitler, if forced to back down, might have altered the course of history. But even *couverture*, the state of armed readiness that would precede a general mobilization, would have cost 30 million francs a day, an expense that would "undoubtedly provoke a run on the franc." And because of the fragility of France's financial position, full mobilization would have led to an immediate "full-scale monetary crisis" and would have "exposed the virtual bankruptcy of the French treasury and toppled the franc." Any doubts about this relationship were erased as capital flight and pressure on the franc increased in the few days before it was known that France would not take any strong measures of resistance. On Sunday, March 8, there were rumors that France might use force against Germany, and on Monday the franc came under pressure in international markets. This pressure did not abate until Wednesday, after the announcement that France would act only with multilateral support and within the framework of the League of Nations, which made it clear that there would be no military response to the German provocation.[48]

Again, twenty-first-century America is not interwar France, just as it is not postwar Britain. But the experience of those countries provides important insights into the types of challenges faced by a country attempting to navigate its grand strategy while nursing a suspect currency. Greater skepticism about the dollar is a new fact of life. Actors may continue to hold their dollars, and even accumulate more of them. But they now do so through gritted teeth. Wariness of the American model adds another stone to the burdens borne by the dollar, the future of which will influence US power in the coming decades. And what can be called the "three Ds"—dollars (so many held abroad), deregulation (still in place) and deficits (federal and current account)—have left the greenback at least as exposed as it was before the crisis. Added to its burdens are the necessary policy responses to the crisis that only increase suspicions about the dollar's long-run health. Meanwhile, potential alternatives loom in the distance. Moreover, and crucially, the dollar no longer enjoys the political "safety net" it once enjoyed. Politics always has and will continue to shape the international monetary order. During the Cold War, monetary squabbles took place between the United States and its strategic allies and military dependencies. No longer.

In sum, the dollar is vulnerable in ways that are unprecedented since before World War *One*. Even in the absence of a major dollar crisis, and even though the greenback will remain the world's most prominent currency, the relative diminution of the dollar's international role will present new constraints on US power. This is because American power has been supplemented and at times facilitated by dollar primacy, which has made it easier to project its power abroad and afforded an assortment of other political perks. Were some dollar diminution to take place, the United States would not only lose that capacity and those perks, it would also face new limitations associated with the macroeconomic management of an international currency in relative decline.

In a scenario in which the dollar's role recedes, and especially as complicated by an increasingly visible overhang problem, American policies would no longer be given the benefit of the doubt. Its macroeconomic management would be subject to intense scrutiny in international financial markets, and its deviations from financial rectitude would start to come at a price. In the past, periods of notable dollar weakness led to US borrowing via mechanisms that involved foreign currency payments that were designed to insure creditors against the possibility of a decline in the value of the dollar. These experimental mechanisms of the late 1960s and 1970s were only used on a modest scale, but they suggest the antecedents of future demands that might be imposed by creditors.[49] It would also become more difficult to reduce the value of US debts via devaluation and inflation, devices that have served the United States well in the past but that in the future would both work less well and further undermine the dollar's credibility.

Reduced autonomy, eroding structural power, vanishing prestige, and a growing overhang problem all suggest a challenging general macroeconomic context for American power in the coming years. More specific problems also loom large, in the form of the risk of a debilitating crisis and vulnerability to economic coercion. The danger of financial crisis remains—the underlying vulnerabilities of the US financial system have not been addressed. Another crisis could come. And it could arrive during a national security crisis.

Dollar Diminution: New Vulnerabilities

In addition to the loss of perks and the consequences of foreign policy inhibitions associated with monetary diminution, the overextended dollar might also leave the United States vulnerable to economic coercion by other states. There is a real threat here, though one less apocalyptic than often suggested by those expressing concerns that China might threaten to dump its enormous dollar holdings as an act of political coercion against the United States. This possibility is severely circumscribed by the fact that it is not in China's interest to do so, leaving this as a mostly empty threat.[50] China now has, as I have argued, "buyer's remorse" with regard to its vast dollar holdings. But it did not accumulate those dollar assets as an act of philanthropy, and it currently finds itself as a major stakeholder in the future of the dollar and the health of the US economy. China would be a big loser in a confrontation that undermined either the greenback or US consumer demand. And despite its remarkable record of economic growth, China's economy has visible fragilities. Significant dollar depreciation would be a blow to China's economy; a collapse in the dollar that reduced American demand for imported goods would be a disaster. Thus China could conceivably dump its dollars, but this would be the economic equivalent of the nuclear option. It is possible to imagine scenarios, especially regarding confrontations over Taiwan, in which China might engage in dollar brinksmanship or even pull the currency trigger; but short of that, China's vested interest in the dollar undercuts the potential political advantages of such a gambit.

But this does not leave the dollar in the clear. China has a more subtle lever of monetary power at its disposal. It has the capacity to modulate the rate at which it acquires dollar assets, as well as the ability to manipulate the timing and publicity associated with the rebalancing of its reserve portfolio, an effort already underway. And this channel of influence is more of a one-way street. A more confident—or more aggrieved—China might use this more subtle technique of monetary power to get the attention of the United States during moments of political conflict. Although the circumstances are (again) notably different, this capacity is parallel to the Franco-British monetary relationship in the late 1920s and early 1930s. In that period, the functioning of the international monetary system gave France the ability to draw gold from Britain virtually at will, threatening the viability of the pound. And France was more than willing to take advantage of this capability to try to influence British behavior whenever the two states came into disagreement on important international political issues.

Again, despite the distinct settings, the parallels are notable and the politics familiar. As always with monetary affairs, disagreements in the 1920s about how best to govern money, and fights over the burdens of adjustment, provided the backdrop against which disputes over the high politics of international security took place. France was the reserve accumulator of the day: in December 1926, France held 7.8 percent of the world's monetary gold reserves. Six years later, more than 27 percent of the world's gold reserves could be found in Paris, leading to inevitable (and, to contemporary eyes, easily recognizable) debates over whether it was Britain or France that was the source of unsustainable distress in the system, and accordingly which of the two should bear the brunt of the adjustment necessary to resolve it.[51]

France held a distinct advantage in these disputes, because "even by remaining passive in the foreign exchange markets . . . [it] was in a strategic position to get gold from abroad," which gave that country a ready lever of power that was recognized by elites in both France and Britain. Bank of England governor Montagu Norman recognized that "the Bank of France has enough sterling to create a situation at any given moment which would endanger the maintenance of the pound on gold." His counterpart in France, Emile Moreau, saw this as a "powerful means of exerting pressure on the Bank of England," power that he was eager to deploy to advance French interests, which Moreau thought fitting, as he saw British monetary and financial policy as "a new kind of imperialism."[52]

France directed its monetary power toward two goals in particular: British recognition of the primacy of French political influence in eastern Europe, and British cooperation in maintaining pressure on Germany. On the former, Moreau wished to "have a serious talk with Mr. Norman" in order to "divide Europe into two spheres of financial influence assigned respectively to France and England." The French central banker was seething at British "financial domination" of Europe, and especially aggrieved by its arrangements with countries such as Poland, Romania, and Yugoslavia. ("If the Bank of England takes away from us these customers, whom we are anxious to hold for political reasons," he wrote in his diary, "I shall show my displeasure by buying gold in London.") On Germany, the two countries clashed routinely on reparations policy and the terms of various arrangements designed to modify and oversee them. In one instance, the Bank of France informed the British treasury that if any attempt was made to modify the terms of the Young Plan, "the French Government would feel it necessary to convert all the sterling held in London by the Bank of France into gold and transfer it to Paris," which, both sides understood, would force the pound off the gold standard.[53]

As seen in chapter 2, France's efforts at monetary diplomacy ultimately backfired and contributed to the collapse of the international financial system, the Great Depression, the radicalization of Germany, and the isolation of eastern Europe—not to mention the elimination of any levers of financial influence it once had. But there are lessons, and warnings, for contemporary politics in this, too. France "never for one moment dreamed that Great Britain would take the final step of going off the gold standard." Throughout, "Mr. Moreau felt more strongly inclined not to throw the pound sterling to earth." France wanted to reveal and exploit British weakness, not cause the collapse of the pound. Indeed, France found itself rushing to support sterling (and ultimately taking considerable financial losses in those efforts), once it realized that the gold link was truly vulnerable. Reversing course, France began buying pounds hastily in August 1931, a month before the pound was forced to break its ties with gold, and participated in two emergency Franco-American loans designed to bolster the British position. These efforts were too little and, especially, too late.[54]

Similarly, simply because China has every incentive to avoid undermining the world economy or bringing down the dollar, such intentions are not necessarily adequate to prevent costly blunders.[55] France did not hesitate to resort to the exercise of monetary power, and it would be naïve to assume that China would abstain from the practice, especially if Sino-American relations deteriorate over economic or international political issues. As I have emphasized, an important difference between the global financial crises of 1931 and 2007 was that, in the former case, the perception of intense security dilemmas across Europe inhibited cooperative efforts that might have contained the crisis and encouraged short-sighted unilateralism that was collectively disastrous. The relatively benign security environment in 2007 contributed to the containment of that crisis. But the possibility of deterioration in the international political environment cannot be dismissed, and if it were to occur, it would be an important destabilizing factor. And the contemporary system might be more fragile than it appears. Those holding large dollar reserves stand to lose from a dollar crisis, but at some point in the middle of such a crisis, they might decide to take, and cut, their losses, adding fuel to that fire.[56]

This may never happen. But it could. More important, even if it does not, the overextended dollar, in addition to losing many of the perks it once enjoyed and becoming a source of pressure in favor of inhibition, austerity, and caution (as opposed to an instrument of power augmentation), will also become, even short of a crisis, more vulnerable to the political manipulation of others. Moreover, as I discuss in the conclusion, all of these new constraints, and more difficult international macroeconomic politics, will be unfamiliar to the United States. Since before World War II—that is, for the entirety of practical and institutional living memory—the international monetary and financial system had served to enhance US power and capabilities in its relations with other states. In the future, however, it may present burdens, constraints, and even sources of weakness; and the contrast between free rides of the past and the tightened belts of the future might make those differences seem particularly punishing.

8

CONCLUSIONS, EXPECTATIONS,
AND SPECULATIONS

Before the financial crisis, trends at home and abroad were already suggestive of new macroeconomic constraints on American power. The global financial crisis of 2007–8 was an inflection point that accelerated those underlying trends, and it has left the United States vulnerable to the possibility that macroeconomic factors will inhibit, rather than enhance, its capabilities on the world stage—a reversal of the experiences of the past seventy-five years. Those new constraints (and more difficult international politics) derive from a basic and generally underappreciated shift in the US engagement with the global macroeconomic order, as well as from new complications regarding the management of the dollar as a global currency. American power will be relatively diminished due to both ideational and material factors.

A central argument of this book is that the crisis will be seen in retrospect as a "learning moment" in world politics, one that shapes the expectations and understandings that actors draw on to help formulate basic decisions about how to orient their policies and politics. The last century has seen two other such learning moments, and choices made by states and decision makers, and the pattern of international economic relations in the periods that followed, are understandable only with reference to those lessons. The first was the Great Depression, which evinced a final revulsion against unmediated laissez-faire capitalism that had devolved into a Dickensian nightmare. Capitalism, left solely to its own devices, was not only unjust, it was inefficient. The final nail in the coffin of laissez-faire was that it failed by its own metric. Free markets needed social safety nets, protective regulations, and supervision—in a word, government—to harness their invaluable and indispensable economic horsepower. The second grand lesson emerged from the inflation of the 1970s and the terrible economic costs of taming it, which powerfully imprinted a hypervigilance against signs of inflationary embers and reoriented macroeconomic policy around suppressing them. Notably, this second moment illustrates that lessons don't have to be "right" to be learned; the economic evidence strongly suggests that, at the very least, the cost of modest levels of inflation are much more benign than the effects of the policies designed to reduce it.[1] But such is the power of formative learning moments in shaping both public policy and widely shared norms about what constitutes legitimate economic management.

The global financial crisis will present another such learning moment in world politics, but much of that learning will take place *outside* of the United States. And that lesson, embraced to a varying extent, import, and consequence in different parts of the world, will be that unbound finance does not work and that the American model associated with the dominance of a large, leading, and liberated financial sector is disreputable. The emergence of what I have called a new heterogeneity of thinking about money and finance will thus mark the end of the second US postwar order. States will experiment with various techniques of financial governance and be more comfortable with controls and less enamored of dazzling complexity, in order to increase their autonomy and insulation from global financial instability and to contain risks that might emanate from their own financial sectors. The delegitimization of the American model will mean that US power and influence will be relatively diminished in this new environment.

Basic material factors will reinforce these developments. The simple fact of the crisis revealed a previously underappreciated vulnerability of the United States to financial crisis. For three-quarters of a century financial crises were things that happened to everybody, everywhere, with the exception, that is, of the United States. This is no longer the case. Assessments of the American economy must now include a weighing of the prospects for a financial crisis. In addition, the steps needed to prevent the recent crisis from triggering a reprise of the Great Depression—more spending, more liquidity—while indisputably essential, nevertheless only reinforced suspicions already harbored about the underlying health of the US economy. More generally and most fundamentally, as we look beyond questions of economic stability, the crisis—or more specifically, the economic aftermath of the crisis—has made more salient and has accelerated a basic trend: the diffusion of the center of global economic gravity away from the United States.

It is essential to be clear that these shifts reflect the *relative* erosion of America's economic status, the implications of which are important, but the magnitude of which is often exaggerated. With alarms about "American decline" routinely sounded in the public domain, it is all too easy to overlook some basic facts: the US economy is colossally large, extremely sophisticated, and remarkably innovative, with rich and robust pools of talent and resources. (The nation will also retain global military predominance. It will not be confronted by a peer military competitor in the foreseeable future.)² America, in short, is not Rome—it is not even postwar Britain. The parlor game of "when exactly will China's economy overtake the US economy in absolute size" is largely meaningless. And, as a political realist, I am very wary of looking at the so-called BRICS (Brazil, Russia, India, China, and South Africa) as a *political* force. These states have at least as much to disagree about among themselves as they have to agree on; they are unlikely to act effectively as a group, nor is it obvious why we should conceive of them as such. Their models of capitalism have little in common, and they each have their own formidable domestic economic and political problems.

Nevertheless, back-of-the-envelope observations about the rise of China and of the increasing importance of economies like those of the BRICS and a host of other states do provide a useful and accurate shorthand for the basic fact that both economic and political power is diffusing in the international system. And economic power provides, in the long run, the basic underpinning of political power and influence. Sometimes faster, sometimes slower, always with twists and turns, and commonly with unpredictable and even counterintuitive consequences for world politics, the basic story is one of diffusion. To observe in the moment that the United States has a very high percentage of the world's largest companies or accounts for a disproportionate share of the world's research and development or to look at some other attribute of the commanding size of the American economy misses the fact that these figures would have been higher in the past and will be lower in the future.

Take the most notable illustration: in the ten years leading up to the global financial crisis (1998–2007), China's economic growth averaged 9.95 percent per year, while that of the United States averaged 3.02 percent. China was becoming an important engine of global economic growth, and the gap between the absolute size of the two economies was narrowing. The crisis only accelerated those trends. Considering, admittedly somewhat arbitrarily, five years as the "postcrisis" era, from 2008–12 the Chinese economy averaged an annual rate of growth of 9.26 percent and the United States 0.58 percent. Put another way, at the end of 2012, China's economy was 55 percent larger than it had been in 2007 while the US economy was not quite 3 percent larger. Once again, it is important not to run ahead of this data. China faces some formidable economic challenges in the coming years. Its rate of economic growth will very likely decelerate. But most projections of economic growth, even those that are cautious about China and optimistic about America, suggest that even if US growth tracks toward the high end of its potential and China's checks in closer to the lower end of its commonly anticipated trajectory, each year (and over the years) China will grow faster than the United States.[3] And it will not be the only country to do so, not by a long shot. In sum, from an American perspective, it is not that "the sky is falling." Growth might even pick up a bit. But the general trend of the diffusion of economic activity throughout the globe, moving toward Asia in particular, will almost certainly continue, and it will have predictable political consequences.

Economics and Politics

These economic trends will also take place in domestic and international political contexts; that is, economic phenomena will be filtered through political processes that will magnify, deflect, or in some cases possibly even mute their implications. I have argued, for example, that one consequence of the delegitimization of the second US order (coupled with the diffusion of global economic power) will be pressure on the dollar's role as an international currency. Political factors will attend to almost every element of this story. Again, the context of this argument needs to be clear: I anticipate a *relative diminution* of the dollar's international role; it will be encroached on especially at the fringes of its influence, on the European periphery, in the Middle East, and in Asia. It continues to be most likely that the dollar will remain the world's most commonly used international currency, but that relative diminution will matter. Managing a currency perceived to be in relative decline will present new complications and challenges and impose on domestic macroeconomic policy autonomy as the dollar and US economic policies are subject to closer and more skeptical scrutiny in world markets. And again, this is fundamentally the opposite of the US experience since the end of World War II.

The financial crisis provided an all-too-painful reminder of the economic illogic of the euro, which has given the dollar some breathing room (and was one of the reasons that the dollar served as a safe haven even during a crisis that originated in the United States). But those fundamental problems will, one way or another, be resolved, and looking toward the future, it would be surprising if the euro did not re-emerge as, at the very least, a plausible hedging alternative, if not full "peer competitor," to the dollar.[4] An increased desire, perhaps most obvious in Asia and especially within the range of China's expanding international economic orbit (but in fact more generally throughout the world) for a more diverse range of currency and reserve options will also work against the greenback. It is also possible to imagine that as the United States becomes increasingly energy independent due to increased domestic gas and oil extraction, Gulf oil states may rethink their exclusive reliance on the dollar, a relationship that to some extent rests on an understanding of an American security guarantee.[5] Although even an energy-independent America would retain a strong interest in assuring the free flow of oil from the Persian Gulf, the United States might (quite plausibly) conclude that the threat of such an interruption has been overstated. At the same time, local actors making similar assessments might come to doubt the wholeheartedness of the US security commitment, especially if it appears that budgetary pressure is forcing the

United States to prioritize its military commitments. With Gulf oil—and Gulf interests—tied up more and more with trading partners in Europe and Asia, over the years currency might follow, leading to a relative rebalancing of monetary holdings and a recasting of monetary understandings.

Even if, as is likely, the dollar remains "first among equals," the relative diminution of its use might cause it to shift from what political scientists call a "top" currency to a "negotiated" currency.[6] This will present new pressures on the management of the dollar, which, although economic in nature, will nevertheless play out on political stages. During times of international crises and confrontation, for example, the dollar may come, uncharacteristically, under pressure on world markets. And, as noted in chapter 7, fragile currencies make for timid statesmen.[7] Certainly some may argue that US foreign policy might be well served by new disincentives to act rashly, but the point remains that in the context of relative dollar diminution, the United States will face constraints and inhibitions during international political crises that it has not previously experienced.

Another political phenomenon likely to become more common, at least from an American perspective, is increased international squabbling over exchange rate issues. States invariably seek to shift the burdens of adjustment abroad; these costs can be quite high and are politically unwelcome. (It bears repeating that much of Europe's current crisis is little more than a fight over how to distribute the burdens of macroeconomic adjustment.) During both its first and second postwar orders, the United States didn't think much about the burdens of adjustment—it just acted unilaterally and left others to deal with the consequences.[8] In an increasingly multipolar international economy, with a relatively diminishing international role for the dollar, this will no longer be the case, and this will compound the new US sensitivity to the presence of external constraints.

A key word here is *new*, and this introduces still another political variable that will interact with (and most likely magnify) the real effects of the diffusion of economic power and the more salient exposure of the United States to pressures for adjustment, new macroeconomic vulnerabilities, and the latent-but-lurking-in-the-minds-of-others danger of financial crisis. These pressures are unfamiliar to the US political system, and that system is already under considerable stress as it deals (or fails to deal) with formidable domestic economic problems, including the need to put government spending and taxation on a sustainable trajectory. The US political system is highly polarized—arguably paralyzed—and the country is just emerging from more than a decade of long, difficult, and costly wars. Faced with new pressures and constraints, commonly frustrated by an inability to have its own way, and in the context of chronic pressures on government spending, the United States might become disenchanted with global leadership.[9]

American elites and citizens are unfamiliar with having to face macroeconomic constraints, which will in itself likely amplify the power of those effects. Moreover, the United States does have a long tradition of isolationism and an even more consistent tradition of unilateralism that is not a vestige of the past but a common attribute of its present. Even in its more modern, internationalist phase—even when generously internationalist—the United States has very rarely been willing to be constrained by binding obligations to others. At the UN, the United States gave itself a veto over deliberations at the Security Council; at the IMF the United States insisted on a voting share that assured it de facto veto power. When the Bretton Woods monetary system became inconvenient, the United States disposed of it. After the end of the Cold War, although the United States often sought UN approval for its military actions abroad, it did not predicate its willingness to use force on the assumption of such approval.

Given the highly charged context of contemporary American politics, and with the fraying of the bipartisan Cold War foreign policy consensus that has left neoisolationist forces in the United States stronger than they have been at any point since the early 1950s, a real possibility exists that new constraints, frustrations, and vulnerabilities will lead to a reassessment of America's engagement with the rest of the world. The domestic political reception of the new challenges that the United States will face may inhibit the exercise of American power—and the reach of its international political influence—to an even greater extent than the imperatives of real economic constraints might imply. Magnified or not, the emerging limits to US power will, over time and by definition, affect the international balance of power, and from there the pattern and disposition of world politics.

The Future's Uncertain

Implicit in this discussion has been an assumption that global developments will be characterized more by continuity with regard to underlying factors than by sudden or discontinuous change. (There are some modest exceptions: China's growth rate will likely decelerate and Europe's will eventually return to normal.) This certainly need not turn out to be the case. Indeed, the most common blunders—often whoppers—by analysts of world politics have been the result of implicitly assuming continuity rather than change with regard to trends that influence international relations.[10] Moreover, even accounting for the possibility of discontinuity and change, my own perspective is to be fundamentally skeptical of the entire predictive enterprise in the social sciences.

Alfred Marshall, one of the founding fathers of modern economic theory—Joseph Schumpeter called him "the great teacher of us all"—was profoundly skeptical of prediction.[11] Marshall explained how the problem of contingency severely circumscribes the prospects for all but the most limited efforts at prediction: "Prediction in economics must be hypothetical. Show an uninterrupted game at chess to an expert and he will be bold indeed if he prophesies its future stages. If either side makes one move ever so little different from what he expected, all the following moves will be altered; and after two or three moves more the whole face of the game will have become different."[12]

This was a perspective shared by our unlikely trio, Keynes, Knight, and Hayek. Just as these very disparate (and often oppositional) economists each saw a world of uncertainty as opposed to risk (and thus would have rejected rational expectations theory and the efficient markets hypothesis), they were also profoundly skeptical, to say the least, of the ability of social scientists to make bold or confident forecasts. Knight saw a belief in prediction as the basic flaw in economic theory; he stressed instead "the inherent, absolute unpredictability" of social scientific phenomena, and he contrasted the prospects of such forecasting "with the scientific judgment in regard to natural phenomena." Hayek also emphasized the distinction between the natural and social sciences, which informed his insistence that "in the study of such complex phenomena as the market," economists could expect to offer no more than "only very general predictions about the kind of events which we must expect in a given situation." Keynes, of course, shared these views. Regarding "the prospect of a European war" or "the price of copper and the rate of interest twenty years hence" or "the obsolescence of a new invention" and the consequences of such developments, he said: "About these matters there is no scientific basis on which to form any calculable probabilities whatever. We simply do not know."[13]

The prospects for prediction are even dimmer in international politics than they are in economics. "The first lesson the student of international politics must learn and never forget," Hans Morgenthau insisted, "is that the complexities of international affairs make simple solutions and trustworthy prophecies impossible." Especially in a political context, one set of unanticipated disturbances or idiosyncratic decisions not only nudges actors toward one path instead of another but also reveals paths previously unseen. What Morgenthau called "the interminable chains of causes and effects" renders efforts at prediction unproductive and, especially when expressed overconfidently, unwise.[14]

Sensitivity to the considerable limits of prediction in international relations informs the way the arguments in this book—and disagreements with those arguments—should be interpreted. The arguments I have made imply certain expectations about the future, but it is the argumentation that matters, not the outcomes. Even in a world of risk (that is, in a world where the underlying probability distribution of outcomes is knowable) the expectations of the best analytical machine (that is, judicious predictions of what will most likely happen) will often, even commonly, be different from the actual events that unfold.[15]

With the logic of the reasoning I have presented in this book more important than the batting average of my predictions, two things come to the foreground for probing the limits to (and potential errors of) my arguments. The first is to fix on the possible sources of analytical error. I have placed great emphasis on a new heterogeneity of thinking about money and finance and the delegitimization of what I have termed the second US postwar order. From these have flowed concepts including "buyer's remorse" on the part of China and reduced American international political influence due to a loss of "hegemonic socialization." This could be wrong. Instead of signaling an inflection point, disenchantment with the American model could be a blip, or a hiccup, but not a lasting disturbance from the original path. After the dust settles, actors outside the United States might decide that the American financial model is indeed the singularly correct one. I don't think they will, but that's exactly the point: if I'm wrong about this, some of the arguments in this book become less compelling.

Similarly, I have assumed that the general trend of the diffusion of global economic activity will continue; that is, as a back-of-the-envelope calculation, US GDP as a share of world product will be lower ten years from now than it is today. I've also suggested that the real implications of this trend will be exacerbated, and thus its implications magnified, by a polarized, if not completely dysfunctional, US polity further stressed by the unfamiliarity of dealing with the challenges of external macroeconomic pressures and constraints. Each of these expectations may also be wrong. On the political side, for example, even if economic trends remain consistent, on paper at least, there are a range of plausible "grand bargains" of tax increases and reforms to the major entitlement programs that would put the government's finances and debt burdens on a sustainable trajectory. America's fiscal problems are not monumental by historical standards, and they are less daunting than those faced by some other states in the contemporary system. Thus a little statesmanship and political functionality might go a long way. Were such a grand bargain to be reached, it would take the edge off, though not eliminate, new constraints on the American economy and mitigate some of the external wariness about its future. It would also likely speak favorably to the prospects for the performance of the economy as a whole, moving forward. Regarding the economy and the force of my argument, if I have overstated the material trends that relatively disfavor the US economy, that would also throw some sand in the gears of my analytical machine.

There are indeed some analysts who are bullish on the prospects for US economic growth. These tend to emphasize various factors in America's favor, including the emergence of very cheap local energy that will present a competitive advantage for domestic industry, as well as favorable demographic trends.[16] And the better the US relative economic performance, the more its relative underlying power will endure; it would also serve to sustain or at least to slow the rate of diminution of the international role of the dollar. Nevertheless, my own view is that, despite reasons for optimism, especially with regard to the trajectory of corporate profits, although it is clearly characterized by obvious strengths, the US economy nevertheless faces daunting challenges. Those challenges, including infrastructure, health care, education, and social mobility, will inhibit the dynamism of and long-term prospects for the US economy, even as GDP continues to recover from the depths of the financial crisis.[17]

The second implication of skepticism about prediction, and to guard against the analytical tyranny of assuming that the future will look like the recent past, is that we should consider counterfactual mental exercises of "anticipation." The goal of such efforts is not to assign relative probabilities, even loosely, to competing scenarios—I cannot emphasize enough that in a world of uncertainty, the probabilities of potential outcomes cannot be assigned, and many outcomes are essentially unforeseeable. Still, there is much to be said for the goal of "trying not to be surprised." That is, there are a number of imaginable futures out there and, most important, a number of imaginable *discontinuities*, which can be anticipated, if not predicted.[18] The goal is not to improve precision in the assigning of odds, but rather to be alert to the possibility that some less likely but potentially very disruptive events might occur. It is not possible to account for all of the wild cards out there, but there are some in the deck that are plainly visible. If any of them are dealt, it is important to understand how they would affect outcomes in world politics and reshape the expectations that I have presented in this book.

If I'd known where it would end, I'd have never let anything start

Major, game-changing discontinuities are plausible, and easily imagined, and would require a reassessment of my conclusions.[19] A major financial crisis with the United States at its epicenter—either a dollar panic or what would become known as "Too Big to Fail Two"—would assure the final dismemberment of the second US postwar order, reduce further US power and influence, and accelerate decline of the dollar as an international currency. The complete implosion of the euro would bolster the dollar as the only safe harbor in sight, though that assumes that such a crisis would not pull down a major US financial institution along with it, which might be wishful thinking. Moreover, the damaging effects on the economies of the United States and China that would result from a deepening of Europe's economic distress should not be underestimated. Finally, it is easy—all too easy—to imagine not simply a deceleration in China's economic growth but its basic interruption. New, sustained economic distress in China would decelerate the shift in the balance of power away from the United States and bolster the international role of the dollar.

Even if the United States performs near the high end of its most likely growth trajectory and China near the lower end of its projected path, China will still, as I have noted, continue to become relatively more important in the world economy. But the wild card remains a more radical, disruptive, indefinitely sustained downshift in China's growth, a possibility that can't be ruled out. Instability in its domestic financial sector, internal labor/migration bottlenecks, and disruptive environmental distress are some of the myriad problems that might cause a major disruption in China's economic growth.[20] This is not something for proponents of American power to root for, even in their most bloodless realpolitik calculations. Given that power in international politics is relative, the United States (and the dollar) would be relatively empowered by a weaker China; but purpose and politics, not simply power, are enormously important, and US interests would not be well served by a wounded China. Recall that the People's Republic is now the world's second-largest importer of other countries' goods, and growth in those states' economies has come to depend on China's large and growing demand for their products. China's economy is now so large that its economic distress would have global spillover effects. Perhaps even worse, the country is, after all, governed by the Communist Party, yet "communism" has not served as the basis of the government's legitimacy for decades: delivering the economic goods has. A staggering economy would bring about a crisis of legitimacy that could lead to domestic political distress, and a government that perceives itself to be under siege would have much less room for maneuverability in international political settings. Indeed, it might try to harness virulent nationalism in an attempt to shore up its relative political power against other actors *within* the country. Thus, although a "successful" China might present challenges in world politics as its ambitions increase with its capabilities, a distressed China would probably be an even more dangerous entity.

The emergence of a more dangerous and destabilizing China might also result from external rather than internal developments. Chronic and irresolvable conflicts with regard to international monetary and financial relations might also cause an unexpected and game-changing crisis in world politics. I have argued that increased friction in these areas is almost certain to occur. That such conflicts could spiral out of control is less likely but certainly possible. Of the many lessons from the Great Depression, one worth recalling here is that international politics not only contributed to the global financial crisis of 1931, and was one of the main reasons why that crisis was uncontained, but that the crisis in turn had tragic effects on the domestic politics of many countries. One reason why the future is always uncertain is that the foreign policies chosen by states are not inevitable: from a range of possibilities, one strategy is settled on after an implicit or explicit debate over competing visions. In the United States, for example, the debate over isolationism versus internationalism was settled differently after World War I than it was after World War II. As Tolstoy described, outcomes seem inevitable as they recede into historical memory.[21] But right there in the moment it is clear things could have been quite different. Part of what determines which foreign policy vision triumphs are perceptions about the international prospects for competing strategies. As we can see most clearly with interwar Japan, the global financial crisis of 1931 foreclosed the prospect for a cooperative strategy envisioned by those advocating for Japan to rise to great power status within the rules and norms of the existing order. In the inhospitable 1930s, liberal internationalists, who had the upper hand in shaping Japanese foreign policy in the 1920s, were removed from the scene. Militarist nationalists took over.[22] Today, China's future is similarly unwritten; once again, we have no way of knowing what is going to happen.[23] But alternative trajectories can be envisioned. And in addition to reckless foreign policy improvisations encouraged by domestic economic distress, an unraveling of the international monetary and financial order might also lead to the emergence of a difficult, even thuggish China that would present alarming challenges—not to the underlying balance of power, but to American interests and to world politics more generally.

Another disruptive, discontinuous change might originate in Europe. I have assumed that the European Union will, however slowly, emerge from its postcrisis difficulties in an orderly fashion: either it will reach new understandings that will stabilize its system, with the euro resuming its trajectory as an increasingly important international currency, or, more dramatically, the eurozone might contract to a hard core of users, with other members of the European Union establishing different types of relationships with the euro in a pattern of concentric circles about that core. But an unraveling of the eurozone might not go smoothly, especially if it is sparked by sovereign debt crises or the disorderly exit of one member that triggers a cascade of self-fulfilling challenges to the credibility of the commitments of other suspect participants. The basic problems of the eurozone are not going away: it is not an optimal currency area—labor mobility is too low and the pooling of fiscal resources inadequate—and it is more coherent as a politically motivated identity project than it is as a single economic unit. The inherent inconsistencies of the common currency, which forced member states to abdicate the levers of monetary and exchange rate policies, has left the tourniquet of austerity as the only policy tool in the medicine bag for states facing distress. All macroeconomic relationships generate disequilibria that require often painful adjustments. But the eurozone system has reduced the parsing out of adjustment costs to their most bitter and naked portions.[24] And as long as participants' identity politics only go so far—that is, as long as individual EU states divide their fellow members, often along north-south lines, into categories of "us" and "them"—these problems are not going to go away. In 2012, the unemployment rate was 24 percent in Greece and 25 percent in Spain; it was 5.5 percent in Germany and 5.3 percent in the Netherlands.[25] Both the very high levels of unemployment in some EU countries and the disparity in unemployment rates between member states are generating powerful political pressures that will not be easy to resolve.

If the euro implodes, that event would presumably bolster the dollar's role as an international currency. But it would not bode well for the United States. The European Union is the world's largest economic entity, and the relationship between the United States and the European Union is also the world's largest: the two economies are intimately enmeshed.[26] Economic distress in Europe is not good for the United States. Moreover, the United States might have more than just a ringside seat if the Continent were rocked by its own financial crisis. The Securities and Exchange Commission, ever so politely, reported in January 2012 that it was "concerned about the risks to financial institutions that are SEC registrants from direct and indirect exposures" to European sovereign debt holdings and that "disclosures about the nature and extent of these exposures . . . have been inconsistent in both substance and presentation."[27]

A final wild card—and one that history suggests shows its face all too often—is another financial crisis with an origin in the United States. In the immediate aftermath of 2007–8, a common assessment, even of informed insiders, was that "unless regulations are changed radically . . . there will continue to be firms that are too big to fail. And when the next, inevitable bubble bursts, the cycle will only repeat itself."[28] Actually, this prediction seems a bit optimistic: the next cycle would probably be worse. On the heels of another crisis, the political will to prevent the financial system from freezing up and the economy from completely cratering might not exist, having been exhausted by the previous efforts that generously saved the industry but showed little empathy for many who became casualties of the Great Recession.

Far from radical change, the United States has emerged from the global financial crisis vulnerable to a repeat performance. Its financial sector is characterized by even fewer, still larger, and highly enmeshed financial behemoths, playing by most of the old rules and, even worse, by all of the old norms.[29] The Dodd-Frank regulatory reforms, and provisions such as the Volcker rule, designed to restrict the types of risky investments that banks would be allowed to engage in, have not simply been watered down, they have been drowned (or at least waterboarded into submission) by a cascade of exceptions, exemptions, qualifications, and vague language. The Volcker rule itself, for example, was originally a ten-page document (based on a three-page memo) that became 298 pages of legislation. And what few teeth remain are utterly dependent for application on the (very suspect) will of regulators.[30]

In sum, in the United States, the "regulatory landscape has been little changed," Paul Volcker observed in August 2013. "Here we are, almost three years after the passage of Dodd-Frank, with important regulatory and supervisory issues arising from the act unresolved."[31] This matters, especially if, as I have argued, the United States is "returning to normal" with regard to the basic level of its exposure to potential financial crises. Recall that for much of the country's history, its unsupervised financial sector was dominated by speculators, innovators, risk takers, and more than a few charlatans and thieves, whose behavior contributed to recurrent crises. The government began to push back against unbridled finance during the Progressive Era, but it took the cataclysm of the Great Depression to create a political climate that produced meaningful regulation and oversight. A long period of stability followed. Even Robert Lucas recently observed, "The fact that during the 66 years that [Glass-Steagall] remained in force the United States did not experience any widespread financial crises commands respect, or at least curiosity."[32] But beginning in the 1980s the regulatory order was dismantled, and finance has grown unchecked, reverting quickly to the behavioral norms of the nineteenth century and the Roaring Twenties, with inevitable, if widely disregarded, consequences for systemic risk. Some observers expected that the 2007–8 crisis would have an effect similar to the Depression and lead to an assertion of political oversight and regulation as in the mid-1930s.[33] But this is not happening, because of the enormous power of the industry, its convergence and enmeshment with Washington, and the ironic success of public policy in limiting the severity of the damage (and thus the political momentum for change) this time around. And so we'll see.

With luck, there won't be a replay of the global financial crisis, Europe will find a way to muddle through its troubles (or even resolve some of them), and China's growth will slow but not stall. But that emerging world—the post–financial crisis international order—will bear less of an American stamp. And the United States, still a great power, perhaps still *the* great power, will find its relative power and influence reduced, and it will be less often able to impose its will, or even, at times, to get what it wants.

Notes

Preface

1. Jonathan Kirshner, "Political Economy in Security Studies after the Cold War," *Review of International Political Economy* 5:1 (Spring 1998): 64–91.

2. See, for example, Charles Kindleberger, *Economic Laws and Economic History* (Cambridge: Cambridge University Press, 1997); and Jonathan Kirshner, "Leadership, Political Economy, and Economic History: The Influence of Charles Kindleberger on International Relations," *Mershon International Review* 41:2 (1997).

3. One of his most famously abused quotes, for example, "in the long run we are all dead," is routinely trotted out as evidence of his short-term thinking. The quote comes from his book *A Tract on Monetary Reform* and was designed to chastise economists who were disregarding the "short run" in their analyses, which, in practice, could be quite some time. The full quote is: "But this long run is a misleading guide to current affairs. In the long run we are all dead. Economists set themselves too easy, too useless a task if in tempestuous seasons they can only tell us that when the storm is past the ocean is flat again." It should also be noted that the *Tract* was published in 1923, well before Keynes became a "Keynesian." Indeed, the *Tract* was, not surprisingly, Milton Friedman's favorite book by Keynes. For an excellent brief introduction to Keynes, see Robert Skidelsky, *Keynes: The Return of the Master* (New York: Public Affairs, 2010).

4. Even passionate anti-Keynesians such as Friedrich von Hayek and Frank Knight share Keynes's views on uncertainty. The optimal level of capital controls is an empirical question that can be settled simply by the evidence. Economism—Keynes was wary of reducing all of life to

an economic calculus—is more of a philosophical position that speaks indirectly to the culture of American capitalism. Ironically, this is a perspective now more commonly associated with the political Right than the political Left.

1. The Global Financial Crisis as World Politics

1. Barry Eichengreen, *Golden Fetters: The Gold Standard and the Great Depression, 1919–1939* (Oxford: Oxford University Press, 1992); Charles P. Kindleberger, *The World in Depression* (Berkeley: University of California Press, 1973); Ben S. Bernanke, *Essays on the Great Depression* (Princeton: Princeton University Press, 2000).

2. Benjamin J. Cohen, *The Geography of Money* (Ithaca: Cornell University Press, 1998); Kathleen McNamara, *The Currency of Ideas: Monetary Politics in the European Union* (Ithaca: Cornell University Press, 1998).

3. Robert Gilpin, *The Political Economy of International Relations* (Princeton: Princeton University Press, 1987), 119.

4. The institution initially envisioned to oversee world trade, the International Trade Organization, never got off the ground, and so the international trade regime was orchestrated by the GATT, which was superseded by the World Trade Organization (WTO).

5. John Gerard Ruggie, "International Regimes, Transactions, and Change: Embedded Liberalism in the Post-War Economic Order," *International Organization* 36 (1982) 379–415.

6. John Maynard Keynes, "Post-War Currency Policy" (September 8, 1941), *The Collected Writings of John Maynard Keynes*, ed. Donald Moggridge and Elizabeth Johnson, 30 vols. (London: Macmillan, 1971–89), 25:21–33 (hereafter cited with original publication date in parentheses followed by *CW* with volume and page numbers).

7. G. John Ikenberry, "A World Restored: Expert Consensus and the Anglo-American Postwar Settlement," *International Organization* 46:1 (1992): 289–323.

8. That is, the probabilities of all possible outcomes are known, like rolling dice. The probability of getting snake eyes is 1 in 36. Seven is the most likely outcome, with a 1/6 chance of occurring.

9. Friedrich von Hayek, "The Pretence of Knowledge," (Nobel memorial lecture, December 11, 1974), Nobel Foundation; Frank Knight, *Risk, Uncertainty and Profit* (1921, repr., Chicago: University of Chicago Press, 1971).

10. Rawi Abdelal, *Capital Rules: The Construction of Global Finance* (Cambridge: Harvard University Press, 2007). It is nevertheless the case, and relevant, that the IMF is incapable of acting against the wishes of the United States, as the institution's voting rules give the Americans an effective veto of its policies. And the US representatives at the IMF were indeed very strongly in favor of the drive to amend the articles.

11. Jonathan Kirshner, ed., *Monetary Orders: Ambiguous Economics, Ubiquitous Politics* (Ithaca: Cornell University Press, 2003).

12. Too much mobility encourages disruptive speculative flows of short-run capital and creates pressure for uniformity across countries' economic policies.

13. Dani Rodrik and Arvind Subramanian, "Why Did Financial Globalization Disappoint?," *IMF Staff Papers* 56:1 (2009).

14. Charles P. Kindleberger, *Manias, Panics, and Crashes: A History of Financial Crises* (New York: Basic Books, 1978); Carmen Reinhart and Kenneth Rogoff, *This Time Is Different: Eight Centuries of Financial Folly* (Princeton: Princeton University Press, 2009).

15. US Treasury, "Deputy Secretary Summers Remarks before the International Monetary Fund," U.S. Treasury Press Release RR-2286, March 9, 1998.

16. Actually, student of the Depression and Federal Reserve chairman Ben Bernanke thought the more recent crisis was the worst in history.

17. Riccardo Rebonato, *Plight of the Fortune Tellers: Why We Need to Manage Financial Risk Differently* (Princeton: Princeton University Press, 2007); Emanuel Derman, *Models Behaving Badly: Why Confusing Illusion with Reality Can Lead to Disaster, on Wall Street and in Life* (New York: Free Press, 2011).

18. Paul Volcker, "Rethinking the Bright New World of Global Finance," *International Finance* 11:1 (2008) 101–107; Raghuram G. Rajan, "Has Financial Development Made the World Riskier?," in *The Greenspan Era: Lessons for the Future, Symposium Sponsored by the Federal Reserve Bank of Kansas City* (Kansas City, MO: Federal Reserve Bank of Kansas City, 2005).

19. Hyman Minsky, *Can "It" Happen Again? Essays on Instability and Finance* (New York: M. E. Sharpe, 1982).

20. Ilene Grabel, "The Rebranding of Capital Controls in an Era of Productive Incoherence," (unpublished paper, 2013).

21. Many scholars hold that the lack of complete capital account openness will prevent the RMB from playing anything more than a minor role as an international currency. This underestimates the extent to which China (and others) will favor not just new options but new models. The American model requires such capital account openness; other models might feature alternate arrangements.

22. Charles Kupchan, *No One's World: The West, the Rising Rest, and the Coming Global Turn* (New York: Oxford University Press, 2012).

23. Albert Hirschman, *National Power and the Structure of Foreign Trade* (Berkeley: University of California Press, 1980). Trade figures are from the World Trade Organization, *International Trade Statistics* (Geneva: World Trade Organization).

24. Joseph Nye, *Soft Power: The Means to Success in World Politics* (New York: Public Affairs, 2004), 7.

25. Benjamin Cohen, "Towards a Leaderless Currency System," in *The Future of the Dollar*, ed. Eric Helleiner and Jonathan Kirshner (Ithaca: Cornell University Press, 2009), 142–63.

26. World Bank, *Global Development Horizons 2011—Multipolarity: The New Global Economy* (Washington, DC: World Bank, 2011). And, if anything, the Bank is likely underestimating these shifts, since its analysis is solely on economic trends and does not account for reassessments by some actors that lead them to recalibrate the extent of their ties to the dollar and the American financial economy more generally.

27. Susan Strange, "Finance, Information and Power," *Review of International Studies* 16:3 (1990): 259–74.

28. Signaling a commitment to orthodoxy will also typically require tight monetary policies that assure creditors and defend exchange rates but are a drag on economic growth.

29. Jonathan Kirshner, *Appeasing Bankers: Financial Caution on the Road to War* (Princeton: Princeton University Press, 2007).

2. Learning from the Great Depression

1. See, for example, Ben S. Bernanke, *Essays on the Great Depression* (Princeton: Princeton University Press, 2004).

2. On Black Friday, October 25, 1929, the Dow Jones Industrial Average closed at 301.22. (It had been as high as 381.17 on September 3.) On November 13, the market closed at 198.60. (It would bottom out at 41.22 on July 8, 1932, having lost almost 90% of its value.)

3. Harold James, *The Creation and Destruction of Value* (Cambridge: Harvard University Press, 2009), 47.

4. Aurel Schubert, *The Cred-Anstalt Crisis of 1931* (Cambridge: Cambridge University Press, 1991), 3–4, 7, 11–12; Michael Bordo and Harold James, "The Great Depression Analogy," *Financial History Review* 17:2 (2011): 128; Iago Gol Aguado, "The Creditanstalt Crisis of 1931 and the

Failure of the Austro-German Customs Union Project," *Historical Journal* 44:1 (2001): 200; Olivier Accominotti, "London Merchant Banks, the Central European Panic, and the Sterling Crisis of 1931," *Journal of Economic History* 72:1 (March 2012): 1–43.

5. Barry Eichengreen, *Golden Fetters: The Gold Standard and the Great Depression, 1919–1939* (Oxford: Oxford University Press, 1992), 259–60.

6. On France's demand for security, see E. H. Carr, *International Relations between the Two World Wars* (London: Macmillan and Co., 1947), 25; and Arnold Wolfers, *Britain and France between the Two World Wars* (New York: W. W. Norton, 1966), 2. On the political roots of financial distress, see, for example, Theo Balderston, "The Banks and the Gold Standard Crisis of 1931," *Financial History Review* 1:1 (April 1994): 65; and George Glasgow, "The Financial and Economic Crisis," *Contemporary Review* 140 (July/December 1931): 140–41.

7. Paul Einzig, *International Gold Movements*, 2nd ed. (London: Macmillan, 1931), 33. Einzig's argument is tested and confirmed in Jonathan Kirshner, *Currency and Coercion: The Political Economy of International Monetary Power* (Princeton: Princeton University Press, 1995), chap. 6. See also Sir Frederick Leith-Ross, *Money Talks: Fifty Years of International Finance* (London: Hutchinson and Co., 1968); and Emile Moreau, *The Golden Franc: Memoirs of a Governor of the Bank of France* (Boulder, CO: Westview, 1991).

8. League of Nations, *World Economic Survey 1931–2* (Geneva: League of Nations, 1932), 72 (quote); Aguado, "Creditanstalt Crisis," 203, 204, 216; Edward W. Bennett, *Germany and the Diplomacy of the Financial Crisis, 1931* (Cambridge: Harvard University Press, 1962), 41, 71, 73, 117, 149–50.

9. Department of State, *Foreign Relations of the United States, 1931*, vol. 1 (Washington, DC: US Government Printing Office, 1946), 23, 24 ("blackmail"), 26 (Stimson); Schubert, *Credit-Anstalt Crisis*, 14–15, 160–61; Bennett, *Germany and the Diplomacy of the Financial Crisis*, 151–52. On the run on the schilling, see Aguado, " Creditanstalt Crisis," 211, 214, 216.

10. Bennett, *Germany and the Diplomacy of the Financial Crisis*, 177–78, 190, 219, 231, 237, 248; *Federal Reserve Bulletin*, November 1930, 383; *Foreign Relations of the United States, 1931*, 1:96; S. V. O. Clarke, *Central Bank Cooperation 1924–31* (New York: Federal Reserve Bank of New York, 1967), 21, 195–96.

11. Eichengreen, *Golden Fetters*; see also Bordo and James, "Great Depression Analogy," 129.

12. Eichengreen, *Golden Fetters*, 187, 18.

13. Vehemently opposed ideas about monetary management were regularly debated in the public sphere. See Royal Institute of International Affairs (RIIA), *The International Gold Problem* (London: Oxford University Press, 1932); and League of Nations, *Report of the Gold Delegation of the Financial Committee* (Geneva: League of Nations, 1932).

14. On economy and orthodoxy, see H. Clark Johnson, *Gold, France, and the Great Depression, 1919–1932* (New Haven: Yale University Press, 1997); Kenneth Mouré, *The Gold Standard Illusion: France, the Bank of France, and the International Gold Standard, 1914–1939* (Oxford: Oxford University Press, 2002); and Julian Jackson, *The Politics of the Depression in France, 1932–1936* (Cambridge: Cambridge University Press, 1985). On the relationship between orthodoxy and national security, see Jonathan Kirshner, *Appeasing Bankers: Financial Caution on the Road to War* (Princeton: Princeton University Press, 2007).

15. Milton Friedman and Anna J. Schwartz, *A Monetary History of the United States, 1867–1960* (Princeton: Princeton University Press, 1963), 111, 133.

16. Benjamin J. Cohen, *The Geography of Money* (Ithaca: Cornell University Press, 1998), 67, 97, 122, 135; Ilene Grabel, "The Political Economy of 'Policy Credibility': The New-Classical Economics and the Remaking of Emerging Economies," *Cambridge Journal of Economics* 24:1 (2000): 1–19; Jonathan Kirshner, "The Inescapable Politics of Money," in *Monetary Orders: Ambiguous Economics, Ubiquitous Politics*, ed. Jonathan Kirshner, 2–15 (Ithaca: Cornell University Press, 2003.

17. Robert Barro and David Gordon, "Rules, Discretion, and Reputation in a Model of Monetary Policy," *Journal of Monetary Economics* 12:1 (1983): 104; Robert Barro, "Inflation and Growth," *Federal Reserve Bank of St. Louis Review* 78:3 (1996): 159. Examples abound of influential macroeconomists and practitioners who fail to find costs of inflation yet push hard for policies designed to suppress even low levels of inflation at almost any cost. The influential authors of one aggressively anti-inflationary guide to policy state plainly that it is "very difficult" to obtain "direct empirical confirmation of a link between inflation and the overall economic performance of the economy." Ben S. Bernanke, Thomas Laubach, Frederic Mishkin, and Adam S. Posen, *Inflation Targeting* (Princeton: Princeton University Press, 1999), 18. Michael Bruno finds "no evidence of a growth-inflation relationship" at annual rates of inflation less than 40 percent. Stanley Fischer argued that a country with a 110% inflation rate will grow more slowly than one with a 10% inflation rate. Incongruously, on the basis of these studies, each of these scholar-practitioners recommends that policies be designed to keep inflation extremely low (on the order of 1–3%). See Stanley Fischer, "Maintaining Price Stability," *Finance and Development* 33:4 (1996): 34–37; Michael Bruno, "Does Inflation Really Lower Growth?," *Finance and Development* 32:3 (1995): 35, 38; and Michael Bruno and William Easterly, "Inflation and Growth: In Search of a Stable Relationship," *Federal Reserve Bank of St. Louis Review* 78:3 (1996): 145. For more on this literature, see Jonathan Kirshner, "The Political Economy of Low Inflation," *Journal of Economic Surveys* 15:1 (2001): 41–70.

18. Richard Cooper, "Prolegomena to the Choice of an International Monetary System," *International Organization* 29:1 (Winter 1975): 63–98; Benjamin J. Cohen, *Organizing the World's Money* (New York: Basic Books, 1977).

19. John Maynard Keynes, *A Treatise on Money: The Applied Theory of Money* (1930, repr., Cambridge: Cambridge University Press, 1971), 272; see also 304.

20. On macroeconomic externalities and their deleterious consequences, see Kenneth A. Oye, *Economic Discrimination and Political Exchange: World Political Economy in the 1930s and 1980s* (Princeton: Princeton University Press, 1992). Again the contrast with trade is illuminating. As Oye argues, if one nation raises its tariffs, even if it does so universally, other states can raise tariffs that directly target the protectionist. They can then bargain bilaterally for market share and would be the sole beneficiaries of anything achieved by their efforts.

21. Charles P. Kindleberger, *The Politics of Money and World Language*, Princeton Essays in International Economics, no. 61, International Finance Section, Princeton University, NJ, August 1967; Gustav Cassel, *The World's Monetary Problems* (London: Constable and Co., 1921), 80.

22. Richard N. Gardner, *Sterling-Dollar Diplomacy in Current Perspective* (New York: Columbia University Press, 1980), 347; Randall Hinshaw, *Toward European Convertibility*, Princeton Essays in International Finance, no. 30, International Finance Section, Princeton University, NJ, November 1958.

23. David Calleo, *The Imperious Economy* (Cambridge: Harvard University Press, 1982); John S. Odell, *US International Monetary Policy* (Princeton: Princeton University Press, 1982); Joanne Gowa, *Closing the Gold Window: Domestic Politics and the End of Bretton Woods* (Ithaca: Cornell University Press, 1983).

24. On hegemonic exploitation, see Andrew Walter, *World Power and World Money* (New York: St. Martin's Press, 1991). On the limits of hegemonic stability theory as applied to money, see Giulio Gallarotti, *The Anatomy of an International Monetary Regime: The Classical Gold Standard, 1880–1914* (Oxford: Oxford University Press, 1995); and Barry Eichengreen, "Conducting the International Orchestra: Bank of England Leadership under the International Gold Standard," *Journal of International Money and Finance* 6:1 (March 1987).

25. On the significance of the realization of British weakness, see Thomas Christensen, *Useful Adversaries: Grand Strategy, Domestic Mobilization, and Sino-American Conflict, 1947–58* (Princeton: Princeton University Press, 1996), chap. 3; and Robert Pollard, *Economic Security and the Origins of the Cold War, 1945–1950* (New York: Columbia University Press, 1985).

26. G. John Ikenberry, "A World Economy Restored: Expert Consensus and the Anglo-American Postwar Settlement," *International Organization* 46:1 (Winter 1992): 289–321; Kathleen McNamara, *The Currency of Ideas: Monetary Politics in the European Union* (Ithaca: Cornell University Press, 1997), 2, 70–71, 171.

27. Susan Howson, *Sterling's Managed Float: The Operations of the Exchange Equalization Account, 1932–39*, Princeton Studies in International Economics, no. 46, International Finance Section, Princeton University, NJ, 1980; Lowell M. Pumphrey, "The Exchange Equalization Account of Great Britain 1932–1939: Exchange Operations," *American Economic Review* 32:4 (1942); and Charles P. Kindleberger, *The World in Depression, 1929–1939* (Berkeley: University of California Press, 1973).

28. David E. Kaiser, *Economic Diplomacy and the Origins of the Second World War* (Princeton: Princeton University Press, 1980); Robert Frankenstein, "The Decline of France and French Appeasement Policies, 1936–9," in *The Fascist Challenge and the Policy of Appeasement*, ed. Wolfgang J. Mommsen and Lothar Kettenacker, 236–45 (London: George Allen and Unwin, 1983); Stephen V. O. Clarke, *Exchange Rate Stabilization in the Mid-1930s: Negotiating the Tripartite Agreement*, Princeton Studies in International Economics, no. 41, International Finance Section, Princeton University, NJ, 1977; Johnson, *Gold, France, and the Great Depression*; Mouré, *Gold Standard Illusion*; Beth Simmons, *Who Adjusts? Domestic Sources of Foreign Economic Policy during the Interwar Years* (Princeton: Princeton University Press, 1994).

29. On these issues, see Ian M. Drummond, *London, Washington, and the Management of the Franc, 1936–1939*, Princeton Studies in International Economics, no. 45, International Finance Section, Princeton University, NJ, 1979, 4, 32, 53; and John Morton Blum, *From the Morgenthau Diaries*, vol. 1 (Boston: Houghton Mifflin, 1959), 140; as well as Kaiser, *Economic Diplomacy*; and Clarke, *Exchange Rate Stabilization*.

30. Einzig, *Behind the Scenes of International Finance* (London: Macmillan, 1931), 145; Kirshner, *Currency and Coercion*, 128, 130–31.

31. Mark Metzler, *Lever of Empire: The International Gold Standard and the Crisis of Liberalism in Prewar Japan* (Berkeley: University of California Press, 2006); Richard J. Smethurst, *From Foot Soldier to Finance Minister: Takahashi Korekiyo, Japan's Keynes* (Cambridge: Harvard University Press, 2007); Kirshner, *Appeasing Bankers*, chap. 3. See also Edward M. Lamont, *The Ambassador from Wall Street: The Story of Thomas W. Lamont, J. P. Morgan's Chief Executive* (Lanham, MD: Madison Books, 1994), esp.157, 195–96, 236–37, 311.

32. Good starting points include Thomas Christensen, "Fostering Stability or Creating a Monster? The Rise of China and US Policy Toward East Asia," *International Security* 31:1 (2006); Aaron Friedberg, "The Future of US-China Relations: Is Conflict Inevitable?" *International Security* 30:2 (2005); and Robert Ross and Zhu Feng, eds., *China's Ascent: Power, Security and the Future of International Politics* (Ithaca: Cornell University Press, 2008).

3. From the First to the Second US Postwar Order

1. On these issues, see Jonathan Kirshner, "John Maynard Keynes and the Crisis of Embedded Liberalism," *Review of International Political Economy* 6:3 (Autumn 1999); Eric Helleiner, *States and the Reemergence of Global Finance* (Ithaca: Cornell University Press, 1994); Mark Blyth, *Great Transformations: Economic Ideas and Institutional Change in the Twentieth Century* (Cambridge: Cambridge University Press, 2002); Rawi Abdelal, *Capital Rules: The Construction of Global Finance* (Cambridge: Harvard University Press, 2007).

2. Greta R. Krippner, *Capitalizing on Crisis: The Political Origins of the Rise of Finance* (Cambridge: Harvard University Press, 2011), 60–61; Ron Chernow, *The House of Morgan* (New York: Atlantic Monthly Press, 1990), 376.

3. John Maynard Keynes (1883–1946) lived a remarkably rich life that defies quick summary. In addition to *The General Theory of Employment, Interest and Money* (1936), his other important books include *The Economic Consequences of the Peace* (1919), *A Tract on Monetary Reform* (1923), and *A Treatise on Money* (1930). But these only scratch the surface of his indefatigable writing and public activity; general readers are especially encouraged to seek out *Essays in Persuasion* and *Essays in Biography*. Closely associated with the Bloomsbury community, Keynes also maintained an active interest in the arts, which informed his perspective on the role of economics and the economist. He founded and managed a theater in Cambridge in 1935 and was later a member of the board of trustees for the National Gallery and chair of the Committee for the Encouragement of Music and Arts. He formally and/or informally served as a government adviser throughout his career. During World War II, Keynes represented the British government in negotiations that shaped the US Lend-Lease Act, the Bretton Woods institutions (World Bank and IMF), and the postwar British loan. Good biographies of Keynes include Roy Harrod, *The Life of John Maynard Keynes* (London: Macmillan, 1951); D. E. Moggridge, *Maynard Keynes: An Economist's Biography* (London: Routledge, 1992); and Robert Skidelsky, *John Maynard Keynes*, 3 vols. (New York: Viking, 1983, 1994, 2000).

4. See, for example, Robert Skidelsky, *Keynes: The Return of the Master* (New York: Public Affairs, 2009); Roger E. Backhouse and Bradley W. Bateman, *Capitalist Revolutionary* (Cambridge: Harvard University Press, 2011); and Peter Clarke, *Keynes: The Rise, Fall and Return of the 20th Century's Most Influential Economist* (New York: Bloomsbury, 2009). Also worth seeking out is Richard Posner, "How I Became a Keynesian," *New Republic*, September 23, 2009.

5. Keynes, "The End of Laissez Faire" (1926), *CW*, 9:287–88; *The General Theory of Employment, Interest and Money* (1936), *CW*, 7:372; and "National Self Sufficiency" (1933), *CW*, 11:239. As Keynes wrote to Hayek, "Your greatest danger ahead is the probable practical failure of the application of your philosophy in the U.S. in a fairly extreme form." (June 28, 1944), *CW*, 27:387.

6. Keynes, "Poverty in Plenty: Is the Economic System Self-Adjusting?"(1934), *CW*, 13:487; *General Theory*, *CW*, 7:379–80; "Am I a Liberal?" (1925), *CW*, 9:304; Harrod, *Life of John Maynard Keynes*, 191; Keynes to Hayek, *CW*, 27:385.

7. John Gerard Ruggie, "International Regimes, Transactions, and Change: Embedded Liberalism in the Post-War Economic Order," *International Organization* 36 (1982): 393. Ruggie initially attributed the concept to Karl Polanyi in his *The Great Transformation*.

8. Keynes, "Post-war Currency Policy" (September 8, 1941), *CW*, 25:31.

9. John Hicks, "Mr. Keynes and the 'Classics': A Suggested Interpretation," *Econometrica* 5:2 (April 1937): 147–59. See also Michel De Vroey and Kevin D. Hoover, *The IS-LM Model: Its Rise, Fall, and Strange Persistence* (Durham: Duke University Press, 2004).

10. Marjorie S. Turner, *Joan Robinson and the Americans* (Armonk, NY: M. E. Sharpe, 1989), 110–12. See also Alan Coddington, "Keynesian Economics: The Search for First Principles," *Journal of Economic Literature* 14:2 (December 1976): 1258–73. Several dissident branches of economics sought to pursue the ideas of the "original Keynes," most notably those known as the post-Keynesians. See Victoria Chick, *Macroeconomics after Keynes: A Reconsideration of the General Theory* (Cambridge: MIT Press, 1983).

11. A. W. Phillips, "The Relationship between Unemployment and the Rate of Change of Money Wage Rates in the United Kingdom, 1861–1975," *Econometrica* 25 (1958): 283–99. Actually, this relationship between the price level and economic activity had been observed by economists in earlier eras, including Irving Fisher, who, in 1926, reported "a genuine and straightforward causal relationship" between employment and the price level. Irving Fisher, "A Statistical Relation between Unemployment and Price Changes," *International Labor Review* 13:6 (1926): 785–92. In 1960 an influential paper by Paul Samuelson and Robert Solow ("Analytical Aspects of Inflation," *American Economic Review* 52:2: 177–94) derived a Phillips curve for the United States

and discussed possible trade-offs attributable to policy (191–93). In retrospect, the argument seems qualified. (Phillips, incidentally, did not hold the view that the relationship he described could be exploited in this way.)

12. Milton Friedman, "The Role of Monetary Policy," *American Economic Review* 53 (1968): 1–17; Edmund S. Phelps, "Phillips Curves, Expectation of Inflation, and Optimal Employment over Time," *Economica* 34 (1967): 254–81.

13. Alan Blinder, "The Anatomy of Double-Digit Inflation in the 1970s," in *Inflation: Causes and Effects*, ed. Robert E. Hall, 261–82 (Chicago: University of Chicago Press, 1982); Olivier Blanchard "Why Does Money Affect Output?" in *Handbook of Monetary Economics*, ed. Benjamin Friedman and Frank Hahn (Amsterdam: Elsevier Science Publishers, 1990), 779–835; Alan Blinder, "The Fall and Rise of Keynesian Economics," *Economic Record* 64 (1988): 281–82. For critiques of the natural rate hypothesis, see George P. Brockway "Are You Naturally Unemployed?," *New Leader* 75:10 (1992); and David M. Gordon, "Six-Percent Unemployment Ain't Natural: Demystifying the Idea of a Rising 'Natural Rate of Employment,'" *Social Research* 52:2 (1987). Critiques of the emergent macroeconomic consensus in general include Gerald Epstein and Herbert Gintis, eds., *Macroeconomic Policy after the Conservative Era* (New York: Cambridge University Press, 1995); and Samuel Bowles, David M. Gordon, and Thomas E. Weisskopf, "Business Ascendency and Economic Impasse: A Structural Retrospective on Conservative Economics, 1979–87," *Journal of Economic Perspectives* 3:1 (1989).

14. Robert Lucas, "Expectations and the Neutrality of Money," *Journal of Economic Theory* 4 (April 1972): 103–24; Robert Lucas, "Econometric Policy Evaluation: A Critique," in *The Phillips Curve and Labor Markets: Carnegie-Rochester Conference Series on Public Policy 1*, ed. Karl Brunner and Allan Meltzer (New York: American Elsevier, 1976),19–46; Thomas Sargent and Neil Wallace, "Rational Expectations, the Optimal Monetary Instrument, and the Optimal Money Supply Rule," *Journal of Political Economy* 83 (April 1975): 241–54; Robert Barro, "Unanticipated Money, Output, and the Price Level in the United States," *Journal of Political Economy* 85 (August 1978): 549–80; Robert Lucas and Thomas Sargent, eds., *Rational Expectations and Econometric Practice* (Minneapolis: University of Minnesota Press, 1981); Preston Miller, ed., *The Rational Expectations Revolution* (Cambridge: MIT Press, 1994).

15. John Muth, "Rational Expectations and the Theory of Price Movements," *Econometrica* 29:3 (July 1961): 316; George Evans and Seppo Honkapohja, "An Interview with Thomas J. Sargent," *Macroeconomic Dynamics* 9 (2005): 566.

16. Robert Lucas and Thomas Sargent, "After Keynesian Macroeconomics," *Federal Reserve Bank of Minneapolis Quarterly Review* 3:2 (1979): 1–16; Thomas Sargent, "Rational Expectations and the Reconstruction of Macroeconomics," *Federal Reserve Bank of Minneapolis Quarterly Review* 4:3 (1980). See also Alan Blinder, "Keynes, Lucas, and Scientific Progress," *American Economic Review* 77:2 (1987): 130–36; Blinder, "Fall and Rise of Keynesian Economics"; R. J. Gordon, "What Is New Keynesian Economics?" *Journal of Economic Literature* 28 (1990): 1115–71.

17. James Tobin, for example, saw very little of Keynes left: "If I had a copyright on who could use the term 'Keynesian' I wouldn't allow them to use it." James Tobin, interviewed in Brian Snowdon, Howard Vane, and Peter Wynarczyk, *A Modern Guide to Macroeconomics: An Introduction to Competing Schools of Thought* (Aldershot, UK: Edward Elgar, 1994), 132. Gregory Mankiw reaches a similar conclusion, but with approval: "Keynes might not recognize the new Keynesians as Keynesians at all." Ibid., 338.

18. See Keynes, *General Theory*, *CW*, 7:156–58 for the "beauty contest" analogy and more; on "animal spirits," *General Theory, CW*, 7:161–62. See also George Akerlof and Robert Shiller, *Animal Spirits* (Princeton: Princeton University Press, 2009), 133–34.

19. Risk means that although the future cannot be predicted with certainty, there are nevertheless distinct, accurate probabilities that can be assigned to all possible outcomes, like the chance of rolling any particular number from the toss of two fair dice.

20. Clarke, *Keynes*, 154; Skidelsky, *Keynes: Return of the Master*, 75, 83; Hyman Minsky, *John Maynard Keynes* (New York: Columbia University Press, 1975), 31; Allan Meltzer, *Keynes' Monetary Theory: A Different Interpretation* (Cambridge: Cambridge University Press, 1988), 9. See also Jochen Runde and Sohei Mizuhara, *The Philosophy of Keynes's Economics: Probability, Uncertainty and Convention* (London: Routledge, 2003).

21. John Maynard Keynes, "The General Theory of Employment," (February 1937), *CW*, 14:122 (quote); see also 113–14, for a discussion of the importance of uncertainty, such as "the prospect of a European war" or "the rate of interest twenty years hence" or "the obsolescence of a new invention," matters of which "there is no scientific basis on which to form any calculable probability whatsoever." See also *General Theory, CW*, 7, chap. 12.

22. Friedrich von Hayek, "The Pretence of Knowledge," Nobel Prize in Economics documents, 1974–2, Nobel Prize Committee; Friedrich von Hayek, "The Use of Knowledge in Society," *American Economic Review* 35:4 (September 1945): 519–30; Frank Knight, *Risk, Uncertainty and Profit* (1921, repr., Chicago: University of Chicago Press, 1971), 19, 20, 198. 232–33, 268, 287–88, 293. See also Roman Frydman and Michael D. Goldberg, *Imperfect Knowledge Economics: Exchange Rates and Risk* (Princeton: Princeton University Press, 2007), 3, 15.

23. Karl Brunner and Allan H. Meltzer, *Money in the Economy: Issues in Monetary Analysis* (Cambridge: Cambridge University Press, 1993), 40, 42, 45, 61; Michael C. Lovell, "Tests of the Rational Expectations Hypothesis," *American Economic Review* 76:1 (1986): 122; Kevin D. Hoover, "Two Types of Monetarism," *Journal of Economic Literature* 22:1 (1984): 70–71. See also James Cover, "Asymmetric Effects of Positive and Negative Money Supply Shocks," *Quarterly Journal of Economics* 107:4 (1992): 1278–79.

24. Thomas Sargent, *The Conquest of American Inflation* (Princeton: Princeton University Press, 1999), 133. Roman Frydman and Michael D. Goldberg, *Imperfect Knowledge Economics: Exchange Rates and Risk* (Princeton: Princeton University Press, 2007), 54; for more discussions of empirical failures, see 106, 113–14, 126, 132, 138, 140, 203; note that this book, with its repeated emphasis on failures "particularly apparent in financial markets" (29), was written before the financial crisis. Not surprisingly, the authors then revisited these themes; see Roman Frydman and Michael Goldberg, *Beyond Mechanical Markets: Asset Price Swings, Risk, and the Role of the State* (Princeton: Princeton University Press, 2011), "gross empirical failures," 52; see also 102, 139, 196.

25. Knight, *Risk, Uncertainty and Profit*, 19, 242; see also 231, 233, 241. See also Jonathan Kirshner, "Rationalist Explanations for War?" *Security Studies* 10:1 (2000): 143–50.

26. David Colander, Michael Goldberg, Armin Haas, Katarina Juselius, Alan Kirman, Thomas Lux, and Brigitte Sloth, "The Financial Crisis and the Systemic Failure of the Economics Profession," *Critical Review* 21:2–3 (2009): 256; Mervyn King, "Monetary Policy: Practice Ahead of Theory," May 17, 2005, reprinted in *Bank of England Quarterly Bulletin* (summer 2005), 4. As one early critic observed, rational expectations assumes "that economic agents not only know the relevant current and past observations, plus the future values of selected time series, but also have whatever additional knowledge is required to transform this information into objectively unbiased conditional expectations of the time series to be predicted." Benjamin Friedman, "Optimal Expectations and the Extreme Information Assumptions of 'Rational Expectations' Macromodels," *Journal of Monetary Economics* 5 (January 1979): 26–27, 38. Recent critics have continued to hammer away at the utter implausibility of these assumptions (to little effect on the discipline as a whole), noting that they imply "all market participants would have discovered an overarching causal mechanism that characterizes aggregate outcomes, as well as how the causal factors evolve over time." Frydman and Goldberg, *Imperfect Knowledge Economics*, 52 (quote), also 4, 6, 8, 28; see also Frydman and Goldberg, *Beyond Mechanical Markets*, 56, 64, 65.

27. Simon Johnson and James Kwak, *13 Bankers: The Wall Street Takeover and the Next Financial Meltdown* (New York: Random House, 2010), 68–70; Sebastian Mallaby, *More Money*

Than God: Hedge Funds and the Making of a New Elite (New York: Penguin, 2010), 105, 107; Frydman and Goldberg, *Beyond Mechanical Markets*, 81–2, 94, 102 (and see esp. additional sources within).

28. John Quiggin, *Zombie Economics: How Dead Ideas Still Walk among Us* (Princeton: Princeton University Press, 2010), 36 (first quote). See also Randall S. Kroszner and Robert J. Shiller, *Reforming US Financial Markets: Reflections before and beyond Dodd-Frank* (Cambridge: MIT Press, 2011) on the efficient markets hypothesis as a cause of deregulation, 21, 22, 30; Paul Davidson, *The Keynes Solution: The Path to Global Economic Prosperity* (New York: St. Martin's, 2009), 1, 2 (second quote).

29. Matthew Sherman, "A Short History of Financial Deregulation in the United States," Center for Economic and Policy Research Report, July 2009, 4–6; Amar Bhidé, "An Accident Waiting to Happen," *Critical Review* 21:2–3 (2009): 228; Krippner, *Capitalizing on Crisis*, 22.

30. Key legislation included the Depository Institutions Deregulation and Monetary Control Act of 1980, which ended interest rate ceilings on deposits, and the Garn-St. Germain Depository Institutions Act of 1982, which deregulated savings-and-loans associations. Sherman, "Short History of Financial Deregulation," 7; Kroszner and Shiller, *Reforming US Financial Markets*, 20, 25; Krippner, *Capitalizing on Crisis*, 58–59, 79, 81, 100.

31. Riccardo Rebonato, *Plight of the Fortune Tellers: Why We Need to Manage Financial Risk Differently* (Princeton: Princeton University Press, 2007), 119–20; Richard S. Grossman, *Unsettled Account: The Evolution of Banking in the Industrialized World since 1800* (Princeton: Princeton University Press, 2010), 266, 272, 281; Financial Crisis Inquiry Commission, *The Financial Crisis Inquiry Report* (New York: Public Affairs, 2011), 36; Sherman, "Financial Deregulation," 8; Bhidé, "Accident Waiting to Happen," 233–34.

32. Peter Truell, "New York Fed Official Resigns over Article in the *Times*," *New York Times*, July 21, 1995; Alan Greenspan, *The Age of Turbulence* (New York: Penguin Press, 2007), 198–99, 257, 375–76 (includes quote from paragraph above). On Gramm-Leach-Bliley and increased systemic risk, see Aigbe Akhigbe and Ann Marie Whyte, "The Gramm-Leach-Bliley Act of 1999: Risk Implications for the Financial Services Industry," *Journal of Financial Research* 27:3 (Fall 2004): 435–46.

33. Katrina Brooker, "Citi's Creator, Alone with His Regrets," *New York Times*, January 3, 2010; Jeff Madrick, "A Big Banker's Belated Change of Heart," *New York Times*, July 29, 2012. On Gramm, who has experienced no change of heart in the wake of the financial crisis, see Eric Lipton and Stephen Labaton, "Deregulator Looks Back, Unswayed," *New York Times* November 17, 2008.

34. Alan Greenspan, "Financial Derivatives," Remarks before the Futures Industry Association, Boca Raton, Florida, March 19, 1999.

35. "Taming the Derivatives Beast: The Dangers of Financial Derivatives," *Economist*, May 23, 1992; US Government Accountability Office (GAO), Report to Congressional Requesters, *Financial Derivatives: Actions Needed to Protect the Financial System* (May 18, 1994), 11, 14–15, 39, 124, 126–27.

36. Floyd Norris, "Orange County Crisis Jolts Bond Market," *New York Times*, December 8, 1994; "Today, Orange County . . . ," *Businessweek*, December 19, 1994; GAO, Report to Congressional Committees, *Financial Derivatives: Actions Taken or Proposed since May 1994* (November 1, 1996), 7, 8, 12, 15, 31, 32, 85.

37. Saul Hansell, "GAO Seeks Sweeping Rules for Derivatives," *New York Times*, May 10, 1994; Lipton and Labaton, "Deregulator Looks Back, Unswayed"; Bethany McClean and Joe Nocera, *All the Devils Are Here: The Hidden History of the Financial Crisis* (New York: Penguin, 2010), 63, 67; Financial Crisis Inquiry Commission, *Financial Crisis Inquiry Report*, 55.

38. Ryan Chittum, "Audit Interview: James L. Bothwell," *Columbia Journalism Review*, July 14, 2009; Sherman, "Financial Deregulation," 10–11; For an example of Born's warnings, see Brett

D. Fromson and Cindy Skrzycki, "CFTC Head Assails Bill Curbing Agency's Powers; Unregulated Markets Called Threat to System," *Washington Post*, February 28, 1997. See also Financial Crisis Inquiry Commission, *Financial Crisis Inquiry Report*, 47–48; McClean and Nocera, *All the Devils Are Here*, 98, 100, 104–6, 109.

39. Alan Greenspan, "The Regulation of OTC Derivatives," Testimony before the Committee on Banking and Financial Services, US House of Representatives," July 24, 1998, 3–5.

40. President's Working Group on Financial Markets, "Over-the-Counter Derivatives Markets and the Commodity Exchange Act," report, November 9, 1999. "William J. Rainer, the new chairman of the Commodity Futures Trading Commission, will leave over-the counter-derivatives alone, a policy that the banking industry has been demanding since last year." Dean Anason, "Futures Commission Head: OTC Oversight Unnecessary," *American Banker*, December 8, 1999.

41. Gramm's wife, Wendy, served on Enron's board of directors and was a member of its audit committee.

42. Chittum, "Audit Interview: James L. Bothwell"; Lipton and Labaton, "Deregulator Looks Back, Unswayed"; Sherman, "Financial Deregulation," 11.

43. Roger Lowenstein, *When Genius Failed: The Rise and Fall of Long-Term Capital Management* (New York: Random House, 2000); Donald MacKenzie, *An Engine, Not a Camera: How Financial Models Shape Markets* (Cambridge: MIT Press, 2006), chap. 8; Sebastian Mallaby, *More Money Than God*, 226.

44. Greenspan, *Age of Turbulence*, 371. In *Citizen Kane* (1941), Boss Jim Gettys tells Charles Foster Kane (Orson Welles), "If it was anybody else, I'd say what's going to happen to you would be a lesson to you. Only you're going to need more than one lesson. And you're going to get more than one lesson."

4. Seeds of Discord: The Asian Financial Crisis

1. Lawrence Summers, "WTO Financial Services Negotiations," talk, Congressional Economic Leadership Institute luncheon, August 12, 1997; Carmen Reinhart and Kenneth Rogoff, *This Time Is Different: Eight Centuries of Financial Folly* (Princeton: Princeton University Press, 2009), 155 (financial crises); Darren McDermott and Leslie Lopez, "Malaysia Imposes Sweeping Currency Controls: Such Capital Restrictions Win Credence in Wake of Financial Turmoil," *Wall Street Journal*, September 2, 1998 (condition of membership).

2. On these themes, see Jonathan Kirshner, ed., *Monetary Orders: Ambiguous Economics, Ubiquitous Politics* (Ithaca: Cornell University Press, 2003).

3. On the central role of ideas and of the elite convergence toward the ideology of capital liberalization, see Rawi Abdelal, *Capital Rules: The Construction of Global Finance* (Cambridge: Harvard University Press, 2007), and also Jeffrey M. Chwieroth, *Capital Ideas: The IMF and the Rise of Financial Liberalization* (Princeton: Princeton University Press, 2010).

4. As Susan Strange argued, financial globalization served to increase US structural power at the expense of other states. Susan Strange, "Finance, Information, and Power," *Review of International Studies* 16:3 (July 1990).

5. The Mexican crisis, which had pronounced similarities with the Asian financial crisis that would soon follow, was famously dubbed at the time the "first financial crisis of the twenty-first century," that is, a crisis associated with massive flows of fast-moving, increasingly uninhibited global financial capital. It was contained in part by massive loan guarantees by the Clinton administration and the IMF. The contrast of the swift and generous aid provided by the United States to Mexico to the harsh conditions imposed on distant Asian nations could only add to the resentments subsequently felt by the latter. Guillermo Ortiz Martinez, "What Lessons Does the Mexican Crisis Hold for Recovery in Asia?," *Finance and Development* 35:2 (June 1998); see also Alexandre Lamfalussy, *Financial Crises in Emerging Markets* (New Haven: Yale University Press, 2000).

6. Alan Greenspan, "The Current Asia Crisis and the Dynamics of International Finance," Testimony before the Committee on Banking and Financial Services, US House of Representatives, January 30, 1998; see also his similar testimony before the Senate Foreign Relations Committee, February 12, 1998.

7. Eisuke Sakakibara, "Reform of the International Financial System," speech, Manila Framework Meeting, Melbourne, Australia, March 26, 1999.

8. The term "Washington consensus," for example, the label used to describe the cocktail of orthodox economic policies prescribed for developing countries, was coined in 1989. See John Williamson, "What Washington Means by Policy Reform," in *Latin American Adjustment: How Much has Happened*, ed. John Williamson (Washington, DC: Institute for International Economics, 1990); see also John Williamson, "The Strange History of the Washington Consensus," *Journal of Post-Keynesian Economics* 27:2 (Winter 2004–5).

9. Nicholas Kristof and David Sanger, "How US Wooed Asia to Let Cash Flow in," *New York Times*, February 16, 1999.

10. Kristof and Sanger, "How US Wooed Asia" (quote); "US to Urge Financial Liberalization at WTO Talks," *Asia Pulse*, August 13, 1997.

11. William Barnes, *South China Morning Post* (Hong Kong), January 19, 1994, 12 (quotes); Paul Jacob, "APEC Finance Ministers to Meet in Hawaii in March," *Straits Times*, January 18, 1994; Sue Kendall, "Bentsen Urges Asian Ministers to Speak Their Mind," Agence France-Presse, March 19, 1994; Tim Cribb, "Thorny Issues Await APEC Finance Ministers," Agence France-Presse, March 20, 1994 (comments of Asian ministers).

12. Anne Davies, "APEC Determined to Avoid Another Mexico," *Sydney Morning Herald*, April 17, 1995 (quotes); Ralf J. Leiteritz, "Ideas, Interests, and Power: The International Monetary Fund and Capital Account Liberalization" (unpublished paper, 2004).

13. Kristof and Sanger, "How US Wooed Asia," (Chile, Korea); Summers, "WTO Financial Services Negotiations," (Summers quotes); Kenneth Klee and Rich Thomas with Stefan Theil, "Defending the One True Faith," *Newsweek,* September 14, 1998, 22 (last quotes).

14. Abdelal, *Capital Rules*, esp. 129, 138, 140–43; Chwieroth, *Capital Ideas*, 186, 191–92.

15. Barry Eichengreen and Harold James, "Monetary and Financial Reform in Two Eras of Globalization," in *Globalization in Historical Perspective*, ed. Michael Bordo, Alan Taylor, and Jeffrey Williamson, 515–44 (Chicago: University of Chicago Press, 2003), 535; Jagdish Bhagwati, "Lessons from the East Asian Experience," in *Building an Infrastructure for Financial Instability*, ed. Eric Rosengren and John Jordan, Federal Reserve Bank of Boston Conference Series, no. 44, June 2000, 25; Robert Wade and Frank Veneroso, "The Gathering World Slump and the Battle over Capital Controls," *New Left Review,* September/October 1998, 13–42 (Volcker); Alan Blinder "Eight Steps to a New Financial Order," *Foreign Affairs* 78:5 (September/October 1999): 57. On Lissakers, see Abdelal, *Capital Rules*, 139; Chwieroth, *Capital Ideas*, 193; and Leiteritz, "Ideas, Interests, and Power," 22. On all of these issues, see also Paul Blustein, *The Chastening: Inside the Crisis That Rocked the Global Financial System and Humbled the IMF* (New York: Public Affairs, 2001), 7, 30, 47, 48.

16. "The Bottom Line," *Banker* 144 (November 1994): 96 (Lipsky); "Communiqué of the Interim Committee of the Board of Governors of the International Monetary Fund," press release no. 95/51, October 8, 1995; "Statement of G7 Finance Ministers and Central Bank Governors," Washington, D.C., April 27, 1997; Alex Brummer, "IMF Aims at Capital Markets," *Guardian,* September, 30, 1996. On the importance of 1995 within the IMF, see Abdelal, *Capital Rules*, 143; and Chwieroth, *Capital Ideas,* 199.

17. "IMF Wins Mandate to Cover Capital Accounts," *IMF Survey*, May 12, 1997, 131–32; "Forces of Globalization Must be Embraced," *IMF Survey*, May 26, 1997; "IMF Given Role in

Fostering Freer Capital Flows," *IMF Survey,* October 6, 1997, esp. 291, 301–2. See also Devesh Kapur, "The IMF: A Cure or a Curse?" *Foreign Policy* 111 (Summer 1998).

18. Econ 102 *might* take on questions of distributive justice that emerge from free trade policy, especially within societies, or issues such as dynamic comparative advantage. But the basic case for free trade in goods is quite robust.

19. Jagdish Bhagwati, "The Capital Myth," *Foreign Affairs* 77:3 (May/June 1998): 9, 12 (quote).

20. Jonathan Kirshner, "The Inescapable Politics of Money," in Kirshner, *Monetary Orders,* 5. It is important to note the qualified nature of this argument. The claim is not that capital flows are bad but rather that completely deregulated capital would lead to a suboptimally high level of flows.

21. Keynes, *Treatise on Money,* vol. 2, *The Applied Theory of Money* (1930), *CW,* 6:272; "Postwar Currency Policy" (September 8, 1941), *CW,* 25:27, 28, 30, 31; "Proposals for an International Currency Union" (November 18, 1941), *CW,* 25:46, 52, 53; "Letter to Roy Harrod" (April 19, 1942), *CW,* 25:149; "Speech before the House of Lords" (May 18, 1943), *CW,* 25:272; "Speech before the House of Lords" (May 23, 1944), *CW,* 26:17. See also Helleiner, *States and the Reemergence,* chap. 2: "Bretton Woods and the Endorsement of Capital Controls," 25–50.

22. See, for example, Barry Eichengreen, James Tobin, and Charles Wyplosz, "Two Cases for Sand in the Wheels of International Finance," *Economic Journal* 105 (1995): 162–72; and Mahbub ul Haq, Inge Kaul, and Isabelle Grunberg, eds. *The Tobin Tax: Coping with Financial Volatility* (New York: Oxford University Press, 1996).

23. Dani Rodrik, "Who Needs Capital-Account Mobility?," in *Should the IMF Pursue Capital-Account Convertibility?,* Essays in International Finance, no. 207, International Finance Section, Princeton University, NJ, May 1998, http://www.princeton.edu/~ies/IES_Essays/E207.pdf, 61.

24. See, for example, Rudiger Dornbusch, "Malaysia: Was It Different?," NBER Working Paper no. 8325, National Bureau of Economic Research, Cambridge, MA, June 2001, http://www.nber.org/papers/w8325.pdf, 3. Another proponent of decontrol does find modest support for a relationship between capital openness and growth, but then only under qualified circumstances. See Sebastian Edwards, "Capital Mobility and Economic Performance: Are the Emerging Economies Different?," NBER Working Paper no. 8076, National Bureau of Economic Research, Cambridge, MA, January 2001, http://www.nber.org/papers/w8076.pdf. For still more skepticism and caution, see Richard N. Cooper, "Should Capital Account Convertibility Be a World Objective?," in Kenen, *Should the IMF Pursue Capital Account Convertibility?*; and Richard N. Cooper, *Should Capital Controls Be Banished?*, Brookings Papers on Economic Activity 1 (1999), http://www.brookings.edu/~/media/projects/bpea/spring%201999/1999a_bpea_cooper.pdf.

25. See, for example, John Williamson and Molly Mahar, *A Survey of Financial Liberalization,* Essays in International Finance, no. 211, International Finance Section, Princeton University, NJ, November 1998, http://www.princeton.edu/~ies/IES_Essays/E211.pdf; Ariel Buria, "An Alternative Approach to Financial Crises," Essays in International Finance, no. 212, International Finance Section, Princeton University, NJ, February 1999, http://www.princeton.edu/~ies/IES_Essays/E212.pdf; Thomas D. Willett, "International Financial Markets as Sources of Crises or Discipline: The Too Much Too Late Hypothesis," Essays in International Finance, no. 218, International Finance Section, Princeton University, NJ, May 2000, http://www.princeton.edu/~ies/IES_Essays/E218.pdf.

26. Jagdish Bhagwati, Testimony before the US House of Representatives, Committee on Financial Services, Subcommittee on Domestic and International Monetary Policy, Trade and Technology Tuesday, April 1, 2003; Dani Rodrik and Arvind Subramanian, "Why Did Financial Globalization Disappoint?," *IMF Staff Papers* 56:1 (2009): 113, 116, 125, 136.

27. Mark Blyth, "The Political Power of Financial Ideas: Transparency, Risk, and Distribution in Global Finance," in Kirshner, *Monetary Orders*; Reinhart and Rogoff, *This Time Is Different*; Charles P. Kindleberger, *Manias, Panics, and Crashes: A History of Financial Crises* (New York: Basic Books, 1978).

28. World Bank, *The East Asian Miracle* (Washington, DC: World Bank, 1993); note, for example, "pragmatic orthodoxy in macroeconomic management," 106–23; Paul Bluestein, *The Chastening: Inside the Crisis that Rocked the Global Financial System and Humbled the IMF* (New York: Public Affairs, 2001), 51, 53 (first quotes). "International Capital Markets Charting a Steadier Course," *IMF Survey*, September 23, 1996, 293, 294 ("resilient," "disciplined"); "ASEAN's Sound Fundamentals Bode Well for Sustained Growth," *IMF Survey*, November 25, 1996, 1; "IMF Wins Mandate," *IMF Survey*, May 12, 1997, 129, 130; Nathaniel Harrison, "IMF Policymakers Weigh Free Capital Flow in Light of Thai Crisis," Agence France-Presse, September 23, 1997.

29. Including from the G24 group of developing nations, which issued a cautionary statement at the Hong Kong meeting. With reference to the ongoing financial crisis, "Ministers emphasize that the capital account liberalization process could put additional stress on the economies that are already straining to adjust to globalization." Intergovernmental Group of Twenty-Four on International Monetary Affairs, "Communiqué," September 20, 1997, http://www.imf.org/external/np/cm/1997/cm970920.htm, 2.

30. Summers, "WTO Financial Services Negotiations"; International Monetary Fund, "*The IMF and Recent Capital Account Crises: Indonesia, Korea, Brazil* (Washington, DC: IMF, 2003), 18 (quote); Abdelal, *Capital Rules*, 156; Chwieroth, *Capital Ideas*, 203.

31. Stanley Fischer, "Capital Account Liberalization and the Role of the IMF," IMF Seminar, Hong Kong, September 19, 1997; Harrison, "IMF Policymakers Weigh Free Capital Flow" (Rubin); John Lipsky, "Causes and Implications of the Asian Currency Crisis," Testimony before House Committee on Banking and Financial Services, November 13, 1997; Louis Uchitelle, "IMF May Be Closer to Lending-Curb Idea," *New York Times* February 3, 1998 (Garten). See also "US to Urge Financial Liberalization at WTO Talks" (following the Thai currency crisis, Summers said, "The view that liberalization would trigger currency speculation is mistaken"); and Lawrence Summers, "Go with the Flow," *Financial Times*, March 11, 1998. "In retrospect, we overshot, and in retrospect there was a certain degree of arrogance," Garten would later observe. Kristof and Sanger, "How the US Wooed Asia."

32. "An 'Irreversible Trend': Seminar Discusses the Orderly Path to Capital Account Liberalization," *IMF Survey*, March 23, 1998, 82; US Treasury, "Deputy Secretary Summers Remarks before the International Monetary Fund," March 9, 1998; Chwieroth, *Capital Ideas*, 204–5; Abdelal, *Capital Rules*, 157–58. Summers told Abdelal that despite continued Treasury support for the amendment, it became a question of allocating "scarce political capital" (159).

33. See, for example, Paul Krugman, "Saving Asia: It's Time to Get Radical," *Fortune*, September 7, 1998; Jonathan Kirshner, "Culprit Is Unregulated Capital," *Los Angeles Times*, September 13, 1998; Robert Reich, "The Real Policy Makers," *New York Times*, September 29, 1998; and analyses in *Asian Wall Street Journal*, September 7, 1998; and *Business Week*, September 28, 1998.

34. James Crotty and Gerald Epstein, "A Defense of Capital Controls in Light of the Asian Financial Crisis," *Journal of Economic Issues* 33:2 (June 1999): 427–33; Barry Eichengreen, *Toward a New Financial Architecture: A Post-Asia Agenda* (Washington, DC: Institute for International Economics, 1999); Paul Krugman, *The Return of Depression Economics* (New York: Norton, 1999); Benjamin Cohen, "Taming the Phoenix? Monetary Governance after the Crisis," in *The Asian Financial Crisis and the Architecture of Global Finance,* ed. Gregory W. Noble and John Ravenhill, 192–212 (Cambridge: Cambridge University Press, 2000).

35. Perhaps an inch at the IMF, but not a foot. On this general continuity, see Chwieroth, *Capital Ideas*, 226, 229.

36. On market fundamentalism, see, for example, *Far Eastern Economic Review*, July 16, 1998, 29. Alan Greenspan, "Do Efficient Financial Markets Mitigate Financial Crises?" remarks, Financial Markets Conference of the FRB of Atlanta, Sea Island, Georgia, October 19, 1999; Greenspan, "The Current Asia Crisis and the Dynamics of International Finance," Testimony before the US House of Representatives, Finance Committee, January 30, 1998; Greenspan, "The Current Asian Crisis and the Financial Resources of the IMF," Testimony before the US House of Representatives, Committee on Agriculture, May 21, 1998.

37. Stanley Fischer, "In Defense of the IMF: Specialized Tools for a Specialized Task," *Foreign Affairs* 77:4 (1998): 105; Fischer, "Proposals and IMF Actions to Reduce the Frequency of Crises," in Rosengren and Jordan, *Building an Infrastructure*. See also "Fischer Presents IMF Perspective on Origins, Implications of Asian Crisis," *IMF Survey*, January 26, 1998; and Fischer, "Capital Account Liberalization and the Role of the IMF," in Kenen, *Should the IMF Pursue Capital Account Convertibility?* On the IMF more generally, see International Monetary Fund, *International Capital Markets: Developments, Prospects, and Key Policy Issues* (Washington, DC: IMF, 1998), esp. 6, 11, 57, 63, 73, 148–50; also International Monetary Fund, *World Economic Outlook: Financial Turbulence and the World Economy* (Washington, DC: IMF, 1998), esp. 16–18, 101–2. It should be noted, however, that in the wake of the crisis the World Bank has been willing to at least address the issue of the possible benefits of some control over short-term capital flows. See World Bank, *Global Economic Prospects and the Developing Countries, 1998/99: Beyond Financial Crisis* (Washington, DC: World Bank, 1999), esp. xi–xii, xxi, 4, 123–24, 128, 142–52; also World Bank, *East Asia: The Road to Recovery* (Washington, Dc: World Bank, 1998), esp. 9–10, 16, 34.

38. Andrew Walter, *Governing Finance: East Asia's Adoption of International Standards* (Ithaca: Cornell University Press, 2008).

39. For early hints of this conflict, see David E. Sanger, "Gaining Currency: The Invisible Hand's New Strong Arm," *New York Times,* September 9, 1998. See also Richard Saludo, "Cold War over Hot Money," *Asiaweek*, September 18, 1998, in which the struggle between laissez-faire liberalism and state-led development is seen as "Cold War 2."

40. Andrew Sheng, *From Asian to Global Financial Crisis: An Asian Regulator's View of Unfettered Finance in the 1990s and 2000s* (Cambridge: Cambridge University Press, 2009), 162; Martin Feldstein, "Refocusing the IMF," *Foreign Affairs* 77:2 (1998): 24, 25, 27, 31, 32; Jeffrey D. Sachs, "Fixing the IMF Remedy," *Banker* (February 1998): 16–18; Bluestein, *Chastening*, 143–44, 155–56.

41. W. Max Corden, "The World Financial Crisis: Are the IMF Prescriptions Right?," in Horowitz and Heo, *International Financial Crisis,* 59–60; T. J. Pempel, conclusion to *The Politics of the Asian Economic Crisis*, ed. T. J. Pempel (Ithaca: Cornell University Press, 1999), 236–37; Ha-Joon Chang, Hong Jae Park, and Chul Gyue Yoo, "Interpreting the Korean Crisis: Financial Liberalization, Industrial Policy, and Corporate Governance," *Cambridge Journal of Economics* 22 (1998): esp. 739; Joseph E. Stiglitz, "Failure of the Fund: Rethinking the IMF Response," *Harvard International Review* (Summer 2001): 17, 18 ("power play"); Robert Gilpin, *The Challenge of Global Capitalism: The World Economy in the 21st Century* (Princeton: Princeton University Press, 2000), 157, 159; Donald Kirk, *Korean Crisis: Unraveling of the Miracle in the IMF Era* (New York: Palgrave, 1999), 35 ("imperialistic"), 36–38, 43, 46; Sheng, *From Asian to Global Financial Crisis*, 40 ("humiliation").

42. See Rawi Abdelal and Laura Alfaro, "Malaysia: Capital and Control," Harvard Business School, case 702-040, April 15, 2002; Marie-Aimée Tourres, *The Tragedy That Didn't Happen: Malaysia's Crisis Management and Capital Controls* (Kuala Lumpur: Institute of Strategic and International Studies, 2003).

43. Michel Camdessus, "Global Capital Flows: Raising the Returns and Reducing the Risks," address, World Affairs Council of Los Angeles, California, June 17, 1997.

44. Robert Wade, "The Asian Crisis and the Global Economy: Causes, Consequences, and Cure," *Current History* 97:622 (November 1998): 368 (Camdessus); International Monetary Fund, World Economic and Financial Surveys, *World Economic Outlook: Financial Turbulence and the World Economy* (October 1998), http://www.imf.org/external/pubs/ft/weo/weo1098/, 4 (setback); Abdelal and Alfaro, "Malaysia: Capital and Control," 11 (Summers); Alan Greenspan, "International Economic and Financial Systems," Testimony before the Committee on Banking and Financial Services, US House of Representatives, September 16, 1998.

45. Beth Duff-Brown, "Malaysia Defies Western Orthodoxy with Unorthodox Currency Controls," Associated Press, September 11, 1999 (aghast). See also Sheng, From Asian to Global Financial Crisis, 189, 194, 212–13, 215 (unanimous); Abdelal and Alfaro, "Malaysia: Capital and Control," 2, 11; Tourres, The Tragedy That Didn't Happen, 3, 104, 229–30, 234–5, 288; Mahani Zainal-Abidin, "Implications of the Malaysian Experience on Future International Financial Arrangements," ASEAN Economic Bulletin 17:2 (2000): esp. 143, 145; Ethan Kaplan and Dani Rodrik "Did the Malaysian Capital Controls Work?," NBER Working Paper no. 8142, National Bureau of Economic Research, Cambridge, MA, February 2001, http://www.nber.org/papers/w8142.pdf, 7; Bhagwati, "Lessons from the East Asian Experience." Contrast these (and a shelf's-worth of other studies) with the very modest fallback positions of the critics. See, for example, Dornbusch, "Malaysia: Was It Different," 4, 13; and especially Akira Ariyoshi, Karl Habermeier, Bernard Laurens, Inci Otker-Robe, Jorge Ivan Canales-Kriljenko, and Andrei Kirilenko, Capital Controls: Country Experiences with Their Use and Liberalization, International Monetary Fund Occasional Paper 190 (May 17, 2000), 15, 30, 31, 54, 101, 104, for the IMF's grudging, reluctant, qualified admission that the controls probably did no harm.

46. Robert Wade and Frank Veneroso, "The Gathering World Slump and the Battle over Capital Controls," *New Left Review* (September/October 1998) (Solomon Brothers, China); Kiichi Miyazawa, "Towards a New Financial Architecture," speech, Foreign Correspondents Club of Japan, December 15, 1998, 3; Christopher Johnstone, "Strained Alliance: US-Japan Diplomacy in the Asian Financial Crisis," *Survival* (Summer 1999): 132; Matthew Montagu-Pollock, "The Real Message in Miyazawa's Plan," *Asiamoney* (February 1999); Abdelal and Alfaro, "Malaysia," 12; Soari N. Katada, "Japan and Asian Monetary Regionalization: Cultivating a New Regional Leadership Role after the Asian Financial Crisis," *Geopolitics* 7:1 (Summer 2002): 87, 97 (cheers).

47. Bhagwati, "Lessons from the East Asian Experience," 22, 28 (quote); Katada, "Japan and Asian Monetary Regionalization," 86. See also Paul Bowles, "Asia's Post-Crisis Regionalism: Bringing the State Back In, Keeping the (United) States Out," *Review of International Political Economy* 9:2 (Summer 2002): 231, 248; Christopher W. Hughes, "Japanese Policy and the East Asian Crisis: Abject Defeat or Quiet Victory?," *Review of International Political Economy* 7:2 (Summer 2000): 241, 242. On Japan and the late 1980s, see Eric Helleiner, "Japan and the Changing Global Financial Order," *International Journal* 47 (Spring 1992): esp. 434–37.

48. Phillip Lipscy, "Japan's Asian Monetary Fund Proposal," *Stanford Journal of East Asian Affairs* 3:1 (Spring 2003): esp. 95–96; Eric Altbach "The Asian Monetary Fund Proposal: A Case Study in Japanese Regional Leadership," *JEI Report* 47 (December 19, 1997), 2, 10, 11; Michael J. Green, *Japan's Reluctant Realism: Foreign Policy Challenges in an Era of Uncertain Power* (New York: Palgrave, 2001), 259–60; Bluestein, *Chastening*, 79, 162, 164, 166; Sheng, *From Asian to Global Financial Crisis*, 33–34, 114; David E. Sanger, "Mr. Rubin's Long March to China," *New York Times,* September 28, 1997 (quote).

49. Alan Greenspan, "The Current Asian Crisis." See also Gary Hamilton, "Asian Business Networks in Transition: Or, What Alan Greenspan Does Not Know about the Asian Business Crisis," in Pempel, *Politics of the Asian Economic Crisis*.

50. Eisuke Sakakibara, "Reform of the International Financial System," speech, Manila Framework Meeting, Melbourne, Australia, March 26, 1999; Sakakibara, "Reform of the

International Financial Architecture," speech, Symposium on Building the Financial System of the 21st Century, Kyoto, Japan, June 25, 1999; Miyazawa, "Towards a New Financial Architecture"; Haruhiko Kuroda (vice-minister of finance), "Information Technology, Globalization, and International Financial Architecture," speech, Foreign Correspondents Club of Japan, June 5, 2000; Masaru Yoshitomi, "Policy Prescriptions for East Asia," in Rosengren and Jordan, *Building an Infrastructure for Financial Stability,* 235. See also Marc Castellano, "Two Years On: Evaluating Tokyo's Response to the East Asian Financial Crisis," *JEI Report* 30 (August 6, 1999); C. Fred Bergsten, "America's Two-Front Economic Conflict," *Foreign Affairs* 80:2 (July/August 1998): 21; Mark Beeson, "Mahathir and the Markets: Globalization and the Pursuit of Economic Autonomy in Malaysia," *Pacific Affairs* 73:2 (2000): 339, 348.

51. David Sanger, "US and Japanese Confer but Differ on Economic Cures," *New York Times,* September 6, 1998; Richard Higgott, "The Asian Economic Crisis: A Study in the Politics of Resentment," *New Political Economy* 3:3 (1998): 333–34, 339, 347, 351; William Grimes, "The Internationalization of the Yen and the New Politics of Monetary Insulation," in Kirshner, *Monetary Orders,* 188; Bowles, "Asia's Post-Crisis Regionalism," 230, 249.

52. Padma Desai, "Why Did the Ruble Collapse in August 1998?" *American Economic Review* 90:2 (May 2000): 52; International Monetary Fund, *Lessons from the Crisis in Argentina,* October 8, 2003, http://www.imf.org/external/np/pdr/lessons/100803.pdf, 3; Bluestein, *Chastening,* 9, 337, 348, 374; Eichengreen and James, "Monetary and Financial Reform," 536.

53. Sidney Weintraub, "Lessons from the Chile and Singapore Free Trade Agreements," in *Free Trade Agreements: US Strategies and Priorities,* ed. Jeffrey Schott, 79–92 (Washington, DC: Institute for International Economics, 2004), 87; Elizabeth Becker and Larry Rohter, "US and Chile Reach Free Trade Accord," *New York Times,* December 12, 2002; Wayne Arnold, "Rift on Capital Controls Snags Singapore Trade Pact," *New York Times,* January 9, 2003; Jagdish Bhagwati and Daniel Tarullo, "Ban on Capital Controls Is a Bad Trade-off," *Financial Times,* March 16, 2003.

5. The New American Model and the Financial Crisis

1. Financial Crisis Inquiry Commission (FCIC), *The Financial Crisis Inquiry Report: Final Report of the National Commission on the Causes of the Financial and Economic Crisis in the Unites States* (New York: Public Affairs, 2011), 354.

2. Following classical economic logic, market failure is grounds for government intervention. Even Adam Smith favored government regulation of interest rates. He thought that, left to its own devices, the free market would skew investment toward suboptimally risky enterprises. See, for example, David Levy, "Adam Smith's Case for Usury Laws," *History of Political Economy* 19:3 (Fall 1987): 18–27.

3. Greta R. Krippner, *Capitalizing on Crisis: The Political Origins of the Rise of Finance* (Cambridge: Harvard University Press, 2011), 3–4, 28–29; Simon Johnson and James Kwak, *13 Bankers: The Wall Street Takeover and the Next Financial Meltdown* (New York: Pantheon, 2010), 60; J. Bradford DeLong and Stephen Cohen, *The End of Influence: What Happens When Other Countries Have the Money* (New York: Basic Books, 2010), 110–11.

4. James Tobin, "On the Efficiency of the Financial System," *Lloyds Bank Review* 153 (July 1984).

5. FCIC, *Financial Crisis Inquiry Report,* xvii, 64–65; Johan A. Lybeck, *A Global History of the Financial Crash of 2007–10* (Cambridge: Cambridge University Press, 2011), 319; Nouriel Roubini and Stephen Mihm, *Crisis Economics: A Crash Course in the Future of Finance* (New York: Penguin, 2010), 68–69, 83.

6. Johnson and Kwak, *13 Bankers,* 5, 60–61, 115; FCIC, *Financial Crisis Inquiry Report,* 61–62; Joseph Stiglitz, *Freefall: America, Free Markets, and the Sinking of the World Economy* (New York: Norton 2010), 247.

7. Karen Ho, *Liquidated: An Ethnography of Wall Street* (Durham: Duke University Press, 2009), 40; Princeton University, Class of 2006 Survey Report; Johnson and Kwak, *13 Bankers*, 117; Roubini and Mihm, *Crisis Economics*, 191; Tobin, "On the Efficiency of the Financial System"; Richard Posner, *A Failure of Capitalism: The Crisis of '08 and the Descent into Depression* (Cambridge: Harvard University Press, 2009), 231.

8. Keynes, "National Self-Sufficiency" (*New Statesman and Nation* July 8 and 15, 1933), *CW*, 21:241, 242; see also Keynes, "My Early Beliefs" (*Two Memoirs* 1949), *CW*, 10:445).

9. Alan Greenspan, *The Age of Turbulence* (New York: Penguin, 2007), 185, 186, 214–18, 222–24, 233.

10. On these issues, see Maurice Obstfeld and Kenneth Rogoff, "The Unsustainable US Current Account Position Revisited," NBER Working Paper no. 10869, National Bureau of Economic Research, Cambridge, MA, October 2004, http://www.nber.org/papers/w10869.pdf; and William R. Cline, *The United States as a Debtor Nation* (Washington, DC: Institute for International Economics, 2005). Trade figures are from US Census Bureau, Foreign Trade Division, June 2012, US Department of Commerce.

11. FCIC, *Financial Crisis Inquiry Report*, 156; see also Herman Schwartz, *Subprime Nation: American Power, Global Capital, and the Housing Bubble* (Ithaca: Cornell University Press, 2009). Savings data are from the US Department of Commerce: Bureau of Economic Analysis, reprinted by the Federal Reserve Bank of St Louis, Economic Research Division.

12. Roubini and Mihm, *Crisis Economics*, 64–65, 69; Stiglitz, *Freefall*, 81–83, 85–87, 90–91, 128, 132; FCIC, *Financial Crisis Inquiry Report*, 38, 45.

13. CDOs, invented at Drexel-Burnham-Lambert in 1987, are assets created from a pool of otherwise unrelated debt instruments of varying risk. SIVs, invented at Citibank in 1988, are highly leveraged products aimed to find profits between the yields of short-term debt instruments and longer-term asset-backed securities. CDSs, invented at J. P. Morgan in 1994, were essentially insurance devices—techniques of spreading and transferring the risks of default. Data on CDS is from Bank for International Settlements, *BIS Quarterly Review* (December 2008): A101.

14. Stiglitz, *Freefall*, 92 (quote); Roubini and Mihm, *Crisis Economics*, 66–67; Johnson and Kwak, *13 Bankers*, 123–24, 126–27, 139.

15. Posner, *Failure of Capitalism*, 93–95, 98 (quote). Ho, *Liquidated*, 164, 252, 257, 290.

16. Ho, *Liquidated*, 298–300; US Senate, Permanent Subcommittee on Investigations, *Wall Street and the Financial Crisis: Anatomy of a Financial Collapse*, April 13, 2011, http://www.hsgac.senate.gov//imo/media/doc/Financial_Crisis/FinancialCrisisReport.pdf, 143, 318; Gillian Tett, *Fool's Gold: The Inside Story of J. P. Morgan and How Wall St. Greed Corrupted Its Bold Dream and Created a Financial Catastrophe* (New York: Free Press, 2009), 64, 92–93, 98–99; FCIC, *Financial Crisis Inquiry Report*, 8, 127, 132, 206.

17. Bethany McClean and Joe Nocera, *All the Devils Are Here: The Hidden History of the Financial Crisis* (New York: Penguin, 2010), 281 (quote); see also 8, 20, 242; Stiglitz, *Freefall*, 160 (second quote); Paul Davidson, *The Keynes Solution: The Path to Global Economic Prosperity* (New York: Palgrave, 2009), 24; Johnson and Kwak, *13 Bankers*, 81, 121; Posner, *Failure of Capitalism*, 41, 49–51, 56–57, 60.

18. Greenspan, *Age of Turbulence*, 372, 373–74 (quotes), also 370, 489–90; Ryan Chittum, "Audit Interview: James L. Bothwell," *Columbia Journalism Review*, July 14, 2009; David Wessel, *In Fed We Trust: Ben Bernanke's War on the Great Panic* (New York, Crown, 2009), 64 (quote); FCIC, *Financial Crisis Inquiry Report*, 28, 189; McClean and Nocera, *All the Devils Are Here*, 243. According to one account, Greenspan said he did not "know why the Federal Reserve has regulatory authority over banks" and questioned the need for margin requirements in stock accounts. Chittum, "Interview: Bothwell."

19. US Senate, *Wall Street and the Financial Crisis*, 40, 41; Greenspan, *Age of Turbulence*, 360, 367 (quotes), also 368, 371, 492; Alan Greenspan, "Economic Flexibility," remarks, National Italian American Foundation, Washington, D.C., October 12, 2005 (last quote).

20. International Monetary Fund (IMF), *Global Financial Stability Report: Market Developments and Issues,* Washington, DC (April 2006), 1, 32, 37, 41, 51, 52, 55–57, 62, 70, 71, 72, 74–76, 78, 81, 133.

21. IMF, *Global Financial Stability Report: Market Developments and Issues,* Washington, DC, (April 2007), 50, 54; IMF, *World Economic Outlook: Spillovers and Cycles in the Global Economy* (Washington, DC: IMF, April 2007), xii (quote), 1, 7, 12 (quote).

22. Douglas Clement, "Interview with Eugene Fama," Federal Reserve Bank of Minneapolis's *The Region* (December 1, 2007).

23. Robert Lucas, "Macroeconomic Priorities," *American Economic Review* 93:1 (March 2003): 1–14; Fama quote is from Clement, "Interview with Eugene Fama."

24. On the convergence (and confidence) of macroeconomic theory, see Michael Woodford, "Convergence in Macroeconomics: Elements of the New Synthesis," *American Economic Journal: Macroeconomics* 1:1 (2009): 267–79; Olivier Blanchard, "The State of Macro," *Annual Review of Economics* 1:1 (2009): 209–28; and Gregory Mankiw, "The Macroeconomist as Scientist and Engineer," *Journal of Economic Perspectives* 20:4 (2006): 29–46. (Mankiw notes the convergence but is less celebratory than the others.)

25. An excellent discussion of these issues can be found in the Senate hearing tasked with evaluating the state of macroeconomic theory in the wake of the crisis. Those providing testimony included Nobel laureate Robert Solow, who offered withering criticism, and one minority witness, V. V. Chari, who acknowledged that "this class of models failed to see the crisis coming" and "tended to deemphasize these kinds of financial crises"; but he nevertheless offered a spirited (if unconvincing) defense of the approach. "Building a Science of Economics for the Real World," Hearing before the Subcommittee on Investigations and Oversight, Committee on Science and Technology, House of Representatives, 111/2, July 20, 2012. See also "Agents of Change," *Economist*, July 22, 2010; Willem Buiter, "The Unfortunate Uselessness of Most 'State of the Art' Academic Monetary Economics," *Financial Times*, ft.com, http://blogs.ft.com/maverecon/2009/03/the-unfortunate-uselessness-of-most-state-of-the-art-academic-monetary-economics/#axzz2pwPvOQ00, March 3, 2009 (Buiter quotes Charles Goodhart on DSGE); Paul Krugman, "How Did Economists Get It So Wrong," *New York Times*, September 6, 2009; Barry Eichengreen, "The Last Temptation of Risk," *National Interest* (May/June 2009); David Colander, Michael Goldberg, Armin Haas, Katarina Juselius, Alan Kirman, Thomas Lux, and Brigitte Sloth, "The Financial Crisis and the Systemic Failure of the Economics Profession," *Critical Review* 21:2–3 (2009): 249–67; Robert Skidelsky, "How to Rebuild a Shamed Subject," *Financial Times*, August 5, 2009.

26. Raghuram G. Rajan, "Has Financial Development Made the World Riskier?" in *The Greenspan Era: Lessons for the Future, Symposium Sponsored by the Federal Reserve Bank of Kansas City* (Kansas City, MO: Federal Reserve Bank of Kansas City, 2005), 315–16 (quote), 318, 332, 336–39, 342, 345–46 (quotes), 350, 359 (quote); Raghuram G. Rajan and Luigi Zingales, *Saving Capitalism from the Capitalists: Unleashing the Power of Financial Markets to Spread Wealth and Create Opportunity* (Princeton: Princeton University Press, 2003).

27. Riccardo Rebonato, *Plight of the Fortune Tellers: Why We Need to Manage Financial Risk Differently* (Princeton: Princeton University Press, 2007), ix–x, 5–7, 137 (quote), 141, 145–46, 178; Emanuel Derman, *Models. Behaving. Badly.: Why Confusing Illusion with Reality Can Lead to Disaster, on Wall Street and in Life* (New York: Free Press, 2011), 153, 185 (quote); Stiglitz, *Freefall*, 94; Posner, *Failure of Capitalism*, 111; Tett, *Fool's Gold*, 34, 102–3 (quote).

28. See the discussants and general discussion following "Has Financial Development Made the World Riskier?" in *Greenspan Era: Lessons for the Future*, 371–97, (Summers quote, 387; Blinder, 394); FCIC, *Financial Crisis Inquiry Report*, 17; Justin Lahart, "Mr. Rajan Was Unpopular (but Prescient) at Greenspan Party," *Wall Street Journal*, January 2, 2009.

29. Edward Cowan, "Bush Group's Proposals on Banking Regulation," *New York Times*, December 24, 1983; Kenneth Noble, "Banking Regulatory Accord Set," *New York Times,* February 1, 1984; "Statement by Paul A. Volcker," House Subcommittee on Banking, Finance and Urban Affairs, April 17, 1985 (also April 24); William Greider, *The Secrets of the Temple: How the Federal Reserve Runs the Country* (New York: Touchstone, 1978), 666 (quotes); Nathaniel Nash, "Bank Curb Eased in Volcker Defeat," *New York Times*, May 1, 1987.

30. Leonard Silk, "Volcker on the Crash," *New York Times*, November 8, 1987.

31. William L. Silber, *Volcker: The Triumph of Persistence* (New York: Bloomsbury, 2012), 10, 275 (quote); Perry Mehrling, "Interview with Paul Volcker," *Macroeconomic Dynamics* 5 (2001): 434–60.

32. Paul A. Volcker, "Rethinking the Bright New World of Global Finance," *International Finance* 11:1 (2008): 101–7.

33. Keynes, *General Theory, CW*, 7:156–58, 161–62.

34. "Finance and Profits: The Changing Nature of American Business Cycles" (1980), 16–18; "The Financial Instability Hypothesis: An Interpretation of Keynes and an Alternative to 'Standard' Theory" (1977), 59–60, 63 (quote), 69; "The Financial Instability Hypothesis: A Restatement" (1978), 91–92, 102, 111 (quote), all reprinted in Hyman P. Minsky, *Can "It" Happen Again? Essays on Instability and Finance* (New York: M. E. Sharpe, 1982).

35. Charles P. Kindleberger, *Manias, Panics, and Crashes: A History of Financial Crises*, 4th ed. (New York: Wiley and Sons, 2000).

36. Carmen M. Reinhart and Kenneth S. Rogoff, *This Time Is Different: Eight Centuries of Financial Folly* (Princeton: Princeton University Press, 2009), xxv, xxvii, 155, 159, 203.

37. Reinhart and Rogoff, *This Time Is Different*, 152–53; On the ubiquity of financial crises throughout modern history, see also Richard S. Grossman, *Unsettled Account: The Evolution of Banking in the Industrialized World since 1800* (Princeton: Princeton University Press, 2010), esp. 297–316 for a catalogue of such crises.

38. Minsky, "Financial Instability Hypothesis," 66; Minsky, "A Restatement," 111; Hyman Minsky, *John Maynard Keynes* (New York: Columbia University Press, 1975); Lybeck, *Global History of the Financial Crash*, 1.

39. Roubini and Mihm, *Crisis Economics*, 8, 16 (quote), 18, 95; Reinhart and Rogoff, *This Time Is Different*, 1, 171–72, 208, 213, 292; Mehrling, "Interview with Paul Volcker." Greatly influenced by Keynes and Kindleberger, in 2006 I wrote that the United States was "at greater risk for a major financial crisis than at any other time since the Second World War." Jonathan Kirshner, "Globalization, Power, and Prospect," in *Globalization and National Security*, ed. Jonathan Kirshner (New York: Routledge, 2006), 337.

40. There is, of course, a massive literature on the crisis. For an overview, see Andrew Lo, "Reading about the Financial Crisis: A Twenty-One-Book Review," *Journal of Economic Literature* 50:1 (March 2012): 151–78.

41. IMF, *Global Financial Stability Report: Navigating the Financial Challenges Ahead*, Washington, DC (October 2009), 9; Bank for International Settlements, 79th Annual Report April 1, 2008–March 31, 2009 (Basel: Bank for International Settlements, June 29, 2009), 7, 8.

42. McClean and Nocera, *All the Devils Are Here*, 111, 112, 117, 124; Tett, *Fool's Gold*, 101; FCIC, *Financial Crisis Inquiry Report*, 118 (quote), 145–47, 210; US Senate, *Wall Street and the Financial Crisis*, 30, 244–46, 274; Mathias Dewatripont, Jean-Charles Rochet, and Jean Tirole, *Balancing the Banks: Global Lessons from the Financial Crisis* (Princeton: Princeton University Press, 2010), 21–22, 28, 46; IMF, *Global Financial Stability Report* (October 2009), 12 ("issuers figured out

how to game the rating agency criteria and were perceived to be receiving structuring advice from the ratings agencies themselves").

43. US Senate, *Wall Street and the Financial Crisis*, 31, 32, 243 ("by the time the ratings agencies admitted their AAA ratings were inaccurate, it took the form of a massive ratings correction that was unprecedented in US financial markets"); McClean and Nocera, *All the Devils Are Here*, 298; FCIC, *Financial Crisis Inquiry Report*, 155.

44. Rawi Abdelal and Mark Blyth argue that although "the CRAs hardly distinguished themselves in the crisis" (to say the least), it was poor public policy that permitted the industry to function as a competition-inhibiting duopoly, and which allowed thinly stretched regulators to rely heavily on CRA ratings. "Just Who Put You in Charge? We Did: CRAs and the Politics of Ratings" (unpublished manuscript, 2013).

45. Wessel, *In Fed We Trust*, 2, 25, 159, 194 (quotes); Henry M. Paulson, Jr., *On the Brink: Inside the Race to Stop the Collapse of the Global Financial System* (New York: Business Plus, 2010), 125, 236, 439–40 (quotes); Dewatripont, Rochet, and Tirole, *Balancing the Banks*, 10, 48.

46. Johnson and Kwak, *13 Bankers*, 6, 9, 96, 192; FCIC, *Financial Crisis Inquiry Report*, 55.

47. Richard A. Oppel, Jr., "Senate Report Says Rubin Acted Legally in Enron Matter," *New York Times*, January 3, 2003; Eric Dash and Julie Creswell, "Citigroup Saw No Red Flags Even as It Made Bolder Bets," *New York Times*, November 22, 2008; "No Line Responsibilities," *Wall Street Journal*, December 3, 2008 (quotes); Posner, *Failure of Capitalism*, 209.

48. Dash and Creswell, "Citigroup Saw No Red Flags"; Jackie Calmes, "Rubinomics Recalculated," *New York Times*, November 23, 2008; Silber, *Triumph of Persistence*, 8 (quote), 296; Robert J. Shiller, "Democratizing and Humanizing Finance," in *Reforming US Financial Markets: Reflections before and beyond Dodd-Frank*, Alvin Hansen Symposium on Public Policy, Harvard University, ed. Benjamin M. Friedman (Cambridge: MIT Press, 2011), 2 (quote), 5, 9.

49. Unless "regulations are changed radically . . . the cycle will only repeat itself," Andrew Ross Sorkin, *Too Big to Fail* (New York: Viking, 2009), 538. If the underlying problems are not fixed, the "world is likely to limp out of this crisis to the next," Robert Skidelsky, *Keynes: The Return of the Master* (New York: Public Affairs, 2009), 183. "Far more radical reforms must be implemented if the financial system is to achieve any semblance of stability in the coming years," Roubini and Mihm, *Crisis Economics*, 210. "The unconditional support provided to the financial system only exacerbated the weaknesses and incentives that created the crisis in the first place," Johnson and Kwak, *13 Bankers*, 174.

50. House Subcommittee on Investigations and Oversight, "Building a Science of Economics for the Real World" (Solow); Johnson and Kwak, for example, propose that no financial institution should be worth more than 4% of GDP (*13 Bankers*, 214–16); on the nondebate, see also Stiglitz, *Freefall*, 44.

6. The Crisis and World Politics

1. Bank for International Settlements, 79th Annual Report April 1, 2008–March 31, 2009 (Basel, Bank for International Settlements, June 29, 2009), 119.

2. Jonathan D. Ostry, Atish R. Ghosh, Karl Habermeier, Marcos Chamon, Mahvash S. Qureshi, and Dennis B. S. Reinhardt, "Capital Inflows: The Role of Controls," IMF Staff Position Note (February 19, 2010), 5 (quote), 15; Olivier Blanchard, Giovanni Dell'Aricca, and Paolo Mauro, "Rethinking Macroeconomic Policy," IMF Staff Position Note (February 12, 2010), 3 ("the crisis clearly forces us to question our earlier assessment"), 11; "Capital Controls: IMF Shifts Its Stance with Plan for Capital Controls," *IMF External Relations Department Morning Press*, April 6, 2011; "Fundamental Questions: The IMF Changes Its Mind on Capital Controls on Capital Inflows," *Economist*, February 18, 2010; IMF, *Global Financial Stability Report*, Washington, D.C., (April 2010), but note the insistence on qualifications at every step, chap. 4, and 1, 6, 12, 18, 30.

Ilene Grabel, "Not Your Grandfather's IMF: Global Crisis, 'Productive Incoherence' and Developmental Policy Space," *Cambridge Journal of Economics* 35 (2011): 812, 814, 816, 817, 825.

3. Moreover, China is a major stakeholder in the stability of the current system and the viability of the US dollar. In this sense especially, it has no incentive to tear down the existing system, even as it seeks greater voice, influence, authority, and autonomy, and even as it anticipates the RMB encroaching on the dollar's influence. I discuss the limits of China's "monetary power" in chapter 7.

4. Inhibits, in that the overriding desire for structural power creates strong disincentives, but this does not rule out the possibly that overt coercive power will be exercised.

5. Jonathan Kirshner, *Currency and Coercion: The Political Economy of International Monetary Power* (Princeton: Princeton University Press, 1995); Albert Hirschman, *National Power and the Structure of Foreign Trade* (1945, repr., Berkeley: University of California Press, 1980); Rawi Abdelal and Jonathan Kirshner, "Strategy, Economic Relations, and the Definition of National Interests," *Security Studies* 9:1–2 (Autumn/Winter 1999–2000): 119–56.

6. Benjamin Cohen emphasizes that this need not be the case. He notes German reluctance, and Japanese ambivalence, regarding the internationalization of their currencies in the 1980s. Eric Helleiner is also skeptical about overstating claims about the inevitability of internationalization, adding US postwar discouragement of Latin American dollarization as another example. These points are well taken, but I would argue that for states with growing international political ambition, the default setting remains that they will seek to extend the influence of their currencies abroad and that exceptions are, indeed, exceptional. For example, had global economic trends from the 1980s continued, it is likely that the yen would have taken on a much larger global role. The foreign policy of postwar Germany was greatly influenced by the fact that it was, in Peter Katzenstein's phrase, a "semi-sovereign state." And while the United States was discouraging Latin dollarization, it was also mounting heroic efforts to organize the entire global monetary order around the dollar as the world's currency.

7. Kirshner, *Currency and Coercion*, chap. 4, also 244, 246, 261, 268; Marcello DeCecco, *The International Gold Standard* (New York: St. Martin's Press, 1984), 44 (quote); Henry Parker Willis, *A History of the Latin Monetary Union* (Chicago: University of Chicago Press, 1901); Emily Rosenberg, "Foundations of United States International Financial Power: Gold Standard Diplomacy, 1900–1905," *Business History Review* 59 (Summer 1985): 169–202.

8. Susan Strange, *Sterling and British Policy: A Political Study of an International Currency in Decline* (Oxford: Oxford University Press, 1971); Andrew Walter, *World Power and World Money: The Role of Hegemony and International Monetary Order* (London: Palgrave Macmillan, 1991).

9. Eric Helleiner, "Below the State: Micro-Level Monetary Power," in *International Monetary Power*, ed. David Andrews (Ithaca: Cornell University Press, 2006), esp. 84. On the increased demand for insulation, see Scott Cooper, "The Limits of Monetary Power: Statecraft within Currency Areas," and Jonathan Kirshner, "Currency and Coercion in the Twenty-First Century," both in Andrews, *International Monetary Power*, 171, 174, 156.

10. William Grimes, "Internationalization of the Yen and the New Politics of Monetary Insulation," in *Monetary Orders: Ambiguous Economics, Ubiquitous Politics*, ed. Jonathan Kirshner (Cornell University Press, 2003), 177, 180, 181 (quote), 183–84, 193–94; C. Randall Henning, "The Exchange-Rate Weapon and Macroeconomic Conflict," in Andrews, *International Monetary Power*, 133 (resentment), 138; Andrew Walter, "Domestic Sources of International Monetary Leadership," in Andrews, *International Monetary Power*, 69. See also Jonathan Kirshner, "Currency and Coercion in the Twenty-First Century," 151; and Saori Katada, "Japan and Asian Monetary Regionalization: Cultivating a New Leadership Role after the Asian Financial Crisis," *Geopolitics* 7:1 (Summer 2002): 86. On the monetary ambitions of a rising Japan, see Eric Helleiner, "Japan and the Changing Global Financial Order," *International Journal* 47:2 (Spring 1992):

esp. 434–37; and Mark Metzler, "The Road to the Dollar Standard: Monetary Hegemony and Japan's Place in the International Order," *Japanese Economy* 30:3 (2002): 74.

11. Carl E. Walter and Fraser J. T. Howie, *Red Capitalism: The Fragile Foundation of China's Extraordinary Rise* (Singapore: Wiley, 2011), ix–x, 3; Rosemary Foot and Andrew Walter, *China, the United States, and Global Order* (Cambridge: Cambridge University Press, 2011), 117, 120, 123; Gregory Chin and Eric Helleiner, "China as a Creditor: A Rising Financial Power?," *Journal of International Affairs* 62:1 (Fall/Winter 2008): 87 (quote), 92, 97–98, 99.

12. Robert Minikin and Kelvin Lau, *The Offshore Renminbi: The Rise of the Chinese Currency and Its Global Future* (Singapore: Wiley, 2013), 4, 53, 73.

13. Geoff Dyer, "Paulson Urges Beijing to Speed Up Reform," *Financial Times*, March 8, 2007; G. John Ikenberry and Charles Kupchan, "Socialization and Hegemonic Power," *International Organization* 44:3 (June 1990): 283–315. Walter and Howie, *Red Capitalism*, 74, 213 ("the global financial crisis eliminated the political consensus in support of the western financial model that had been in place since 1992"); Foot and Walter, *China, the United States, and Global Order*, 265, 270. (From the late 1990s to 2007 China saw the US banking system as "the exemplar towards which the Chinese financial system should gradually converge." This "greatly eroded" in 2008–9.) Chin and Helleiner, "China as a Creditor," 96 (regulator quotes).

14. Yu Yongding, "Further Discussion on the Internationalization of the RMB," *International Economic Review* 5 (November/December 2011) (first quote); Zhang Ming, "Reform of the International Monetary System under the Global Financial Crisis," Chinese Academy of Social Sciences, Institute of World Economics and Politics, Research Center for International Finance, Working Paper no. 0919 (December 21, 2009) (second quote); see also Kenneth Lieberthal and Wang Jisi, *Addressing US-China Strategic Distrust* (Washington, DC: Brookings Institution, 2012) on concerns for the future of the dollar and "some urgency to internationalize the Renminbi," 15.

15. Li Ruogu, "The Financial Crisis and International Monetary System Reform," *China Finance* 5, (2010); Li Yang, "Reform of the Global Financial System and Asia's Choices: We Need Deeper Thinking," *Studies of International Finance* 10, (2010); Qu Fengjie, "Trends of Change in the International Financial System and China's Policy Responses," *New Finance* 5 (2009) ("restraints"); Li Daokui and Yin Xingzhong, "New Structure of the International Monetary System: Research on the Post-Financial Crisis Era," *Journal of Financial Research* 2 (2010).

16. Wu Xinbo, "Understanding the Geopolitical Implications of the Global Financial Crisis," *Washington Quarterly* 33:4 (October 2010): 157 (quote), 159 (quote), 161; Lieberthal and Wang, *Addressing US-China Strategic Distrust*, 15 (hegemony); Song Guoyou, "The International Financial System Shows Signs of Being Remolded," *Western Forum* 11 (2008); World Bank, *Global Development Horizons 2011–Multipolarity: The New Global Economy* (Washington, DC: World Bank, 2011), 7, 126; Lu Qianjin, "Discussion of International Financial System Reform and RMB Internationalization Strategy," *Social Science* 4, (April 2009) ("establishing a diverse international monetary system is the realistic choice. . . . Mutual restraint and competition among currencies will be good"); Li and Yin, "New Structure of the International Monetary System" ("the foundations of US credit have already entered a long path of decline"); Qu, "Trends of Change in the International Financial System " ("financial and monetary cooperation in Asia will grow stronger, and the RMB's status as a regional currency will rise"); Zhang, "Reform of the International Monetary System."

17. Chen Siqing, "Deeper-Level Analysis of the Reasons for the US Financial Crisis and Its Lessons for China's Banking Industry," *Studies of International Finance* 12 (2008); Li, "The Financial Crisis and International Monetary System Reform"; Yu Yongding, "US Subprime Crisis: Background, Causes and Development," Chinese Academy of Social Sciences, Institute of World Economics and Politics, Research Center for International Finance, Working Paper no. 0817 (October 8, 2008) (Anglo-Saxon); Xia Bin, "China's Development and the International Monetary

Order," *Theoretical Horizon* 1 (2011) (Harvard). See also Zhang, "Reform of the International Monetary System," ("one of the root causes of the subprime crisis was that global financial regulatory authorities held a laissez-faire attitude about financial innovations").

18. Joon-Kyung Kim and Chung H. Lee, "Between Two Whales: Korea's Choice in the Post-Crisis Era," in *Strategic Asia 2009–10: Economic Meltdown and Geopolitical Stability*, ed. Ashley Tellis, Andrew Marble, and Travis Tanner (Seattle: National Bureau of Asian Research, 2009), 153, 162–63; Pieter Bottelier, "China and the International Financial Crisis," in Tellis, Marble and Tanner, *Strategic Asia*, 71, 100 ("from China's perspective, the United States has lost credibility in the economic and financial arena. The crisis has confirmed Chinese leaders in their belief that they were correct in resisting US pressure"); John Williamson, "Is the 'Beijing Consensus' Now Dominant?," *Asia Policy* 13 (January 2012), 3 ("discredit Western views"); Nancy Birdsall and Francis Fukuyama, "The Post-Washington Consensus: Development after the Crisis," *Foreign Affairs* 90:2 (March/April 2011): 3 ("the American version of capitalism is, if not in full disrepute, then at least no longer dominant"); Foot and Walter, *China, The United States, and Global Order*, 271 ("major blow to the credibility and legitimacy"); see also Walter and Howie, *Red Capitalism*, 74, 213; and Chin and Helleiner, "China as a Creditor," 96.

19. Williamson, "Is the 'Beijing Consensus' Now Dominant?," 15; see also Birdsall and Fukuyama, "Post-Washington Consensus," 47. On China's bending toward the American model and subsequent pause, see Walter and Fraser, *Red Capitalism*, 10, 13, 14.

20. Benjamin Cohen, "The China Question: Can Its Rise Be Accommodated?" in *The Great Wall of Money: Politics and Power in China's International Monetary Relations*, ed. Eric Helleiner and Jonathan Kirshner (Ithaca: Cornell University Press, 2014).

21. Minikin and Lau, *Offshore Renminbi*, 10, 204, 213; Gregory Chin also sees a "significant shift" in Beijing's disposition with regard to international monetary reform more generally in the wake of the crisis; "China's Rising Monetary Power," in Helleiner and Kirshner, *Great Wall of Money*. On the demand side, see Injoo Sohn, "Towards Normative Fragmentation: An East Asian Financial Architecture in the Post-Global Crisis World," *Review of International Political Economy* 19:4 (October 2012): 591; Miguel Otero-Iglesias and Federico Steinberg, "Reframing the Euro vs. Dollar Debate through the Perceptions of Financial Elites in Key Dollar-Holding Countries," *Review of International Political Economy* 20:1 (February 2013): 200.

22. The special drawing right (SDR) is a reserve asset created by the International Monetary Fund.

23. Zhou Xiaochuan, "Reform of the International Monetary System," People's Bank of China, March 23, 2009; David Barboza, "China Urges New Money Reserve to Replace Dollar," *New York Times*, March 24, 2009; Gregory Chin and Wang Yong "Debating the International Currency System: What's in a Speech?," *China Security* 6:1 (2010): 4, 5, 11, 12.

24. Chin and Wang, "Debating the International Currency System," 14; Zhang Yuyan, "Internationalization of the RMB: Endorse or Oppose?" *International Economic Review* 1 (2010) (Chinese economists). Zhang also adds that "a significant majority of Chinese economists support the internationalization" of the RMB. Zhang, "Reform of the International Monetary System," (aim of the strategy); Zhang Yuyan and Zhang Jingchun, "International Currency's Costs and Benefits," *World Affairs* 21 (2008) (major power). See also Lu Qianjin, "Discussion of International Financial System Reform"; Xia Bin, "China's Development"; and Wu Xinbo, "Understanding the Geopolitical Implications of the Global Financial Crisis." All of these authors advocate for a greater international role for the yuan. Wu, (writing in an American outlet), argues that the global financial crisis marked the end of the post–Cold War order, invalidated the American economic model at home and the one size fits all Washington consensus it aggressively proffered abroad, and anticipates that "China's deepening economic connections with its regional partners promise to expand its political clout in East Asia," 155, 156, 160 (quote).

25. Eric Helleiner and Anton Malkin, "Sectoral Interests and Global Money: Renminbi, Dollars, and the Domestic Foundations of International Currency Policy," *Open Economies Review* 23:1: 49, 50, 52. (This argument assumes, of course, that domestic sectoral politics is an important factor in explaining currency internationalization.) Walter and Fraser, *Red Capitalism*, 25, 27, 38, 77–78, 80, 138–39; Michael F. Martin, "China's Banking System: Issues for Congress," CRS Report for Congress, February 20, 2012, http://www.fas.org/sgp/crs/row/R42380.pdf.

26. See, for example, Sebastian Mallaby and Olin Wethington, "The Future of the Yuan: China's Struggle to Internationalize Its Currency," *Foreign Affairs* 91:1 (January/February 2012): 136, 137; Jeffrey Frankel, "Historical Precedents for Internationalization of the RMB," Council on Foreign Relations, November 2011, http://www.cfr.org/china/historical-precedents-internation alization-rmb/p26293, 13; World Bank, *Global Development Horizons 2011*, 139; Bottelier, "China and the International Financial Crisis,"100; Takatoshi Ito, "The Internationalization of the RMB: Opportunities and Pitfalls," Council on Foreign Relations, November 2011, http://www.cfr.org/ china/internationalization-rmb-opportunities-pitfalls/p26287, 11 (quote).

27. And this position would appear to be gaining a toehold on legitimacy. See, for example, Olivier Jeanne, Arvind Subramanian, and John Williamson, *Who Needs to Open the Capital Account?* (Washington, DC: Peterson Institute for International Economics, 2012). On the relationship between internationalization and liberalization, see also Dong He, "Renminbi Internationalization: A Primer," Hong Kong Institute for Monetary Research, July 31, 2012; and Christopher A. McNally, "Abstract Sino-Capitalism: China's Reemergence and the International Political Economy," *World Politics* 64:4 (October 2012): 760–62.

28. Zhou Xiaochuan, "Several Issues in the Establishment and Implementation of Financial Industry Standards," *China Finance*, January 5, 2012. On internationalization ahead of liberalization, see Robert N. McCauley, "Internationalizing the Renminbi and China's Financial Development Model," Council on Foreign Relations, November 2011, http://www.cfr.org/china/ renminbi-internationalization-chinas-financial-development-model/p26290, 1, 3 ("in internationalizing the Renminbi within a system of capital controls, the Chinese authorities set out on a path with no signposts"), 13, 21; Barry Eichengreen, "When Currencies Collapse: Will We Replay the 1930s or the 1970s?," *Foreign Affairs* 91:1 (January/February 2012): 129, 130 (infrastructure, vehicle, reserves, swaps); World Bank, *Global Development Horizons 2011*, 140.

29. Note that the new heterogeneity implies the search for (and willingness to embrace) a variety of alternatives; it does not require the development of, and certainly not convergence around, a specific competing model. Matt Ferchen, "Whose China Model Is It anyway? The Contentious Search for Consensus," *Review of International Political Economy* 20:2 (April 2013): 390–420. See also Sophie Meunier, "The Dog That Did Not Bark: Anti-Americanism and the 2008 Financial Crisis in Europe," *Review of International Political Economy* 20:1 (February 2013), which distinguishes between "Anti-Americanism" and postcrisis disenchantment with the US economic model.

30. Ming Zhang, "China's New International Financial Strategy amid the Global Financial Crisis," *China and World Economy* 17:5 (2009): 23, 24, 27, 29, 31; Pieter Bottelier, "Future of the Renminbi as an International Currency," ChinaUsfocus.com, April 29, 2011, http://www.chinaus focus.com/finance-economy/future-of-the-renminbi-as-an-international-currency/; Keith Bradsher, "In Step to Enhance Currency, China Allows Its Use in Some Foreign Payments," *New York Times*, July 7, 2009; George Koo and Henry Tang, "How Shall America Respond to Chinese Yuan as a Global Currency?" ChinaUsFocus.com, February 29, 2012, http://www.chinaus focus.com/finance-economy/how-shall-america-respond-to-chinese-yuan-as-a-global-currency/; Thaksin Shinawatra, "An Asia Bond Could Save Us from the Dollar," *Financial Times*, October 6, 2008, quote.

31. Ito, "Internationalization of the RMB," 2 (quotes), 4–5, 16; Koo and Tang, "Yuan as a Global Currency"; Edward Wong and Natasha Singer, "Currency Agreement for Japan

and China," *New York Times*, December 27, 2011; Simon Rabinovitch, "China and Japan Agree on Currency Push," *Financial Times*, December 27, 2011; Wang Xiaotian and Gao Changxin, "China-Japan Currency Deal Ushers in a New Era," ChinaDaily.com.cn, May 30, 2012, http://europe.chinadaily.com.cn/business/2012-05/30/content_15418505.htm; "China and Australia in $31bn Currency Swap," *Financial Times*, May 22, 2012; "China and Brazil in $30bn Currency Swap Agreement," *BBC News*, June 22, 2012, http://www.bbc.co.uk/news/business-21949615.

32. Kosuke Takahashi, "Japan and China Bypass US in Direct Currency Trade," *Asia-Pacific Journal* 24:3 (June 11, 2012); Chin and Wang, "Debating the International Currency System," 13; Ito, "Internationalization of the RMB," 8; Bottelier, "Future of the Renminbi"; Zhang, "Internationalization of the RMB," 6; Gregory Chin, "Off to the RMB Races: The Singapore Stock Exchange," Cigionlone.org, July 23, 2012, http://www.cigionline.org/publications/2012/7/rmb-races-%E2%80%94-singapore-stock-exchange. As one banker notes, "Very soon, all companies trading with China will have a "renminbi moment," when they realise that the internationalisation of the Chinese currency is not a matter of long-term strategising, but something on which they have to act here and now." Mike Rees, "Renminbi's Rapid Rise Concentrates Minds," Financial Times, ft.com, December 19, 2012, http://www.ft.com/intl/cms/s/0/0592b99a-3af0-11e2-bb32-00144feabdc0.html.

33. There are many historical examples of important regional and global monetary arrangements that have been designed and operated in the absence of full capital account convertibility; indeed, in some cases, these arrangements have had substantial illiberal qualities. This is not to suggest that China's approach to an internationalized RMB will not (or should not) be market friendly; but history suggests that there are many different ways to orchestrate such arrangements. See Kirshner, *Currency and Coercion*, chap. 4. McNally also suggests divergence from the US model; see "Abstract Sino-Capitalism," 763–64. An example of the more skeptical perspective is Yang Jiang, "The Limits of China's Monetary Diplomacy," in Helleiner and Kirshner, *Great Wall of Money*.

34. See, for example, Menzie Chinn and Jeffrey Frankel, "Why the Euro Will Rival the Dollar," *International Finance* 11:1 (2008): 49–73; and Adam S. Posen, "Why the Euro Will Not Rival the Dollar," *International Finance* 11:1 (2008): 75–100.

35. World Bank, *Global Development Horizons 2011*, 3, 126; also Benjamin Cohen, "Towards a Leaderless Currency System," in *The Future of the Dollar*, ed. Eric Helleiner and Jonathan Kirshner (Ithaca: Cornell University Press, 2009).

36. Not to be forgotten is the fact that a monetary hegemon can be a source of instability and exploitation.

37. Wayne M. Morrison and Marc Labonte, "China's Currency: An Analysis of the Economic Issues," CRS Report for Congress, August 3, 2011, http://www.fas.org/sgp/crs/row/RS21625.pdf, 1–2, 13; Morris Goldstein and Nicholas R. Lardy, *The Future of China's Exchange Rate Policy*, Washington, DC, Institute for International Economics, July 2009, 18, 26–27, 33, 52, 85–86.

38. US Treasury, "Report to Congress on International Economic and Exchange Rate Policies," May 2005, http://www.treasury.gov/resource-center/international/exchange-rate-policies/Documents/Treasury_ReportToCongressOnInternationalEconomicAndExchangeRatePolicies-2004H2_2005%20May%2017.pdf (quotes); "Statement of Secretary John W. Snow on the FOREX Report," May 17, 2005, US Treasury, press release js-2449; National Association of Manufacturers, "Treasury's Failure to Cite China on Currency Dismays NAM," NAM press release 05–384, November 28, 2005.

39. Including j-curve effects, local price adjustments that would postpone and mitigate the exchange rate effects, and the diminished effect on final prices due to unaffected imported intermediate components.

40. Statement of Douglas Holtz Eakin, director, Congressional Budget Office, "Economic Relationships between the United States and China," before the Committee on Ways and Means, US House of Representatives, April 14, 2005. See also the similar conclusion in "Report to Congress on International Economic and Exchange rate Policies," US Department of the Treasury, Office of International Affairs, October 15, 2009, 14; and Morrison and Labonte (also representing a US government agency), "China's Currency," 17, 19, 22.

41. C. Fred Bergsten, "What to Do about the US-Japan Economic Conflict," *Foreign Affairs* 60 (Summer 1982): 1059, 1065–66; Robert V. Roosa, *The United States and Japan in the International Monetary System, 1946–1985* (New York: Group of Thirty, 1986), 1; Koichi Hamada and Hugh Patrick, "Japan and the International Monetary Regime," in *The Political Economy of Japan*, vol. 2, ed. Takashi Inoguchi and Daniel Okimoto (Stanford: Stanford University Press, 1988), 118–19; Robert C. Angel, *Explaining Economic Policy Failure: Japan in the 1969–71 International Monetary Crisis* (New York: Columbia University Press, 1991), 38; Ronald McKinnon and Kenichi Ohno, *Dollar and Yen: Resolving Economic Conflict between the US and Japan* (Cambridge: MIT Press, 1997), 10, 205; William Grimes, *Unmaking the Japanese Miracle: Macroeconomic Politics 1985–2000* (Ithaca: Cornell University Press, 2001), 125, 132.

42. On concerns for instability and fragility, see, for example, Susan Shirk, *China: Fragile Superpower* (Oxford: Oxford University Press, 2007); C. Fred Bergsten, Bates Gill, Nicholas Lardy, and Derek Mitchell, *China: The Balance Sheet* (New York: Public Affairs, 2006), chap. 3. On banking sector instability, see also Goldstein and Lardy, *Future of China's Exchange Rate Policy*, 46, 49; and Morrison and Labonte, "China's Currency," 28.

43. Ronald I. McKinnon, *Exchange Rates under the East Asian Dollar Standard: Living with Conflicted Virtue* (Cambridge: MIT Press, 2005), 10–11, 129–30, 147, 151–53, 248; McKinnon, "China's New Exchange Rate Policy: Will China Follow Japan into a Liquidity Trap?," *Economists' Voice* 3:2 (2006).

44. David Calleo, "Twenty-First Century Geopolitics and the Erosion of the Dollar Order," in Helleiner and Kirshner, *Future of the Dollar*, 186. On political foundations of monetary order, see Robert Gilpin, *Global Political Economy: Understanding the International Economic Order* (Princeton: Princeton University Press, 2001).

45. Hubert Zimmerman, "Ever Challenging the Buck? The Euro and the Question of Power in International Monetary Governance," in *Governing the EMU*, ed. Francisco Torres, Amy Verdun, and Hubert Zimmerman (Florence, ITL: EUI, 2004); European Central Bank, *The International Role of the Euro*, July 2009, http://www.ecb.europa.eu/pub/pdf/other/euro-international-role201307en.pdf, 14. See also Saori Katada, "Japan and Asian Monetary Regionalization: Cultivating a New Regional Leadership Role after the Asian Financial Crisis," *Geopolitics* 7:1 (Summer 2002); and Paul Bowles, "Asia's Post-Crisis Regionalism: Bringing the State Back In, Keeping the (United) States Out," *Review of International Political Economy* 9:2 (Summer 2002).

7. The Crisis and the International Balance of Power

1. Even when China's economy surpasses America's in aggregate size, with four times the population of the United States, it will still be, for some time, a developing country with a relatively modest per capita income. The eurozone remains the aggregation of its constituent member economies.

2. On these central issues, see Robert Gilpin, *War and Change in World Politics* (Cambridge: Cambridge University Press, 1981).

3. As noted in chapter 6, China often gets the lion's share of attention in discussions of changes to the balance of international power because of its obvious size and importance. But China is not at all the only moving piece on this chessboard. Even if China, like Japan in the

1990s, were to have its rising star unexpectedly burn out, unlike the 1990s, there is a crowd of middle-sized states that are also emerging on the scene. On this point, see Charles Kupchan, *No One's World: The West, the Rising Rest, and the Coming Global Turn* (New York: Oxford University Press, 2012).

4. Maurice Obstfeld and Kenneth S. Rogoff, *Global Current Account Imbalances and Exchange Rate Adjustments*, Brookings Papers on Economic Activity 1 (2005), http://www.brookings.edu/~/media/projects/bpea/spring%202005/2005a_bpea_obstfeld.pdf; Jeffrey Frankel, "Could the Twin Deficits Jeopardize US Hegemony?," *Journal of Policy Modeling* 28 (2006): 653–63; Robert Hunter Wade, "The Invisible Hand of the American Empire," *Ethics and International Affairs* 17:2 (2003): 77–88. See also Helen Thompson, "Debt and Power: The United States' Debt in Historical Perspective," *International Relations* 21:3 (2007): 305–23. Others were less pessimistic; see, for example, Richard N. Cooper, *Living with Global Imbalances*, Brookings Papers on Economic Activity 2 (2007), http://www.brookings.edu/~/media/projects/bpea/fall%202007/2007b_bpea_cooper.pdf, 91–108.

5. Jonathan Kirshner, "Globalization and American Power," workshop memo, April 16, 2004. See also my "Globalization, Power, and Prospect," in *Globalization and National Security*, ed. Jonathan Kirshner (Routledge, 2006), 337. I was in good company: Paul Volcker estimated there was a 75% chance of a dollar crisis within five years, "Checking the Depth Gauge: How Low Might the Dollar Sink?," *Economist,* November 11, 2004; see also William R. Cline, *The United States as a Debtor Nation,* (Washington, DC: Institute for International Economics, 2005), 175, 180, 236.

6. Recall Carmen Reinhart and Kenneth Rogoff, *This Time Is Different: Eight Centuries of Financial Folly* (Princeton: Princeton University Press, 2009); Charles P. Kindleberger, *Manias, Panics, and Crashes: A History of Financial Crises* (New York: Basic Books, 1978); and Richard S. Grossman, *Unsettled Account: The Evolution of Banking in the Industrialized World since 1800* (Princeton: Princeton University Press, 2010).

7. Yukio Hatoyama "A New Path for Japan," *New York Times,* August 27, 2009.

8. G. John Ikenberry and Charles Kupchan, "Socialization and Hegemonic Power," *International Organization* 44:3 (June 1990): 283–315. For more on the loss of legitimacy, see, for example, Wu Xinbo, "Understanding the Geopolitical Implications of the Global Financial Crisis," *Washington Quarterly* (October 2010): 161; and Andrew Sheng, *From Asian to Global Financial Crisis: An Asian Regulator's View of Unfettered Finance in the 1990s and 2000s* (Cambridge: Cambridge University Press, 2009), 123.

9. China's continued economic growth is by no means guaranteed, and this raises a host of other important questions, which I consider in chapter 8.

10. Joseph S. Nye, Jr., *The Future of Power* (New York: Public Affairs, 2011); Kupchan, *No One's World.*

11. See, for example, Benjamin Cohen, "Towards a Leaderless Currency System," in *The Future of the Dollar*, ed. Eric Helleiner and Jonathan Kirshner (Ithaca: Cornell University Press, 2009).

12. Takatoshi Ito, "The Internationalization of the RMB: Opportunities and Pitfalls," Council on Foreign Relations, November 2011, http://www.cfr.org/china/internationalization-rmb-opportunities-pitfalls/p26287, 2, 16 (quote); Steven E. Halliwell, "Russia and the Global Crisis: Consequences of Delayed Reform," in *Strategic Asia 2009–10: Economic Meltdown and Geopolitical Stability*, ed. Ashley Tellis, Andrew Marble, and Travis Tanner (Seattle: National Bureau of Asian Research, 2009), 191–94. Bessma Momani, "Gulf Cooperation Council Oil Exporters and the Future of the Dollar," *New Political Economy* 13:3 (September 2008): 293–314; David Spiro, *The Hidden Hand of American Hegemony: Petrodollar Recycling and International Markets* (Ithaca: Cornell

University Press, 1999); R. Taggart Murphy, "East Asia's Dollars," *New Left Review* 40 (July/August 2006): 43, 62 (quote).

13. In 2012, the official reserves of China were about $3.3 trillion, Japan $1.3 trillion, Saudi Arabia $625 billion, Russia $500 billion (IMF Statistics Department COFER database, https://www.imf.org/external/data.htm). It is estimated that 70% of China's reserves are held in dollars, and the dollar accounts for 60% of the world's reserves.

14. World Bank, *Global Development Horizons 2011–Multipolarity: The New Global Economy* (Washington, DC: World Bank, 2011), 7, 13, 126, 131, 140, 144, 152 (quote). Menzie Chinn and Jeffrey Frankel, "Why the Euro Will Rival the Dollar," *International Finance* 11:1 (2008): 49–73; Adam S. Posen, "Why the Euro Will Not Rival the Dollar," *International Finance* 11:1 (2008): 75–100. Barry Eichengreen and Marc Flandreau, "The Rise and Fall of the Dollar (or When Did the Dollar Replace Sterling as the Leading Reserve Currency?)," *European Review of Economic History* 13 (2009): 379–80, 403–4. See also Charles P. Kindleberger, *The Politics of International Money and World Language,* Essays in International Finance, no. 61, International Finance Section, Princeton University, August 1967.

15. Rawi Abdelal argues that the framers of the eurozone understood that eventually and inevitably some sort of reckoning would force a reassessment of monetary arrangements in Europe. But they also understood that it would take some sort of crisis (if not quite this big) to propel the union forward. Rawi Abdelal, *Capital Rules: The Construction of Global Finance* (Cambridge: Harvard University Press, 2007), chap. 4.

16. For a good short discussion of many of these basic problems, see Martin Feldstein, "The Failure of the Euro: the Little Currency That Couldn't," *Foreign Affairs* 91:1 (January/February 2012): 105–16. But even Feldstein expects the eurozone to endure, largely intact (116). See also Kevin H. O'Rourke and Alan M. Taylor, "Cross of Euros," *Journal of Economic Perspectives* 27:3 (Summer 2013): 167–92.

17. See, for example, Richard N. Cooper, "The Future of the Dollar," Policy Brief 09-21, Peterson Institute for International Economics, September 2009, http://www.piie.com/publications/interstitial.cfm?ResearchID=1290; Matthias Matthijs, "The Dollar Paradox: America Caught between Managing Decline and Enjoying Exorbitant Privileges," in *Festschrift for David Calleo,* ed. John Harper (Bologna, ITL: SAIS, Johns Hopkins University, 2013).

18. Rebecca M. Nelson, Paul Belkin, Derek E. Mix, and Martin A. Weiss, "The Eurozone Crisis: Overview and Issues for Congress," CRS Report for Congress R42377, Congressional Research Service, February 29, 2012, 10 (quote); see also Raymond J. Ahearn, James K. Jackson, Derek E. Mix, and Rebecca M. Nelson, "The Future of the Eurozone and US Interests," CRS Report for Congress R41838, Congressional Research Service, January 17, 2012.

19. Benjamin J. Cohen, *The Future of Money* (Princeton: Princeton University Press, 2004); Kathleen R. McNamara and Sophie Meunier, "Between National Sovereignty and International Power: What External Voice for the Euro?" *International Affairs* 78:4 (2002): 849–68; Barry Eichengreen, "Sterling's Past, Dollar's Future: Historical Perspectives on Reserve Currency Competition," NBER Working Paper no. 11336, National Bureau of Economic Research, Cambridge, MA, May 2005, http://www.nber.org/papers/w11336.pdf, 7–8. On the euro as a potential peer competitor, see C. Fred Bergsten, "The Dollar and the Euro," *Foreign Affairs* 76:4 (July/August 1997): 83; C. Randall Henning and Pier Carlo, *Transatlantic Perspectives on the Euro* (Washington, DC: Brookings, 2000), 22–28; and C. Randall Henning, "The Exchange-Rate Weapon and Macroeconomic Conflict," in *International Monetary Power,* ed. David Andrews (Ithaca: Cornell University Press, 2006), esp. 130.

20. Cohen, in contrast, positions himself in the middle ground between optimists and pessimists, who tend to assume the euro must change, one way or another. He expects the euro to

muddle through as is. Benjamin J. Cohen, "The Future of the Euro: Let's Get Real," *Review of International Political Economy* 19:4 (October 2012): 689–700.

21. For a recent comprehensive overview of this issue, see Benjamin J. Cohen, "The Benefits and Costs of an International Currency: Getting the Calculus Right," *Open Economies Review* 23:1 (February 2012): 13–31.

22. Cohen, "Benefits and Costs," 16; and World Bank, *Global Development Horizons,* 126, 135, provide various calculations. Cohen also emphasizes costs and concludes that "no definitive answer" can be given to the question of whether it pays to issue international money, 20, 28 (quote). On the investment differential/premium, see Pierre-Olivier Gourinchas and Hélène Rey, "From World Banker to World Venture Capitalist: US External Adjustment and the Exorbitant Privilege" NBER Working Paper 11563, August 2005, http://www.nber.org/papers/w11563.pdf. Interest in the seigniorage gain was high during debates about the dollar's "exorbitant privilege" in the late Bretton Woods era. See Ronald McKinnon, *Private and Official International Money: The Case for the Dollar*, Essays in International Finance, no. 74, International Finance Section, Princeton University, NJ, April 1969: 5, 17, 21–22; Herbert G. Grubel, "The Distribution of Seigniorage from International Liquidity Creation," in *Monetary Problems of the International Economy*, ed. Robert A. Mundell and Alexander K. Swoboda (Chicago: University of Chicago Press, 1969); Benjamin J. Cohen, "The Seigniorage Gain of an International Currency: An Empirical Test," *Quarterly Journal of Economics* 85 (1971): 494–507; E. S. Kirschen, "The American External Seigniorage," *European Economic Review* 5 (1974): 355–78.

23. See Benjamin Cohen, "The Macrofoundations of Monetary Power," in Andrews, *International Monetary Power*.

24. William A. Salant, "The Reserve Currency Role of the Dollar: Blessings or Burden to the United States?," *Review of Economics and Statistics* 46:2 (May 1964): 165–66 (quotes); Robert Z. Aliber, "The Costs and Benefits of the US Role as a Reserve Currency Country," *Quarterly Journal of Economics* 78:3 (August 1964): 445, 454; Jacques Rueff and Fred Hirsch, "The Role and the Rule of Gold," Essays in International Finance, no. 47, International Finance Section, Princeton University, NJ, June 1965, 2–3.

25. On US pressure, see Francis J. Gavin, *Gold, Dollars, and Power: The Politics of International Monetary Relations, 1958–1971,* (Chapel Hill: University of North Carolina Press, 2004); and Hubert Zimmermann, *Money and Security: Troops and Monetary Policy in Germany's Relations to the United States and the United Kingdom, 1950–71* (Cambridge: Cambridge University Press, 2002).

26. Susan Strange, "Finance, Information, and Power," *Review of International Studies* 16:3 (July 1990): 259–74.

27. As noted in chapter 2, Treasury Secretary John Connolly once cheerfully told US allies, "The dollar may be our currency, but it is your problem." Privately, his sentiments were even less cheerful. According to Connolly, his "basic approach [was] that the foreigners are out to screw us. Our job is to screw them first." John Odell, *US International Monetary Policy* (Princeton: Princeton University Press, 1982), 263.

28. Susan Strange, "The Persistent Myth of Lost Hegemony," *International Organization* 41:4 (Autumn 1987): 569; see also David P. Calleo, *The Imperious Economy* (Cambridge: Harvard University Press, 1982), 63, 65, 78; and Henry G. Aubrey, "Behind the Veil of International Money," Essays in International Finance, no. 71, International Finance Section, Princeton University, NJ, January 1969, 16.

29. Susan Strange, *States and Markets* (New York: Basil Blackwell, 1988), 25; see also Susan Strange, "Finance and Capitalism: The City's Imperial Role Yesterday and Today," *Review of International Studies* 20:4 (October 1994): 407–10; Strange, "Finance, Information and Power"; and Eric Helleiner, "Below the State: Micro-Level Monetary Power," in Andrews, *International Monetary Power*, esp. 73–76.

30. Albert O. Hirschman, *National Power and the Structure of Foreign Trade* (Berkeley: University of California Press, 1980); Jonathan Kirshner, "The Theory of Monetary Dependence," chap. 5 in *Currency and Coercion: The Political Economy of International Monetary Power* (Princeton: Princeton University Press, 1995); Rawi Abdelal and Jonathan Kirshner, "Strategy, Economic Relations, and the Definition of National Interests," *Security Studies* 9.1–2 (Autumn/Winter 1999–2000): 119–56. States that accumulated dollars in the 1960s found themselves with a considerable stake in the viability of the dollar; see, for example, Salant, "Reserve Currency Role," 170; and Cooper, "Future of the Dollar," 11.

31. Joseph S. Nye, Jr., *Bound to Lead: The Changing Nature of American Power* (New York: Basic Books, 1990); Nye, *Soft Power: The Means to Success in World Politics* (New York: Public Affairs, 2004).

32. Gregory Chin and Eric Helleiner, "China as a Creditor: A Rising Financial Power?," *Journal of International Affairs* 62:1 (Fall/Winter 2008): 87 (quote), 99. This latter possibility is consistent with the conclusion of Eichengreen and Flandreau, who argue that "the possibility of a sharp shift in reserve composition cannot be discounted." "Rise and Fall of the Dollar," 404.

33. The United States would also enjoy reduced international monetary power, that is, the ability to advance its interests by taking advantage of its position in the international monetary system. For a thoughtful overview of the nature of monetary power, see David Andrews, "Monetary Power and Monetary Statecraft," in Andrews, *International Monetary Power*; see also Cohen, "Macrofoundations of Monetary Power," esp. 31, 36, 45; and Kirshner, *Currency and Coercion*.

34. World Trade Organization, *International Trade Statistics, 2009* (Geneva: WTO, 2009); IMF, *Direction of Trade Statistics, Yearbook 2009* (Washington, DC: IMF, 2009). He Li, "China's Growing Interest in Latin America and Its Implications," *Journal of Strategic Studies* 30:4–5 (August/October 2007): 842–43. To take one example, exports from Brazil to China rose from $2.3 billion in 2001 to $56 billion in 2011. Robert Minikin and Kelvin Lau, *The Offshore Renminbi: The Rise of the Chinese Currency and Its Global Future* (Singapore: Wiley, 2013), 137.

35. Hirschman, *National Power*, 29 (quote); see also Gary S. Becker, "A Theory of Competition among Pressure Groups for Political Influence," *Quarterly Journal of Economics* 98 (August 1983): 373–400; Charles P. Kindleberger, "Group Behavior and International Trade," *Journal of Political Economy* 59 (February 1959): 30–47; and the illustrations in Kirshner and Abdelal, "Strategy, Economic Relations, and the Definition of National Interests."

36. David Shambaugh, "China Engages Asia: Reshaping the Regional Order," *International Security* 29 (Winter 2004–5): 83, 85 (quote); Michael Vatikiotis, "A Too-Friendly Embrace," *Far Eastern Economic Review* (June 17, 2004): 20–22; Howard W. French and Norimitsu Onishi, "Economic Ties Binding Japan to Rival China," *New York Times*, October 31, 2005; Nicholas Lardy, "China, the Great New Economic Challenge?" in *The United States and the World Economy: Foreign Economic Policy for the Next Decade*, ed. C. Fred Bergsten (Washington, DC: Institute for International Economics, 2005), 122–24, 127–28; Stephanie Hemelryk and Robert Benewick, *The State of China Atlas: Mapping the World's Fastest Growing Economy* (Berkeley: University of California Press, 2005), 14–15, 96–97; Thomas Lum, Wayne Morrison, and Bruce Vaughn, "China's 'Soft Power' in Southeast Asia," CRS Report for Congress RL34310, Congressional Research Service, January 4, 2008, http://www.fas.org/sgp/crs/row/RL34310.pdf, 4, 9, 11, 14. See also (with a more qualified view of the political consequences) Robert Ross, "Balance of Power Politics and the Rise of China: Accommodation and Balancing in East Asia, *Security Studies* 15:3 (July/September 2006): 365–66, 376, 378.

37. In theory, with floating rates, the "overhang" can be ignored and excess currency "mopped up" by depreciation. In practice, states are very sensitive to the management of this type of problem even in the absence of fixed rates. On the overhang, its previous application to the American case, and concerns for new vulnerabilities, see Susan Strange, "The Politics of International Currencies," *World Politics* 23:2 (January 1971): 219, 225; Fred Bergsten, "New Urgency for International

Monetary Reform," *Foreign Policy* 19 (Summer 1975): 80, 83; and Benjamin J. Cohen, "Europe's Money, America's Problem," *Foreign Policy* 35 (Summer 1979): 42.

38. Kirshner, *Currency and Coercion,* 64–70; Harold Macmillan, *Riding the Storm* (New York: Harper and Row, 1971), 164. See also Diane B. Kunz, *The Economic Diplomacy of the Suez Crisis* (Chapel Hill: University of North Carolina Press, 1991); Lewis Johnman, "Defending the Pound: The Economics of the Suez Crisis, 1956," in *Post-War Britain, 1945–64: Themes and Perspectives,* ed. Anthony Gorst, Lewis Johnman, and W. Scott Lewis (London: Pinter, 1989); and Howard J. Dooley, "Great Britain's 'Last Battle' in the Middle East: Notes on Cabinet Planning during the Suez Crisis of 1956," *International History Review* 11:3 (August 1989).

39. Phillip Darby, *British Defence Policy East of Suez, 1947–68* (London: Oxford University Press, 1973), 293; Michael Chichester and John Wilkinson, *The Uncertain Ally: British Defence Policy, 1960–1990* (Aldershot, UK: Grower, 1982), 9–10; Jeremy Fielding, "Coping with Decline: US Policy Toward the British Defense Reviews of J. Néré, *The Foreign Policy of France from 1914–1945* 66," *Diplomatic History* 23:4 (Fall 1999): 633–37, 645; "Memorandum from President Johnson to Secretary of the Treasury Fowler," *Foreign Relations of the United States: 1964–1968,* vol. 7 (Washington, DC: US Government Printing Office, 1998), 173.

40. Clive Ponting, *Breach of Promise: Labour in Power, 1964–1970* (London: Hamish Hamilton, 1989), 55; Darby, *British Defence Policy,* 283, 304; Fielding, "Coping with Decline," 634–36, 651; Michael Dockrill, *British Defence since 1945* (Oxford: Basil Blackwell, 1988), 94–5, 97, 101, 103; J.C. Hurewitz, "The Persian Gulf: British Withdrawal and Western Security," *Annals of the American Academy of Political and Social Science* 401 (May 1972): 107, 114; Chichester and Wilkinson, *Uncertain Ally,* 20, 23, 31–32.

41. Kathleen Burk and Alec Cairncross, *Goodbye Great Britain: The 1976 IMF Crisis* (New Haven: Yale University Press, 1992), 20, 78, 105; Dockrill, *British Defence* 104, 106, 107; Chichester and Wilkinson, *Uncertain Ally,* 47–48; 53; "Britain's Defensive World Role," *Economist,* November 24, 1979, 27.

42. Jonathan Kirshner, *Appeasing Bankers: Financial Caution on the Road to War* (Princeton: Princeton University Press, 2007).

43. H. Clark Johnson, *Gold, France, and the Great Depression, 1919–1932* (New Haven: Yale University Press, 1997); Kenneth Mouré, *The Gold Standard Illusion: France, the Bank of France, and the International Gold Standard, 1914–1939* (Oxford: Oxford University Press, 2002); Martin Wolfe, *The French Franc between the Wars, 1919–1939* (New York: Columbia University Press, 1951), esp. 35, 83.

44. Kenneth Mouré, *Managing the Franc Poincaré: Economic Understanding and Political Constraint in French Monetary Policy, 1928–1936* (Cambridge: Cambridge University Press, 1991), 17–18, 22, 27, 121; Barry Posen, *The Sources of Military Doctrine: France, Britain, and Germany between the World Wars* (Ithaca: Cornell University Press, 1984), 20. Robert Murray Haig, "The National Budgets of France, 1928–1937," *Proceedings of the Academy of Political Science* 17:4 (1938): 26, 29; Talbot Imlay, *Facing the Second World War: Strategy, Politics, and Economics in Britain and France, 1938–1940* (Oxford: Oxford University Press, 2003), 25; Bradford Lee, "Strategy, Arms, and the Collapse of France 1930–40," in *Diplomacy and Intelligence during the Second World War,* ed. Richard Langhorne (Cambridge: Cambridge University Press, 1985), 59, 63, 64, 65.

45. Mouré, *Managing the Franc,* 151; Emile Moreau, *The Golden Franc: Memoirs of a Governor of the Bank of France* (Boulder, CO: Westview, 1991), 128, 513–15, 517–18; J. Néré, *The Foreign Policy of France from 1914 to 1945* (London: Routledge & Kegan Paul, 1975), 127, 129–30; Anthony Adamthwaite, *France and the Coming of the Second World War,* (London: Routledge, 1977), 27 ("the franc was the Achilles heel of French Policy"); Haim Shamir, *Economic Crisis and French Foreign Policy, 1930–1936* (Leiden, NLD: E. J. Brill, 1989), 16–17, 26, 44; Paul Einzig, *France's Crisis* (London: Macmillan, 1934), viii, ix, 12, 102 (quote), 119.

46. Nere, *French Foreign Policy,* 152; Rene Girault, "The Impact of the Economic Situation on the Foreign Policy of France, 1936–9," in *The Fascist Challenge and the Policy of Appeasement,* ed. Wolfgang Mommsen and Lothar Kettenacker (London: George Allen and Unwin, 1983), 223 (quote), 214, 216; Shamir, *Economic Crisis,* 133, 211, 215; Robert Frankenstein, "The Decline of France and French Appeasement Policies, 1936–9," in Mommsen and Kettenacker, *Fascist Challenge,* 237.

47. R. A. C. Parker, "The First Capitulation: France and the Rhineland Crisis of 1936," *World Politics* 8:3 (April 1956): 367, 371; Néré, *French Foreign Policy,* 186–89; Raphaelle Ulrich, "Rene Massigli and Germany, 1919–1938," in Boyce, *French Foreign and Defence Policy,* 143; James Thomas Emmerson, *The Rhineland Crisis 7 March 1936: A Study in Multilateral Diplomacy* (Ames: Iowa State University Press, 1977), 39, 41, 47; Shamir, *Economic Crisis,* 218.

48. Emerson, *Rhineland Crisis,* 78 (quotes), 105, 111, 247. Stephen Schuker, "France and the Remilitarization of the Rhineland, 1936," *French Historical Studies* 14:3 (Spring 1986): 304, 330, 334, 335 (quotes); Brendan Brown, *The Flight of International Capital* (London: Routledge, 1987), 71; "French Financial Weakness," *Economist,* March 28, 1936, 711.

49. John Makin, "Swaps and Roosa Bonds as an Index of the Cost of Cooperation in the 'Crisis Zone,'" *Quarterly Journal of Economics* 85:2 (May 1971); Anna Schwartz, "From Obscurity to Notoriety: A Biography of the Exchange Stabilization Fund," *Journal of Money, Credit, and Banking* 29:2 (May 1997).

50. Daniel Drezner, "Bad Debts: Assessing China's Financial Influence in Great Power Politics," *International Security* 34:2 (2009); also Chin and Helleiner, "China as a Creditor."

51. Gold holdings calculated from *Federal Reserve Bulletin,* June 1933, http://fraser.stlouisfed.org/docs/publications/FRB/1930s/frb_061933.pdf, 368. These active debates took place in regular meetings at the Royal Institute for International Affairs and Financial Committee of the League of Nations. See Royal Institute of International Affairs (RIIA), *The International Gold Problem* (London: Oxford University Press, 1932); League of Nations, *Report of the Gold Delegation of the Financial Committee* (Geneva: League of Nations 1932); and *Selected Documents Submitted to the Gold Delegation of the Financial Committee* (Geneva: League of Nations 1931, 1930). For an illustration of the contrasting British and French positions, compare Albert Aftalon, "The Causes and Effects of the Movement of Gold into France," with T. E. Gregory, "The Causes of Gold Movements into and out of Great Britain, 1925–29," both in *Selected Documents* (1931).

52. William A. Brown, Jr., *The International Gold Standard Reinterpreted, 1914–34,* 2 vols. (New York: National Bureau of Economic Research, 1940), 766 (first quote); Henry Clay, *Lord Norman* (London: Macmillan, 1957), 231 (Norman quote); Moreau, *Golden Franc,* 430 (quote); Andrew Boyle, *Montagu Norman: A Biography* (London: Cassell & Co., 1967), 198–99; Susan Strange, *Sterling and British Policy* (London: Oxford University Press, 1971), 52; see also Charles P. Kindleberger, "The International Monetary Politics of a Near Great Power: Two French Episodes, 1926–36 and 1960–70," *Economic Notes* 11: 2–3 (1972), reprinted in Kindleberger, *Keynesianism versus Monetarism* (London: George Allen and Unwin, 1985), 121; and Paul Einzig, *Behind the Scenes of International Finance* (London: Macmillan, 1932).

53. Moreau, *Golden Franc,* 430 (Moreau followed through with his threat); Boyle, *Montagu Norman,* 225–26; S. V. O. Clarke, *Central Bank Cooperation, 1924–31* (New York: Federal Reserve Bank of New York, 1967), 146; Frederick Leith-Ross, *Money Talks: Fifty Years of International Finance* (London: Hutchinson & Co., 1968), 124 (Leith-Ross was on the receiving end of the French threat).

54. Edward W. Bennett, *Germany and the Diplomacy of the Financial Crisis, 1931* (Cambridge: Harvard University Press, 1962), 105 ("never dreamed"), 113; Brown, *International Gold Standard,* 458 ("strongly inclined").

55. Aaron Friedberg, "Implications of the Financial Crisis for the US-China Rivalry," *Survival* 52:4 (August/September 2010). As Friedberg argues, just because a situation of MAD (mutually

assured destruction) exists, there is no guarantee it can't happen (40–41). Daniel Drezner also sees international political conflict as the one reason why a sudden shift from the dollar might take place; Daniel W. Drezner, "Will Currency Follow the Flag?," *International Relations of the Asia-Pacific* 10 (2010), 407.

56. Chinn and Frankel, "Why the Euro Will Rival the Dollar," 67.

8. Conclusions, Expectations, and Speculations

1. Jonathan Kirshner, "The Political Economy of Low Inflation," *Journal of Economic Surveys* 15:1 (February 2001): esp. 47–50. See also Olivier Blanchard, Giovanni Dell'Ariccia, and Paolo Mauro, "Rethinking Macroeconomic Policy," IMF Staff Position Note SPN/10/03, February 10, 2010 (http://www.imf.org/external/pubs/ft/spn/2010/spn1003.pdf), a remarkable post–financial crisis paper that suggests the post-1970s suppression of inflation might have been taken too far.

2. Barry R. Posen, "Command of the Commons: The Military Foundation of US Hegemony," *International Security* 28:1 (Summer 2003): 5–46. The benefits of sustaining such dominance, it should be noted, are not necessarily obvious. See Robert Jervis, "International Primacy: Is the Game Worth the Candle?" *International Security* 17:4 (Spring 1993): 52–67; and Daniel Drezner, "Military Primacy Doesn't Pay (Nearly as Much as You Think)" *International Security* 38:1 (Summer 2013): 52–79.

3. Growth rates from 1998 to 2012 are from the World Bank. For examples of projected rates of growth, see, Congressional Budget Office, *The Budget and Economic Outlook: Fiscal Years 2013–2023* (February 2013), 64; and National Intelligence Council, *Global Trends 2030: Alternative Worlds* (December 2012).

4. Benjamin J. Cohen, *The Future of Money* (Princeton: Princeton University Press, 2004); Kathleen R. McNamara and Sophie Meunier, "Between National Sovereignty and International Power: What External Voice for the Euro," *International Affairs* 78:4 (2002): 849–68; C. Randall Henning, "The Exchange-Rate Weapon and Macroeconomic Conflict," in *International Monetary Power*, ed. David Andrews (Ithaca: Cornell University Press, 2006).

5. David Spiro, *The Hidden Hand of American Hegemony: Petrodollar Recycling and World Politics* (Ithaca: Cornell University Press, 1999).

6. Eric Helleiner, "Enduring Top Currency, Fragile Negotiated Currency: Politics and the Dollar's International Role," in *The Future of the Dollar*, ed. Eric Helleiner and Jonathan Kirshner (Ithaca: Cornell University Press, 2009); Susan Strange, *Sterling and British Policy: A Political Study of an International Currency in Decline* (London: Oxford University Press, 1971).

7. Jonathan Kirshner, *Appeasing Bankers: Financial Caution on the Road to War* (Princeton: Princeton University Press, 2007).

8. Often, it should be noted, that unilateralism was generous in nature, especially in the 1940s and 1950s.

9. Aaron Friedberg, "Implications of the Financial Crisis for the US-China Rivalry," *Survival* 52:4 (2010): 35–36. On the possibility that American politics might magnify new constraints on US power, Gideon Rachman notes that "the United States is, in many ways, psychologically ill-prepared for the end of American Hegemony." *Zero Sum World* (London: Atlantic Books, 2010), 259.

10. Arguably the single most influential book in international relations theory, *Theory of International Politics* by Kenneth Waltz predicted in 1979 that the bipolar world would endure indefinitely, because he projected that the smaller Soviet Union would grow a bit faster than the larger United States, and no other state could mount much of a challenge to either. In a decade, of course, bipolarity ended as the Soviet Union collapsed. Predictions didn't get much better from there. In the late the 1980s, one common topic of discussion was when (not if) Japan's GDP would overtake that of the United States. Other examples of erroneous forecasting based on extending trends indefinitely abound.

11. Joseph Schumpeter, "Alfred Marshall's Principles: A Semi-Centennial Appraisal," *American Economic Review* 31:2 (June 1941): 248.

12. Alfred Marshall, "Fragments," in *Memorials of Alfred Marshall*, ed. A. C. Pigou (London: Macmillan, 1925), 360 (quote); Alfred Marshall, *Principles of Economics*, 8th ed. (London: McMillan, 1920), esp. book 1, chap. 3, "Economic Generalizations or Laws," 30–33.

13. Frank Knight, *Risk, Uncertainty, and Profit* (1921, repr., Chicago: University of Chicago Press, 1971), 241, 311; see also Frank Knight, " 'What Is Truth' in Economics?," *Journal of Political Economy* 48:1: 29–31; Friedrich Hayek, "The Pretence of Knowledge," (Nobel memorial lecture, December 11, 1974), Nobel Foundation; John Maynard Keynes, "The General Theory of Employment," *Quarterly Journal of Economics* 51:2 (February 1937), *CW*, 14:113–14 (quotes), 122.

14. Hans J. Morgenthau, *Politics among Nations: The Struggle for Power and Peace*, 3rd ed. (New York: Knopf, 1960), 20 (quote), 21; Hans J. Morgenthau, *Scientific Man vs. Power Politics*, (Chicago: University of Chicago Press, 1946), 129 (quote), 139, 146–48, 150, 220, 221. Morgenthau echoed the admonitions of Knight and Hayek about failing to appreciate the difference between the natural sciences and the social sciences, and was highly critical of "the illusion of a social science imitating a model of the natural sciences" (*Scientific Man,* 121, 139). Similarly, Robert Gilpin stresses how "unique and unpredictable sets of developments" render prediction beyond the means of the student of world politics. *War and Change in World Politics* (Cambridge: Cambridge University Press, 1981), 3.

15. It is wise to guess that the roll of two dice will yield a sum higher than five. But 25% of the time, that guess will be wrong.

16. See, for example, Susan Lund, James Manyika, Scott Nyquist, Lenny Mendonca, and Sreenivas Ramaswamy, *Game Changers: Five Opportunities for US Growth and Renewal* (n.p.: McKinsey Global Institute, 2013). For an optimistic take on the future of American power and prospects for the dollar order, see Doug Stokes, "Achilles' Deal: Dollar Decline and US Grand Strategy after the Crisis," *Review of International Political Economy* (May 8, 2013), http://dx.doi.org/10.1080/09692290.2013.779592.

17. On these issues, see, for example, Edward Luce, *Time to Start Thinking: America in the Age of Descent* (New York: Atlantic Monthly Press, 2012). Timothy Noah, *The Great Divergence: America's Growing Inequality Crisis and What We Can Do about It* (New York: Bloomsbury, 2012).

18. That is, the goal is not to say, there is a 20 percent chance of war, but rather we should not be surprised if a war occurs, and that would change our expectations in the following ways.

19. Thus, in the subhead above, the sentiment expressed by Orson Welles's character in his film, *The Lady from Shanghai* (Columbia, 1947).

20. Susan Shirk, *China: Fragile Superpower: How China's Internal Politics Could Derail Its Peaceful Rise* (Oxford: Oxford University Press, 2007).

21. Leo Tolstoy, *War and Peace*, trans. Richard Pevear and Larissa Volokhonsky (New York: Random House, 2007), 1202.

22. Mark Metzler, *Lever of Empire: The International Gold Standard and the Crisis of Liberalism in Prewar Japan* (Berkeley: University of California Press, 2006); Richard J. Smethurst, *From Foot Soldier to Finance Minister: Takahashi Korekiyo, Japan's Keynes* (Cambridge: Harvard University Press, 2007).

23. Jonathan Kirshner, "The Tragedy of Offensive Realism: Classical Realism and the Rise of China," *European Journal of International Relations,* 18:1 (March 2012): 52–74. Political scientists holding to deterministic models—that is, the idea of a known future—can reach different conclusions. See, for example, John Mearsheimer, *The Tragedy of Great Power Politics* (New York: Norton, 2001).

24. On "the politics of permanent austerity" in Europe, see Mark Blyth, *Austerity: The History of a Dangerous Idea* (Oxford: Oxford University Press, 2013), chap. 2.

25. Unemployment figures are from the European Commission.

26. Rebecca M. Nelson, Paul Belkin, Derek E. Mix, and Martin A. Weiss, "The Eurozone Crisis: Overview and Issues for Congress," CRS Report for Congress R42377, Congressional Research Service, February 29, 2012, 10.

27. Securities and Exchange Commission, Division of Corporation Finance, "CF Disclosure Guidance: Topic No. 4 European Sovereign Debt Exposures," January 6, 2012.

28. Andrew Ross Sorkin, *Too Big To Fail* (New York: Viking, 2009), 538.

29. Simon Johnson and James Kwak, *13 Bankers: The Wall Street Takeover and the Next Financial Meltdown* (New York: Pantheon, 2010), esp. 202, 205; Phillip Mirowski, *Never Let a Serious Financial Crisis Go to Waste: How Neoliberalism Survived the Financial Meltdown* (London: Verso, 2013).

30. James B. Stewart, "Volcker Rule, Once Simple, Now Boggles," *New York Times,* October 21, 2011; William L. Silber, *Volcker: The Triumph of Persistence* (New York: Bloomsbury, 2012), 296; James Barth, Gerard Caprio, Jr., and Ross Levine, *Guardians of Finance: Making Regulators Work for Us* (Cambridge: MIT Press, 2012), 172, 214.

31. Paul Volcker, "The Fed and Big Banking at the Crossroads," *New York Review of Books* 60:13 (August 15, 2013), 33. As one scholar observes, "post-crisis developments seem to indicate that the privileged position of banks has been entrenched rather than diminished." Andrew Baker, "Restraining Regulatory Capture? Anglo-America, Crisis Politics, and Trajectories of Change in Global Financial Governance," *International Affairs* 86:3 (2010): 655.

32. Robert Lucas, "Glass-Steagall: A Requiem," *American Economic Review* 103:3 (May 2013): 43.

33. See, for example, Charles R. Geisst, *Wall Street: A History,* updated ed. (Oxford: Oxford University Press, 2012).

INDEX

Asian financial crisis of 1997–98, 60–61,
70–73; China after, 9, 13, 77, 113; failure
to anticipate, 8; ideological fissures in
wake of, 61, 77–79; IMF's response
to, 8–9, 61, 62, 65, 71–76, 78, 79, 115,
183n5; interpretations of, 73–79; US
response to, 9, 53, 61, 74, 78–79, 112,
183n5; World Bank after, 187n37
Asian Monetary Fund initiative, 77–78
austerity: Asian financial crisis and, 9, 76;
global financial crisis and EU policies
of, 139, 170; Great Depression and, 3,
26; international currency in decline
and, 17, 147, 148; Keynes on, 85
Austria, Great Depression and, 22,
23–24

balance-of-payments flexibility, US, 16,
140, 141, 143
balance of power: and financial liberaliza-
tion, 62; global financial crisis and, 2,
15, 131; and IMF structure, 6; relative de-
cline of American power and, 107, 116,
131, 163, 199n3
Bank for International Settlements, 99, 106
Banking Act of 1933. *See* Glass-Steagall Act
Barings Bank, 55
Bear Stearns, 100
Bentsen, Lloyd, 63
Bernanke, Ben, 82, 100, 174n16
Bhagwati, Jagdish, 65, 66–67, 69, 77
Blinder, Alan, 65, 94
Blyth, Mark, 193n44
Born, Brooksley, 56
Brazil: capital controls in, 107; trade with
China, 144
Bretton Woods system, 33, 37–38, 110,
141; collapse of, 31, 38, 111, 127, 141,
142, 163
Britain: and France, monetary relation-
ship in interwar years, 153–55; Great
Depression and, 22, 23–24, 33, 34; after
World War II, 31, 32, 146–49
British pound sterling: crises after World War
II, 146–49; international use of, 110, 111
Bush, George H. W., deregulation under,
11, 62, 94

Bush, George W.: global financial crisis
and, 100; tax cuts under, 85–86

Calleo, David, 129
Camdessus, Michel, 64, 65, 71, 72, 74, 76
capital controls: after Asian financial crisis,
73, 76–77, 187n37; Bhagwati on, 69;
China and, 80, 113, 120; first US postwar order and, 6; after global financial
crisis, 13, 107; ideas about, 66–67; IMF
and, 6, 44, 107, 188n45; IMF's push
for dismantling of, 7–8, 9, 59–60, 61,
64–66, 70, 72; Keynes on, 6, 68; Malaysia
and, 76–77; World Bank and, 187n37
capital mobility: Asian elites on, 79;
and economic growth, 8, 69–70; and
financial crises, 8, 60, 70; as negative
externality, 68–69. *See also* financial
liberalization
Carter, Jimmy, 52, 62, 116
CDOs. *See* collateralized debt obligations
CDSs. *See* credit default swaps
Chari, V. V., 191n25
Chen Siqing, 117
Chile: trade with China, 144; US push for
financial deregulation in, 64, 80
Chin, Gregory, 113–14, 119
China: Asian financial crisis and, 9, 13,
61, 77, 113; capital controls in, 80, 113,
120; dollar holdings by, 13, 113, 114,
115, 152–53, 201n13; exchange rate
policies of, 125–26, 128; fragilities
of, 128, 160, 199n1; global financial
crisis and, 13–14, 107, 108, 114, 116; as
importer, 144, 168; monetary ambitions
of, 14, 108–9, 111, 113–17, 113–23, 136,
196n24; monetary power of, potential
exercise of, 153, 155; rise of economic
and political power of, 15, 116, 134–35,
143–45, 159, 160; structural power of,
trajectory for, 143–45; trading partners
of, 121, 144, 203n34; uncertainty about
future of, 36, 167–68, 169; and US,
relationship of, 13, 21, 125–26, 153, 168,
194n3. *See also* RMB
Chwieroth, Jeffrey, 64
Citigroup, 53, 102–3